Advance Praise

School leaders can play powerful roles in igniting student learning, but all too often policy-makers have advocated technical approaches to leadership development that are blind to the cultural and contextual dynamics of schools. *Leading Futures* provides the intellectual armamentarium for a refreshing contrast to this general pattern. Based upon an ambitious international study of school leadership practices—including those in under-investigated nations such as Indonesia, Malaysia and Russia—the authors provide a series of nuanced analysis in a single book that will catapult the whole field of educational leadership forward. This book is true tour de force that will be read and re-read many times by all of us endeavouring to keep abreast of the exciting new transformations in education around the world today.

Dennis Shirley
Editor-in-Chief, *Journal of Educational Change*
Professor, Lynch School of Education, Boston College
Co-author of *The Global Forth Way*

Leadership is undoubtedly one of the most important factors in producing successful and widespread educational change. But leadership does not look the same in all contexts and cultures. *Leading Futures* brings together scholars and writers on educational leadership from around the world to remind us that more and better comparative studies are needed that look at leadership from many angles. The editors of this book are themselves leaders of change on a global scale. Like them, this book challenges all of us to rethink all the things we thought were universally true about leadership and its effectiveness. A mustread for anyone who wants to extend their understanding of leadership beyond their own domain.

Andy Hargreaves
Brennan Chair, Lynch School of Education, Boston College
Adviser to the Premier and Minister of Education of Ontario
Co-author of *Professional Capital*

While it has been readily acknowledged for some time that school leaders play a significant role in educational success, their roles and quality of leadership have become even more significant in the present context of important new demands being made on schools, teachers and pupils. Significant and ambitious reform initiatives are being launched by governments globally in response to globalization's opportunities and challenges.

Leading Futures is a very welcome contribution to studying leadership challenges in this new context. Drawing on an international study of school leadership, its careful attention to the interplay of culture and context throws up interesting insights, which will move the study and practice of school leadership forward in significant ways.

An important new book that deserves wide readership and careful study.

S. Gopinathan
Adjunct Professor, Lee Kuan Yew School of Public Policy,
National University of Singapore
Founding Editor, *Asia Pacific Journal of Education*

LEADING
FUTURES

LEADING FUTURES

Global Perspectives on
Educational Leadership

EDITED BY

Alma Harris | Michelle S. Jones

 www.sagepublications.com
Los Angeles • London • New Delhi • Singapore • Washington DC

First published in 2016 by

 SAGE Publications India Pvt Ltd
B1/I-1 Mohan Cooperative Industrial Area
Mathura Road, New Delhi 110 044, India
www.sagepub.in

SAGE Publications Inc
2455 Teller Road
Thousand Oaks, California 91320, USA

SAGE Publications Ltd
1 Oliver's Yard, 55 City Road
London EC1Y 1SP, United Kingdom

SAGE Publications Asia-Pacific Pte Ltd
3 Church Street
#10-04 Samsung Hub
Singapore 049483

Published by Vivek Mehra for SAGE Publications India Pvt Ltd, typeset in 11/13 Adobe Garamond Pro by RECTO Graphics, Delhi and printed at Chaman Enterprises, New Delhi.

Library of Congress Cataloging-in-Publication Data Available

ISBN: 978-93-515-0255-5 (HB)

The SAGE Team: Shambhu Sahu, Saima Ghaffar, Apeksha Sharma, Nand Kumar Jha and Ritu Chopra

To Adam, Christopher, Charlotte and Jaime
Be ambitious about your future.

Thank you for choosing a SAGE product!
If you have any comment, observation or feedback,
I would like to personally hear from you.
Please write to me at **contactceo@sagepub.in**

Vivek Mehra, Managing Director and CEO, SAGE India.

Bulk Sales

SAGE India offers special discounts
for purchase of books in bulk.
We also make available special imprints
and excerpts from our books on demand.

For orders and enquiries, write to us at

Marketing Department
SAGE Publications India Pvt Ltd
B1/I-1, Mohan Cooperative Industrial Area
Mathura Road, Post Bag 7
New Delhi 110044, India

E-mail us at **marketing@sagepub.in**

Get to know more about SAGE

Be invited to SAGE events, get on our mailing list.
Write today to **marketing@sagepub.in**

This book is also available as an e-book.

Contents

Acknowledgements

This book would not have been possible without the enthusiasm and professionalism of Nicola Everett at SAGE. We are indebted to Professor Suria Baba for so many things but her introduction to Nicola was a catalyst for this book. We are also grateful to all our chapter authors for their thought provoking contributions that collectively provide a powerful account of educational leadership around the globe. To our amazing team at the Institute of Educational Leadership, University of Malaya, we say 'thank you' for all that you do to support us and particularly for helping us make the 'Asia Leadership Summit 2014' a reality. Thanks also to Jacqueline Perera for proofreading the book in its final stages. Finally, to all those supporting and developing future leaders around the globe, we wish you every success.

International Comparisons: Critique, Culture and Context

Alma Harris and Michelle S. Jones

Globalization continues to drive the development of new educational reform policies and securing better educational outcomes remains an imperative for policy-makers. Pressure to change, transform and improve educational systems has never been so acute or so highly prized. Better 'teacher quality' and 'leadership quality' remain the mantra of the moment and, it is argued, the pathway to improve the performance of education systems (Mourshed et al., 2010). International benchmarks such as the 'Programme for International Student Assessment' (PISA), the 'Progress in International Reading Literacy' (PIRLS) and the 'Trends in International Mathematics and Science Study' (TIMSS) have been global game changers. The rise of international comparisons to their current position of international influence can be explained by the positive relationships between educational attainment and economic development (Meyer and Benavot, 2013). Consequently, these international large-scale assessments studies (LSAs) of student attainment continue to have a significant impact upon education policy and heavily influence national agendas for educational improvement (Caro et al., 2014).

International comparative data have been a significant wake-up call for those education systems that were complacent about their performance and those that felt unashamedly superior. The 'big-brother' scrutiny of comparative advantage has galvanized education policy-makers in different countries to re-evaluate system performance and to put in place new approaches to improve outcomes. Of all these international benchmarks, PISA is the most dominant. Launched in 1997, PISA is conducted in cycles of three years and examines reading literacy, mathematical and scientific competency of national samples of 15-year-old students. Its prime aim is to 'allow national policy-makers to *compare* the performance of their education systems with those of other countries' (Organisation for Economic Cooperation and Development [OECD], 1999:7). As a consequence, most of official reporting is in the form of comparative league tables that present the rankings of each country, in each of the three subject areas.

The imperative to compare and contrast educational performance is one major by-product of PISA. It has afforded the opportunity to look beyond country borders and to scrutinize the performance of other education systems (OECD, 2011; Tucker, 2011). On the positive side, LSAs have advanced our understanding of the factors associated with better student outcomes and have provided a much needed basis for country-by-country comparison. Conversely, on the minus side there are some serious critiques of the theoretical and methodological approaches deployed by LSAs, and in particular those associated with PISA (Caro et al., 2014). Although the critiques of PISA have received significantly less airtime than the popular accounts and various descriptions of the 'best-performing' systems based on its data, they are nonetheless important and worth consideration.

Critique

PISA league tables are based on the rankings derived from the average performance scores of students in tests of reading, and mathematical and scientific literacy. The accuracy of this ranking depends a great deal on what is tested, who is tested and which tests are used. It also depends on what kinds of analyses are performed on the data. In order to accurately compare the results obtained from different groups or countries, the tests must first be able to measure the same competencies or features within each participating country. This is an issue of 'cultural fit'. Such a requirement is important for two reasons: First, to guarantee the fidelity of the measure and the precision of any subsequent comparison and second, because PISA is much, much more than just an international benchmark.

PISA has clearly established its role in policy formation and this goes far beyond the boundaries of measurement. Its intentions have been stated as that of 'providing high quality data to support policy formation and review' (OECD, 2003:3). As such, PISA findings are increasingly used to justify, change or provide support for the existing policy direction in both the domestic and international contexts (Gaber et al., 2012; Sjøberg, 2012). Hence concerns about the accuracy of its data and the validity of its countrywide comparisons are even more important.

The weight of evidence about the methodological, statistical and theoretical limitations of PISA is increasing and the voices of dissent are slowly getting heard. The critical discourse surrounding PISA is gaining momentum as secondary analyses are presented and new insights are shared. There is now a considerable amount of literature on PISA that challenges the legitimacy of the entire comparative exercise and calls into question the wisdom of relying on PISA as a reliable comparative measure (Eivers, 2010; Fiscbach et al., 2010; Lenkeit & Caro, 2014; Murphy, 2014). There are also questions about PISA's role and functions within the policy arena and the extent of its impartiality (Feniger and Lefstein, 2014; Grek, 2009).

PISA is now a highly influential instrument of policy and, it has been advocated, part of the new global apparatus of governance (Murphy, 2010). Sahlberg (2014) uses the term 'global education reform movement' or GERM to refer to a set of policies that have increasingly been advocated and adopted in many parts of the world as a direct result of successive PISA findings. These policies are:

1. *The standardization of education*: The setting of performance standards and testing to evaluate student attainment through frequent external assessment measures.

2. *Increased focus on literacy and numeracy:* Basic knowledge and skills are considered the most important and are also more suited to standard testing and comparison.
3. *Consequential accountability:* The tying of school performance to the processes of accrediting, promoting, inspecting and rewarding or punishing schools and teachers.

These policies have become integral to the globalization of education policy along with decentralization, privatization and the drive for increased efficiency in school systems (Knodel et al., 2013). They are advocated on the basis that the education systems that 'outperform others' embrace such policies and that this largely explains their success (Barber and Mourshed, 2007; Mourshed et al., 2010). Over the last decade, the number of countries with standardized national testing has increased significantly and the indisputable convergence around the policies associated with GERM has strengthened. At the present time, PISA remains a major influence on policy-making around the world. Its findings and recommendations carry great weight and continue to shape national agendas for educational improvement and change (Hanberger, 2014; Waldow et al., 2014).

Despite such global influence, there are some worrying 'blind spots' in the PISA methodology and analysis, which are not high on the international radar. For example, Murphy (2014:913) proposes that some negative PISA findings have been ignored or 'deliberately downplayed' to suit broader policy imperatives and purposes. His work highlights 'inconsistent use of statistical methods in PISA 2006 analysis and selective reporting of its 2009 analysis'. This secondary data analysis shows how 'attention has been drawn to positive findings for school autonomy, competition and accountability measures while negative results for consequential accountability policies have been hidden' (Murphy, 2014:913). In other words, there has been partial reporting of the evidence with the positive aspects of certain policy-drivers being shared but not the negative aspects. The inference drawn by Murphy (2014) is that PISA is supporting certain schooling policies over others, largely those associated with GERM.

Another important 'blind spot' concerns the marginalization of culture or context as an important explanatory factor of educational performance. Even though PISA tests more than a million students in more than 60 countries, there are no cultural-specific measures. Therefore, it is questionable how far the test remains exactly the same when translated into other languages and introduced into different cultures, contexts and systems? How far is there real equivalence across the tests? Kankaraš and Moors (2013) conclude from their analysis that 'in-equivalence occurred in a majority of test questions in all three (PISA 2009) scales researched and is, on average, of a moderate size. It varies considerably both across items and across countries'. If the PISA test is not testing the same thing in different countries (i.e., equivalency) but instead there is wide variability (i.e., in-equivalency), then how can valid comparisons be made? Furthermore, Kankaraš and Moors (2013) suggest that the 'scores of Southeast Asian countries or territories increase when accounting for in-equivalence in the scales'. In short, with such differences in the data the validity of country-to-county comparisons is questionable and the accuracy of the comparison is inevitably reduced (Kreiner and Christensen, 2014). While the debate about PISA takes various lines of argument, the critiques converge around one common issue—the wisdom of relying on PISA as *the* indicator of comparative country performance rather than just a measure.

Another critique of PISA is the total bypassing in the data collection of important cultural and structural factors that differ considerably from country to country, for example, the influence of socio-economic factors on educational attainment. PISA simply removes such cultural 'white noise' from its analysis, providing a series of league tables of countries according to certain PISA questions or categories of questions. Yet a careful look across these different league tables reveals that without adequate contextualization, these tables are relatively meaningless plus they often contradict each other as countries frequently change place depending on the scale or question.

Reflecting upon Teaching and Learning International Study (TALIS), another international comparative survey, Fullan (2014)[1]

---

[1] http://www.michaelfullan.ca/wp-content/uploads/2015/01/15_Worlds-of-Education.pdf (last accessed on 12 April 2015).

highlights the importance of interpreting quantitative data very carefully to avoid 'half-truths'. He says,

> [A] dangerous half-truth is a finding or statement that has some merit, but falls short because it fails to state under what conditions it is true. Such findings can be easily misinterpreted by eager or biased policy-makers who rush to put policies in place that turn out to be superficial or harmful to the cause of student learning.

Taking a comparative perspective without taking full account of the context or conditions in which certain findings are 'true' can lead to unintended consequences. Blindly copying the practices, approaches and policies of those systems deemed to be performing at a higher level without adequate contextualization is not a sensible option. Yong Zhao puts this point very strongly in Chapter 1 of this book. Equally, if comparison is based on little more than country-specific stories or narratives, any findings or recommendations must be treated with caution.

The Book

This book is not a cross-cultural analysis and does not claim to be. There is no overarching analytical framework or any underlying empirical design that would warrant this label. The assembling of different accounts from various countries at best affords a comparative perspective but a cross-cultural analysis cannot be claimed. A cross-cultural approach requires much more than geographical diversity or the sequencing of country-specific narratives, as the major comparative project by House et al. (2004) has clearly shown. In contrast, this book offers empirical, theoretical and analytical accounts of educational leadership from different perspectives, diverse countries and differentially performing education systems. Its prime intention is to inform rather than to advise.

With so many books on the subject of educational leadership and a much cluttered marketplace, why another book on this topic? The rationale for this book is pretty straightforward. First, this book aims to add to the contemporary, comparative knowledge base about educational leadership by drawing together writers from different contexts and countries. It deliberately brings together a wide range of scholars and commentators who offer their own particular stance on educational leadership, that is, from a policy, practice or research perspective. Second, this book aims to explore leadership practice at different levels (system, professional and leader or earner) from the vantage point of very different systems and countries. Third, this book aims to offer contemporary insights into the ways in which very different systems are actively working to build the leadership capacity for change and transformation.

Leadership capacity is certainly a buzzword of the moment and has been repeatedly underscored as an important prerequisite of better system improvement and sustainable transformation (Barber et al., 2013). Capacity building, however, is much more than just routine reskilling or upskilling. As Fullan (2010:57) argues, 'Capacity building concerns competencies, resources and motivation'. Individuals and groups are high in capacity if they possess and continue to develop the knowledge and skills, and if they are committed to putting the energy to get important things done collectively and continuously. At the system level, capacity building 'is a highly complex, dynamic, knowledge-building process, intended to lead to increased student achievement in every school' (Sharrat and Fullan, 2009:8).

Evidence shows that even the best policies cannot succeed without qualified, dedicated and skilled personnel to deeply implement them (Jensen, 2012). It highlights that without effective leadership at all levels in the system, sustainable change and improvement is less likely to occur (Harris et al., 2014). OECD country evaluations as well as the latest TALIS[2] report have recently highlighted the importance of leadership in supporting school improvement and teacher learning (OECD, 2013), but this relationship between leadership and organizational improvement is far from new. It has been examined and empirically tested for over four decades (Hallinger, 2011), and the findings are worth revisiting.

---

[2] http://www.oecd.org/edu/school/talis.htm (last accessed on 12 April 2015).

Leading Improvement

There are things that are categorically known about the relationship between educational leadership and organizational performance. Those researching and writing in the leadership field have repeatedly substantiated the contribution of leadership to better organizational performance and outcomes (Hallinger, 2000, 2003; Hargreaves & Fullan, 2012; Leithwood et al., 2008). An array of international research evidence demonstrates the impact of leadership on the school as an organization, its culture and performance (Day et al., 2009, 2010). A great deal of research has focused upon the leadership behaviours, practices and actions associated with improving schools and school systems (Leithwood et al., 2008). A review of educational leadership effects by Hallinger and Heck (1999) underscored the centrality of leadership in achieving better student and organizational outcomes. Increasingly, comprehensive and systematic reviews of the evidence have identified the impact of effective leadership upon student outcomes (Louis et al., 2010a, 2010b).

A substantial body of evidence also points towards the importance of leadership capacity building as a means of creating and sustaining school improvement (Fullan, 2001; Sergiovanni, 1999, 2001). It has been argued that at the core of the capacity-building model there is distributed leadership along with social cohesion and trust (Harris, 2010; Spillane, 2006; Spillane et al., 2001, 2004). Leadership, from a distributed perspective, is proposed to reside in the human potential available to be released within an organization. It also provides a basis for measuring and investigating a more comprehensive and complex set of leadership practices that go far beyond a set of standards or the checklists of characteristics, skills and strategies that remain a resilient part of the leadership field (Harris, 2014).

The empirical evidence underlines the simple but unequivocal fact that school improvement can be achieved by changing key organizational processes, such as leadership, and by building improvement capacity (Hallinger, 2011). The core message from the research base is that leadership is an important catalyst for change and an essential component of school or system improvement. The importance of

the school leader as a factor in school effectiveness has been corrobo-
rated by the substantial school effectiveness research base (Reynolds,
2010) and has consistently been reinforced by the empirical evidence
from the school improvement field (Day et al., 2001). Despite some
variability in the quality of findings, the research base on school
leadership has provided empirical confirmation on two things: First,
leaders make a difference to system, school and student outcomes,
and second, leadership is both culturally and contextually defined.

Culture

Commercial organizations have been quick to take advantage of the
fact that leaders make a difference but have been more reluctant
to deal, in any serious way, with the issue of cultural or contextual
influences. Inevitably, this is a complex and contested territory, but
contemporary accounts of 'high performance' devote limited attention to the fact that cultural factors are powerful and pervasive.
Providing neatly packaged 'solutions' to the challenge of organizational change and system improvement has meant sidestep-
ping messy or confusing cultural factors (Barber et al., 2013). The
inconvenient truth is that culture affects behaviour, understanding and action, but this is evaded in much of the contemporary
writing about system reform. Many of the commentaries on 'high-
performing' systems offer rather romantic views, devoid of any deep
cultural analysis (Stewart, 2013). They talk a great deal about leadership capacity building but far less about the cultural aspects that
heavily define how leadership is understood, enacted and practised
in various systems and countries.

The issue of culture is also a significant gap in the educational
leadership research base for a number of important reasons. First,
the majority of the studies in the educational leadership field have
concentrated attention on the school level and have been largely
preoccupied with establishing a relationship between leadership and
school-specific outcomes (Hallinger, 2011). Consequently, most
of the available empirical evidence focus on the operational issues

of school-level change rather than cultural aspects or influences. Second, the development of leadership theory within the field has focused largely on an individual leader. Stemming from an initial interest in personality or trait theories of leadership, the theoretical models of leadership have subsequently moved to behavioural theories of leadership, then situational leadership and subsequently transformational leadership, placing the leader as a change agent within his or her own cultural context (Leithwood et al., 2008). While contemporary writers have taken a different theoretical framing on educational leadership (Harris, 2014; Spillane et al., 2001), there is still a fixation with the actions and effect of the individual leader.

Third, it is not surprising that in the face of so much empirical attention on a single leader there has been a parallel growth and interest in patterns of leadership preparation and development (Walker et al., 2013). This literature has provided the best opportunity yet to look beyond the school gates and to investigate leadership and leadership development in different contexts. In their work, Walker et al. (2013) provide a useful analysis of five leadership programmes through a detailed documentary analysis. Similarly, Huber and West (2002) offer a critical review of the development of school leaders by providing descriptive accounts of school leader preparation in 11 different countries. Other comparative work undertaken by Huber (2004) pulls together different descriptions of the current leadership practice from around the world with some general commentary and analysis. The 'International Research on Principal's Work' has produced an anthology of research on leadership development in different countries (Ärlestig et al., 2015). This collection outlines the research activity that has been devoted to school leadership in 24 countries. It focuses particularly but not exclusively on the research evidence pertaining to the role and work of the principal in each individual country.

Despite these cross-country contributions, the field of educational leadership is still missing three important cultural strands in its substantial empirical base. First, it lacks contemporary, comparative empirical accounts of leadership and leadership development from a system perspective. Second, it still misses out on authentic cross-cultural empirical studies focusing upon leadership research, practice and development. Third, in relatively short supply are research studies that deliberately factor in contextual and cultural analysis as potential explanatory factors of successful leadership.

7 System Leadership Study

In 2012, a research project was established with the prime aim of looking at leadership in different cultures and contexts. The 7 system leadership study (7SLS) is a comparative analysis of different education systems.[3] It is a detailed and systematic comparative analysis of the approaches to leadership development in systems of varying nature, scale and scope. The study is empirically mapping the way in which different education systems develop school leaders and the impact these programmes have on a principals' leadership practice. The primary goal of this empirical study is to collect primary data about the leadership development strategies deployed in different education systems and, where possible, to compare the leadership practices of school principals within the seven systems. The 7SLS is a mixed method, cross-cultural empirical study comprising quantitative and qualitative data collection methods.[4]

This research study involves seven education systems that are all at various stages in their enactment and implementation of leadership development. Australia has introduced standards for school leaders and has a national body for teaching and school leadership.[5] In Malaysia there is a 'National Professional Qualification for Educational Leaders' (NPQEL)[6] that is mandatory. This qualification is based upon the 'National Professional Qualification for Headship' (NPQH)[7] in England. In Singapore and Hong Kong

---

[3] In this study, system means both the national education system (Singapore, Hong Kong and England) and the sub-education syst ems, that is, states, municipalities, regions (Russia, Australia, Malaysia and Indonesia).

[4] For more information -7systemleadershipstudy@gmail.com #7systemstudy.

[5] Australian Institute for Teaching and School Leadership.

[6] http://aplikasi.iab.edu.my/npqel/default2.aspx (last accessed on 12 April 2015).

[7] https://www.gov.uk/national-professional-qualification-for-headship-npqh (last accessed on 12 April 2015).

there are well-established, internationally known and highly effective programmes of leadership preparation (Ng, 2012; Pang, 2006). In Russia, programmes of leadership development and preparation are offered at the regional and municipality levels but there is no national programme or qualification. In Indonesia, a national qualification for all school leaders has been introduced.

The genesis of this book stems from the 7SLS and a major leadership summit (Asia Leadership Summit, 2014, Kuala Lumpur). The prime aim of both the 7SLS and the Asia Leadership Summit (ALS 2014) was to offer genuine comparative perspectives on leadership practice and development. The ALS, hosted by the University of Malaya in January 2014, was a conference designed to focus on the contemporary issues and challenges in the field of educational leadership and leadership development. The questions posed at the conference came directly from school students who opened the event by raising issues that they wanted the conference to address. Their questions form the structure for the conference and also, in part, inform the structure of this book.

Many of the contributors who feature in this book are expert advisors to the 7SLS and also participated in this Summit. However, this is not a conference book. While parts of the discussion from the study and the Summit will be covered in some of the chapters that follow, all the chapters have been written primarily to provide contemporary perspectives on educational leadership from very different settings and contexts.

The book is organized into three sections and some of the questions raised by the students underlie each section.

System Level

Leading Futures: System Transformation

1. How can policy be developed and implemented so that it impacts positively on future practice? What form of leadership will this require?

2. How do we make stronger connections between policy and practice?
3. What evidence do we have about the outcomes of a strong policy/practice relationship?
4. What type of leadership will secure transformation on a national and global scale?
5. Who will be the future leaders of system transformation?
6. What type of leadership will system transformation necessitate?

Professional Level

Leading Futures: Collaborative Professional Learning

1. How do we ensure professional learning with impact?
2. What are the implications for leadership and leaders who support effective professional learning?
3. What type of leadership does effective collaborative professional learning require?
4. How can we lead educational networks most effectively?
5. What are the skills of the network leader?
6. What are the future challenges of those leading networks within, between and across schools?

Leader and Learner Level

Leading Futures: Redefining Educational Leadership

1. What models or forms of leadership are most likely to capture and describe leadership practice in the future?
2. How will context and culture shape educational leadership?
3. What are the core principles of 21st century leadership?
4. What is needed to be a 21st century leader in very different contexts?
5. How far will the role of the principal be part of a future educational landscape?

6. How will principal certification assist in raising standards and performance?
7. What will be the challenges of leading global pedagogy?
8. What will learning in an open world look like?
9. What does 'new' in the new technologies imply for the classroom of the future?
10. What does effective pedagogy entail?

In the chapters that follow, such questions will be considered, debated and reflected from the perspective of different cultures and contexts. The aim of the book is also to open up a comparative debate about educational leadership and not just to offer country-specific accounts or stories. The core objective of this book is to offer different intellectual views and perspectives on leadership in order to gain a better understanding of the way in which leadership can contribute to better student outcomes. By looking across systems and countries and taking a more contextualized view there is the possibility of understanding why some education systems *really* outperform others.

While it is self-evident that no single country or system has all the answers to contemporary educational challenges, by taking a legitimate comparative perspective, finding a productive way forward will be more likely. We undoubtedly need more longitudinal studies that go beyond providing a snapshot of educational attainment every few years. As Goldstein (2008) has argued, 'to make comparisons in terms of the effects of education systems it is necessary (although not sufficient) to have longitudinal data and it remains a persistent weakness of all existing large-scale international comparative assessments that they make little effort to do this'. In other words, we need to track individuals through different education systems in order to sort out the effects of different types of influences on subsequent educational attainment.

While the superior performance of certain education systems can be explained in part by their policies, improvement strategies, implementation processes and their inherent ability to develop human capital, this is certainly not the entire story. Explanations of high performance cannot be attributed to these explanations alone, however powerful and persuasive their proponents might be. Cultural and contextual factors play a very important part in explanations of educational performance despite their notable absence from many contemporary analyses. This is not to dismiss the benefits of international comparative data altogether but rather to take a more circumspect view.

Before the advent of international comparative data, there was a tendency for systems to be ethnocentric and to not look outside their geographical boundaries. The international benchmarks have certainly encouraged countries to take a more critical view of performance, which is a good thing. However, they have also fuelled a view that culture is a relatively unimportant factor and that there are common strategies that will guarantee system success (Mourshed et al., 2010; Stewart, 2012). Undoubtedly, caution is needed when explaining the success of any education system. More independent detailed, empirical studies are needed that go beyond simple causal attributions or decontextualized accounts of 'high performance'. Yet, around the world, education systems are busily copying things that the 'better systems' supposedly deploy, even though wisdom of this approach is debatable and the exact return on this investment is often difficult to see.

Context

It is unlikely that the pressure for better system outcomes and better educational performance is unlikely to abate any time soon (Jensen, 2012). As argued at the start of this introduction, international benchmarking has gained such prominence that education is now, more than ever before, a global commodity. In the rush to ratchet up system performance, policy-makers are fixated with finding simple solutions and are actively encouraged to borrow policies from systems that perform at a 'higher' level (Mourshed et al., 2010; Stewart, 2012). This global drive is not helped by analyses of 'high performance' that reduce contextual influences on educational attainment to little more than mood music or background noise. The resulting causal attributions follow a simple formula: To get higher performance, we must follow what the 'best systems' do or rather what we are told that they do.

This logic not only oversimplifies the complex nature of educational change but also neatly factors out any possibility that culture or context could be powerful explanatory variables of better system performance. Moreover, this rationale takes zero account of the fact that educational outcomes emanate from the interactions and inter-related decisions of different educational actors (students, parents, teachers, school leaders, governors, etc.) within a particular context. It is as if decades of research on effective learning, teaching and schooling has ceased to exist. Left in its place is the practice of 'fishing for correlations' (Caro et al., 2014) and generating standardized policy frameworks that are not only compelling in their simplicity but are ultimately damaging if superimposed on a system without any consideration of contextual differences.

The continued influence of OECD's education policy work depends, to a significant effect, on stressing the importance of policy factors above the effects of cultural and social contexts (Ozga, 2012; Sellar and Lingard, 2013a, 2013b, 2013c). Using cultural and contextual factors to explain the success of education systems cannot be subsequently packaged into a set of reforms for other countries to implement. While learning from other policy contexts is clearly important, it is also imperative that any of the comparative analysis take appropriate account of culture and context. Policy-makers have been encouraged to look towards the 'high-performing systems', such as Shanghai or South Korea, for policy solutions (Tucker, 2011). However if some of the cultural aspects that define educational practice in those systems were more widely shared and known, such policy options might be considered less palatable (Ripley, 2013).

Ultimately, the critical issue is not whether certain educational policies matter more or less than their social and cultural contexts, but to ask 'how policy and culture connect together' (Feniger and Lefstein, 2014). Exploring the way in which culture interacts with a policy to shape educational opportunity will require a more in-depth analysis that moves away from simplistic cultural stereotyping. In reality, cultural and contextual influences are diverse, complex and multifaceted, as the chapters in this book will illuminate.

References

Arlestig, H., Day, C. and Johansson, O. (eds.). (2015). *Research on Principals and Their Work: Cross Cultural Perspectives.* Dordrecht: Springer. (In Press).

Barber, M. and Mourshed, M. (2007). *How the world's best-performing school systems come out on top.* London: McKinsey and Company, Retrieved from www.mckinsey.com/App_Media/Reports/SSO/Worlds_School_Systems_Final.pdf (last accessed on 12 April 2015).

Barber, M., Whelan, F., and Clark, M. (2010). Capturing the leadership premium: How the World's Top School Systems are Building Leadership Capacity for the Future. McKinsey & Company. Retrieved from http://mckinseyonsociety.com/capturing-the-leadership-premium/ (last accessed 8 July 2015).

Caro, D. H., Sandoval-Hernadez, A. and Ludtke, O. (2014). Cultural, social, and economic capital constructs in international assessments: An evaluation using exploratory structural equation modelling. *School Effectiveness and School Improvement, 25(3),* 433–450.

Day, C., Harris, A. and Hadfield, M. (2001). Challenging the orthodoxy of effective school leadership. *International Journal of Leadership in Education, 4(1),* 39–56.

Day, C., Sammons, P., Hopkins, D., Harris, A., Leithwood, K., Gu, Q., Brown, E., Ahtaridou, E. and Kington, A. (2009). *The impact of school leadership on pupil outcomes.* London: DCSF.

Day, C., Sammons, P., Leithwood, K., Hopkins, D., Harris, A., Gu, Q. and Brown, E. (2010). *Ten strong claims about successful school leadership.* Nottingham: NCSL.

Eivers, E. (2010). PISA: Issues in implementation and interpretation. *The Irish Journal of Education: Iris Eireannach an Oideachais,* 94–118.

Feniger, Y. and Lefstein, A. (2014). How not to reason with PISA data: An ironic investigation. *Journal of Education Policy, 29(6),* 845–855.

Fischbach, A., Keller, U., Preckel, F., and Brunner, M. (2013). PISA proficiency scores predict educational outcomes. *Learning and Individual Differences, 24,* 63–72.

Fullan, M. (2001). *Leading in a culture of change.* San Francisco, CA: Jossey-Bass.

———. (2010). *All systems go: The imperative for whole system reform,* Thousand Oaks, CA/ Toronto: Corwin Press/Ontario Principals Council.

———. (2014). Worlds of Education. *Education International,* Issue No 44.

Gaber, S., Cankar, G., Umek, L. M. and Tašner, V. (2012). The danger of inadequate conceptualisation in PISA for education policy. *Compare: A Journal of Comparative and International Education, 42(4),* 647–663.

Goldstein, H. (2008). Evidence and education policy–some reflections and allegations. *Cambridge Journal of Education, 38(3),* 393–400. Cambridge: University of Cambridge.

Grek, S. (2009). Governing by numbers: The PISA 'effect' in Europe. *Journal of Education Policy, 24(1),* 23–37.

Hallinger, P. (2000). *A review of two decades of research on the principalship using the Principal Instructional Management Rating Scale.* Paper presented at the annual meeting of the American Educational Research Association, Seattle, WA.

———. (2003). Leading educational change: Reflections on the practice of instructional and transformational leadership. *Cambridge Journal of Education, 33*(3), 329–351.

———. (2011). Leadership for learning: Lessons from 40 years of empirical research. *Journal of Educational Administration, 49*(2), 125–142.

Hallinger, P. and Heck, R. H. (1999). Can leadership enhance school effectiveness? In Bush et al. (Eds.). *Educational management: Redefining theory, policy and practice*, 178–190. London: Paul Chapman.

Hanberger, A. (2014). What PISA intends to and can possibly achieve A critical programme theory analysis. *European Educational Research Journal, 13*(2), 167–180.

Hargreaves, A. and Fullan, M. (2012). *Professional capital: Transforming teaching in every school.* New York: Teachers College Press.

Hargreaves, A., Boyle, A. and Harris, A. (2014). *Uplifting leadership.* San Francisco: Wiley Press.

Harris, A. (2010). Distributed leadership: evidence and implications. In T. Bush, L. Bell and D. Middlewood (eds.), *The Principles of Educational Leadership and Management*, 55–69. London: SAGE.

———. (2014). *Distributed leadership matters.* California: Corwin Press.

Harris, A., Jones, M. S., Adams, D., Perera, C. J., and Sharma, S. (2014). High-Performing Education Systems in Asia: Leadership Art meets Implementation Science. *The Asia-Pacific Education Researcher, 23*(4), 861–869.

House R.J., Hanges, P.J., Javidan, M., Dorfman, P.W., and Gupta, V. (2004). *Culture, Leadership, and Organizations: The GLOBE Study of 62 Societies.* Thousand Oaks, CA: SAGE.

Huber, S. G. and West, M. (2002). Developing school leaders: A critical review of current practices, approaches and issues, and some directions for the future. In P. Hallinger and K. Leithwood (eds.), *Second International Handbook of Educational Leadership and Administration* (pp. 1071–1101). Netherlands: Springer.

Huber, S. G. (2004). School leadership and leadership development: Adjusting leadership theories and development programs to values and the core purpose of school. *Journal of Educational Administration, 6*(42), 669–684.

Jensen, B. (2012). *Learning from the best school systems in Asia: KOF Index of Globalisation.* Grattan Report. Retrieved from http://globalization.kof.ethz.ch/static/pdf/rankings_2012.pdf (last accessed on 12 April 2015).

Kankaraš, M. and Moors, G. (2013). Analysis of cross-cultural comparability of PISA 2009 scores. *Journal of Cross-Cultural Psychology, 45*(3), 381–399.

Knodel, P., Martens, K. and Niemann, D. (2013). PISA as an ideational roadmap for policy change: exploring Germany and England in a comparative perspective. *Globalisation, Societies and Education, 11*(3), 421–441.

Kreiner, S., and Christensen, K. B. (2014). Analyses of model fit and robustness. A new look at the PISA scaling model underlying ranking of countries according to reading literacy. *Psychometrika, 79*(2), 210–231.

Leithwood, K., Harris, A. and Hopkins, D. (2008). Seven strong claims about successful school leadership. *School leadership and management, 28*(1), 27–42.

Lenkeit, J. and Caro, D. H. (2014). Performance status and change: Measuring education system effectiveness with data from PISA 2000–2009. *Educational Research and Evaluation, 20(2)*, 146–174.

Louis, K. S., Dretzke, B. and Wahlstrom, K. (2010a). How does leadership affect student achievement? Results from a national US survey. *School Effectiveness and School Improvement, 21(3)*, 315–336.

Louis, K. S., Leithwood, K., Wahlstrom, K. L. and Anderson, S. E. (2010b). *Learning from leadership: Investigating the links to improved student learning*. Minneapolis: The Wallace Foundation. Retrieved from www.cehd.umn.edu/carei/Leadership/Learning-from-Leadership_Final-Research-Report_July-2010.pdf (accessed 14 August 2011).

Meyer, H.-D. and Benavot, A. (2013). *PISA, power, and policy: The emergence of global educational governance*. London: Symposium.

Mourshed, M., Chinezi, C. and Barber, M. (2010). *How the world's most improved school systems keep getting better*. London: McKinsey & Company.

Murphy, D. (2014). Issues with PISA's use of its data in the context of International Education Policy Convergence. *Policy Futures in Education, 12(7)*, 893–916.

Murphy, S. (2010). The pull of PISA: Uncertainty, influence, and ignorance. *Inter-American Journal of Education for Democracy, 3(1)*, 27–44.

OECD. (1999). *Measuring student knowledge and skills: A new framework for assessment*. Paris, France: OECD Publishing.

———. (2003). *Student Engagement at School: A Sense of Belonging and Participation: Results from PISA 2000.*, Paris: OECD.

———. (2011). *Lessons from PISA for the United States, strong performers and successful reformers in education*. OECD Publishing. Retrieved from http://dx.doi.org/10.1787/9789264096660-en (last accessed on 12 April 2015).

———. (2013). *Synergies for better learning: an international perspective on evaluation and assessment*. Retrieved from http://www.oecd.org/edu/school/Evaluation_and_Assessment_Synthesis_Report.pdf (last accessed on 12 April 2015).

Ozga, J. (2012). Introduction: Assessing PISA. *European Educational Research Journal, 11(2)*, 166–171.

Pang, N. S. K. (2006). *Globalization: Educational research, change and reform*. Hong Kong: Chinese University Press.

Reynolds, D. (2010). *Failure free education*. London: Routledge.

Ripley, A. (2013). *The smartest kids in the world and how they got that way*. New York: Simon and Schuster.

Sahlberg, P. (2014). *Finnish Lessons 2.0: What can the world learn from educational change in Finland?* New York: Teachers College Press.

Sellar, S. and Lingard, B. (2013a). Looking East: Shanghai, PISA 2009 and the reconstitution of reference societies in the global education policy field. *Comparative Education, 49(4)*, 464–485.

———. (2013b). The OECD and the expansion of PISA: New global modes of governance in education. *British Educational Research Journal, 40(6)*, 917–936.

———. (2013c). The OECD and global governance in education. *Journal of Education Policy, 28(5)*, 710–725.

Sergiovanni, T. (1999). *Rethinking leadership: A collection of articles*. Arlington Heights, IL: Skylight Professional Development.

———. (2001). *Leadership: What's in it for schools?* London: Routledge.

Sharratt, L. and Fullan, M. (Eds.). (2009). *Realization: The change imperative for deepening district-wide reform*. Thousand Oaks: Corwin Press.

Sjøberg, S. (2012). PISA: Politics, fundamental problems and intriguing results. *Recherches en Education, 14(1)*, 1–21.

Spillane, J. P. (2006). *Distributed leadership*. San Francisco, CA: Jossey-Bass.

Spillane, J. P., Halverson, R. and Diamond, J. B. (2004). Towards a theory of leadership practice: A distributed perspective. *Journal of Curriculum Studies, 31(1)*, 3–34.

Spillane, J. P., Halverson, R. and Drummond, J. (2001). Investigating school leadership practice: A distributed perspective. *Educational Researcher, 30(3)*, 23–28.

Stewart, V. (2012). *A World Class Education-learning from international models of excellence and innovation*. Alexandria, VA: ASCD.

Stewart, W. (2013). *Is Pisa fundamentally flawed?* Retrieved from http://www.tes.co.uk/article.aspx?storycode=6344672 (last accessed on 12 April 2015).

Tee Ng, P. (2012). Mentoring and coaching educators in the Singapore education system. *International Journal of Mentoring and Coaching in Education, 1(1)*, 24–35.

Tucker, M. (2011). *Surpassing Shanghai: An agenda for American education built on the world's leading systems*. Cambridge: Harvard Education Press.

Walker, A., Bryant, D. and Lee, M. (2013). International patterns in principal preparation: Commonalities and variations in pre-service programmes. *Educational Management Administration and Leadership, 41(4)*, 405–434.

Waldow, F., Takayama, K. and Sung, Y. K. (2014). Rethinking the pattern of external policy referencing: Media discourses over the 'Asian Tigers', PISA success in Australia, Germany and South Korea. *Comparative Education, 50(3)*, 302–321.

SECTION 1

System Level

Leading Futures:
System Transformation

As the tide turns in the ocean, the movement might not be apparent or indeed visible to the naked eye. Yet a major shift is quietly and irrecoverably taking place. More than a decade into the new millennium little, it appears, has radically changed in many educational systems around the world despite much speculation about the potential potent forces of global, economic and technological changes. Many of our schools and school systems look largely as they did a decade or so before. But the underlying pace of technological change is quickening and with it the absolute certainty that dramatic change is inevitable. The question is not *if* the educational tide will turn, but it is exactly *when*.

Even though we glibly accept that 21st century learning will require different skills from those cherished only a few decades ago, many countries and systems are still holding fast to the educational practices and pedagogies of a previous age. Conversely, countries such as Singapore, Indonesia and Hong Kong have changed their curriculum to make more room for creativity and innovation. In contrast other systems are relentlessly increasing the external pressure on professionals in the vain hope of securing better outcomes. The Global Education Reform Movement (GERM) with its emphasis on standards and standardization seems an unstoppable force. While accountability in and of itself is not necessarily a bad thing, countries that have used external accountability and standardization to secure lasting improvement, such as England and the USA, are yet to see a sustainable return on this investment.

In the East, the pressure to perform at the highest level is even more acute than in systems in the West. The innate and fierce desire among parents, teachers and young people to succeed is far more powerful than any external driver or accountability measure. The expectations of educational success in Singapore, Hong Kong, Shanghai and Korea define not only what young people do in life but also their worth as a human being. Some would argue that this pressure is too great and that young people are locked into 'educational misery' (Zhao, 2014).

So is it just an accident that most of the 'top-performing' education systems in the world are located in Asia? Is it just serendipity that more Asian young people are destined for higher education than their Western counterparts? Chapter 1 of this book sheds some light on these questions and Yong Zhao lays down in it the gauntlet by challenging the way in which Programme for International Student Assessment (PISA) scores and international rankings are driving educational policy. Using China as a reference point, he offers an important critique of the inaccuracies of the assumption made about its education system and raises some important questions about the nature and consequences of PISA tests. The main question he raises is how far policy-makers and policy-making should be guided by international benchmarking that paradoxically could restrict innovation and change. He also calls into question, how far 'educational authoritarianism' should be glorified and celebrated.

In Chapter 2, Janet H. Chrispeels looks at policy formation and enactment in various countries and compares Singapore and the USA in order to illustrate how policy formation and enactment varies across systems. This chapter looks at the issue of creating a strong policy–practice connection and also focuses on the facilitation of policy implementation. A comparison is made between three different education systems: Ontario, Singapore and California. This analysis underlines the need for policy coherence and argues for focused professional development to support the policy, if it is to influence practice. This chapter concludes that the most effective policy-making must be a co-constructed process, with educators playing a centrally important role in shaping design and implementation.

In Chapter 3, Isak Froumin and Anatoly Kasprzhak continue the discussion about co-construction of a policy. They focus on the way in which innovative schools have played an important role in educational policy-making in Russia. In contrast to the 'top-down' or linear model of policy-making, innovative schools are charged with the responsibility of breaking new ground, experimenting and bringing forward new ideas for the entire system. To work effectively, they argue that this model necessitates that the innovative schools have to have a strong alliance with the government. In other words, they have to be part of a co-construction of policy-making in order to transform the system. Often there is a delineation made between 'top-down' and 'bottom-up' policy-making processes. In this chapter, the authors argue that innovative schools provide an integration of these two approaches and offer other systems an example of how to engage practitioners authentically and effectively in the policy-making process.

In Chapter 4, Paula Kwan traces the history of policy-making in Hong Kong since the handover to China in 1997. She looks at the policies on leadership development to highlight some gaps in the 'policy to practice' relationship and argues that policies need to really take account of how far they achieve the desired outcomes. She argues that over the past two decades, Hong Kong has undergone a large number of changes against a unique politically transitional context as well as introducing a number of reform initiatives that mirror international trends. She notes that some of the initiatives are meant to serve political rather than educational purposes. She outlines how policies concerning leadership preparation, for example, are constrained by school-specific circumstances and context. This chapter concludes by offering some prospective thoughts on ways of improving leadership development for all leaders in the system while noting that the group-oriented and high power distance culture in Hong Kong schools constitutes a considerable impediment to innovative leadership practices.

Chapter 5 by Anthony Mackay and Albert Bertani explores the challenges of leadership in the 21st century. The authors call for a new paradigm of leadership where school leaders as system leaders are pivotal in transformation and change. They argue that new educational leaders must create the conditions for radical transformation and to meet the needs of a changing society. In short, they must have a range of skills and attributes that ensure that they can innovate within the system to improve the system. Like the previous chapter, the emphasis is placed upon leadership as activism and school leaders being the drivers of policy formation and implementation. The authors conclude that the new system leaders will need to take risks and to overcome the entrenched position of policy-makers in order to truly transform the system.

Chapter 6 by Carol Campbell provides a master class in how to secure reform at scale. It provides an analysis of system wide improvement in Ontario and argues that while the governance of education may function in a tri-level manner (government, district/network, school), the nature, influence and practices of professionals should not be confined to, or constrained by, structural notions of 'top', 'middle' or 'bottom' in the leadership of educational change. The lessons from Ontario underline that system improvement involves leadership through both formal governance structures and through more organic professional networks connecting individual and collective leadership throughout the entire education system.

Reference

Zhao, Y. (2014), *Who's Afraid of the Big Bad Dragon: Why China has the Best (and Worst) Education System in the World*, San Francisco: Jossey-Bass.

1

Who's Afraid of PISA: The Fallacy of International Assessments of System Performance*

Yong Zhao

PISA might have met its waterloo in Shanghai. The international assessment programme operated by Organisation for Economic Cooperation and Development (OECD) that has evolved into a de facto shadow government shaping an education policy around the world may soon see its force disappearing, even ending. Ironically, what is poised to undo PISA's influence is its newly minted and massively celebrated education star—Shanghai, which is considering dropping out of the programme. While PISA had always been criticized and questioned, it was not until Shanghai was granted the best education system by PISA in 2008 that the criticism and questioning began to gain momentum. More importantly, while prior questioning was mostly about its technical inadequacies, Shanghai exposed PISA's fundamental flaw: an outdated definition of educational quality.

---

* Adapted from the book by Zhao, *Who's Afraid of Big Bad Dragon: Why China Has the Best (and Worst) Education in the World*.

When Finland was the superstar in the PISA world, most people accepted it and the Finns were mostly in agreement and proud. But when Shanghai replaced Finland, there were more doubts outside and little celebration inside China. The Chinese parents, students, teachers, education leaders, researchers and policy-makers generally hold a much less rosy view of their education than OECD. In fact, the Chinese education, Shanghai included, has been cursed as the world's worst education system for a long time. Numerous efforts have been devised and implemented to reform the system, aiming to dismantle the very elements that PISA has praised as primary contributing factors of Shanghai's success.

Illusion of Excellence

In other words, the Shanghai success is but an illusion created by PISA. Supporting the illusion are simply three test scores. It is utterly shocking and embarrassing to see some otherwise rational and well-educated people (or at least they should be) in powerful positions believe that these three test scores show the quality of their education systems, the effectiveness of their teachers, the ability of their students and the future prosperity of their society. Nonetheless, PISA has somehow garnered the power to create arresting illusions of excellence in the education universe.

The power originates from its bold claim to assess "the extent to which students near the end of compulsory education have acquired key knowledge and skills that are essential for full participation in modern societies" (OECD, 2013:15). Moreover, PISA claims to find educational stars by identifying which education systems better prepare their children for 'full participation in modern societies', as measured by PISA scores. The goal is for educational systems to learn from "the highest-performing and most rapidly improving school systems" (OECD, 2013:15).

The claims are as bold as they are illusory, but what if there are *serious problems* with the PISA data? What if the statistical techniques used to compile them are *utterly wrong* and based on a *profound conceptual error?* Suppose the whole idea of being able to accurately rank such diverse education systems is *meaningless, madness* (Stewart, 2013). The answers are sadly yes to all these questions. PISA has major technical and conceptual flaws in its composition of the tests, administering of the tests, use of statistical techniques to generate country rankings and definition of education outcomes. Svend Kreiner, Professor of biomedical statistics at the University of Copenhagen, questions the appropriateness of the model that PISA uses to produce its country rankings. PISA uses the Rasch model, a widely used psychometric model named after the late Danish mathematician and statistician Georg Rasch. For this model to work properly, certain requirements must be met. But according to Kreiner, who studied under Rasch and has worked with his model for 40 years, PISA's application does not meet those requirements. In an article published in *Psychometrika*, Kreiner and Karl Bang Christensen show that the Rasch model does not fit the reading literacy data of PISA, and thus the resulting country rankings are not robust. As a result, rankings of countries can vary a great deal over different subsets. Denmark, for example, can rank anywhere between the 5th and 36th position out of 56 countries (Kreiner and Christensen, 2014). This means that (PISA) comparisons between countries are meaningless.

Kreiner was not the first or the only scholar to raise questions about PISA's technical flaws. In 2007, a collection of nearly 20 independent scholars took apart PISA's methodology, examining how it was designed; how it sampled, collected and presented data and what its outcomes were. Then the researchers compared the test's real-life validity to its claims (Hopmann et al., 2007). Almost all of them "raise[d] serious doubts concerning the theoretical and methodological standards applied within PISA, and particularly to its most prominent by-products, its national league tables or analyses of school systems" (Hopmann et al., 2007:10). Some of their conclusions were as follows:

1. PISA is by design culturally biased and methodologically constrained to a degree which prohibits accurate representations of what actually is achieved in and by schools. Nor is there any

proof that what it covers is a valid conceptualization of what every student should know.

2. The products of most public value, the national league tables, are based on so many weak links that they should be abandoned right away. If only a few of the methodological issues raised in this volume are on target, the league tables depend on assumptions about the validity and reliability which are unattainable.

3. The widely discussed by-products of PISA, such as the analyses of 'good schools', 'good instruction' or differences between school systems, go far beyond what a cautious approach to these data allows for. They are more often than not speculative (Hopmann et al., 2007:12–13).

While the dispute over PISA's technical flaws continues, some argue that even if PISA did everything right technically, it 'still' could not possibly claim to be measuring the quality of entire education systems, let alone their students' ability to live in the modern world. "There are very few things you can summarise with a number and yet PISA claims to be able to capture a country's entire education system in just three of them," wrote Dr Hugh Morrison of Queen's University Belfast in Northern Ireland. "It can't be possible. It is madness" (Morrison, 2013). Morrison, a mathematician, does not think that the Rasch model should be used at all. He argues that "at the heart of Rasch, and other similar statistical models, lies a fundamental, insoluble mathematical error that renders PISA rankings 'valueless' and means that the programme 'will never work'" (Stewart, 2013). The problem of PISA, according to Morrison, violates a central principle of measurement drawn from physicist Niels Bohr's work: The entity measured cannot be divorced from the measuring instrument. Morrison illustrates his point with an example. Suppose Einstein and a student both produced a perfect score on a test. "Surely to claim that the pupil has the same mathematical ability as Einstein is to communicate ambiguously?" The unambiguous communication would be: "Einstein and the pupil have the same mathematical ability relative to this particular test. Mathematical ability, indeed any ability, is not an intrinsic property of the individual; rather, it's a joint property of the individual and the measuring instrument" (Morrison, 2013). In a nutshell, Morrison's point is that PISA scores students' ability to complete tasks included in the test, *not* their general ability to understand and succeed.

Even if PISA did measure cognitive abilities as accurately as it claims to, those abilities only span three domains: math, reading and science. PISA makes the assumption that these skills are universally valuable. In other words, as Svein Sjøberg, Professor of science education at Norway's University of Oslo, points out that PISA "assumes that the challenges of tomorrow's world are more or less identical for young people across countries and cultures" and, thus, promotes "kind of universal, presumably culture-free, curriculum as decided by the OECD and its experts." This assumption is mistaken. "Although life in many countries do [sic] have some similar traits, one can hardly assume that the 15-year olds in e.g. Japan, Greece, Mexico and Norway are preparing for the same challenges and need identical life skills and competencies" (Sjøberg, 2012:7).

Even if cognitive skills in math, science and reading were the most important skills in the universe, they would not—'could' not—be the only skills that an educational system should cultivate. Skills and knowledge in other domains, such as the humanities, social sciences, foreign languages, history, geography, physical education, etc. (Sjøberg, 2012:3), play a crucial role if citizens of any country are to live a fulfilling life. So do non-cognitive skills: social-emotional skills, curiosity, creativity, resilience, engagement, passion and a host of other personality traits. In fact, many would argue that talents, skills, knowledge and creativity in domains outside math, science and reading are at least as important, perhaps even more important, to live successfully in the new world. Henry Levin, Professor of economics of education at Teachers College, Columbia University, reviews empirical evidence that shows the essential value of non-cognitive skills to work and life in his article 'More Than Just Test Scores' published in the journal *Prospects: Quarterly Review of Comparative Education* (Levin, 2012).

Thus, even if PISA were methodologically sound, conceptually correct and properly administered, its only unambiguous conclusion would be that 15-year-old students in any education system received the highest scores in math, reading and science in 2009 and 2012. Leaping from the highest PISA score in three subjects to the best education system in the world is too big a jump for any logical person—unless the purpose of education is defined as doing well on the PISA.

Since no one, not the Chinese and not even the PISA team (I hope), would define the purpose of education as achieving good PISA scores, making China the world's model of educational excellence just because some of its 15 year olds received the highest PISA scores is not only inaccurate but misleading. The excellence is a simple illusion created by the PISA league tables.

Romanticized Misery

PISA's explanation of what contributed to Shanghai's excellence is considered delusional. The factors promoted by PISA operators have been identified as the culprits of China's education miseries. Andreas Schleicher, for example, has on many occasions promoted the idea that Chinese students take responsibilities for their own learning, while in 'many countries, students were quick to blame everyone but themselves'. France is his prime example:

> More than three-quarters of the students in France ... said the course material was simply too hard, two-thirds said the teacher did not get students interested in the material, and half said their teacher did not explain the concepts well or they were just unlucky.

Students in Shanghai felt just the opposite, believing that "they will succeed if they try hard and they trust their teachers to help them succeed." Schleicher maintains that this difference in attitude contributed to the gap between Shanghai, ranked 1st, and France, ranked 25th. "The fact that students in some countries consistently believe that achievement is mainly a product of hard work, rather than inherited intelligence, suggests that education and its social context can make a difference in instilling the values that foster success in education" (Schleicher, 2013a).

Self-condemnation Does Not Lead to High Scores

Schleicher got the numbers right, but his interpretation is questionable. There are plenty of countries that have higher PISA rankings than France, yet reported similar attitudes. For example, more students in 8th ranked Liechtenstein and 9th ranked Switzerland (over 54%, in contrast to 51% in France) said their teachers did not explain the concepts well.[1] The percentage of students attributing their math failure to 'bad luck' was almost identical across the three countries: 48.6 per cent in Liechtenstein, 48.5 per cent in Switzerland and 48.1 per cent in France. The difference in the percentage of students claiming the course material was too hard was not that significant: 62.2 per cent in Liechtenstein, 69.9 per cent in Switzerland and 77.1 per cent in France. Neither was the difference in the percentage of students saying that "the teachers did not get students interested in the material": 61.8 per cent in Liechtenstein, 61.1 per cent in Switzerland and 65.2 per cent in France.

Moreover, the PISA report seems to contradict Schleicher's reasoning because it finds that students with lower scores tend to take more responsibility. Overall, the groups of students who tend to perform more poorly in mathematics—girls and socio-economically disadvantaged students—feel more responsible for failing mathematics tests than students who generally perform at higher levels (OECD, 2013:62).

The degree to which students take responsibility for failing in math or blaming outside factors does not have much to do with their PISA performance. Conversely, countries where students are more likely to blame teachers are not necessarily poor performers.

Using Shanghai as the cut-off, the countries with the lowest percentage (below 35%) of students blaming their teachers for failing to explain the concepts well are Korea, Kazakhstan, Japan, Singapore, Malaysia, Russian Federation, Chinese Taipei, Albania, Vietnam and Shanghai. An almost identical list of countries has the lowest percentage (below 41%) of students blaming their teachers for not getting their students interested in the material: Kazakhstan, Japan, Albania, Singapore, Thailand, Malaysia, Russian Federation,

Montenegro and Shanghai. Combining responses to both questions, that is, "my teacher did explain the concept well this week" or "my teacher did not get students interested in the material", results in a list of top 10 countries where students are least and most likely to blame their teachers. Among the countries whose students are least likely to blame teachers are some of the best (Shanghai, Japan, Korea, Singapore, Taipei and Vietnam), worst (Kazakhstan, Albania and Malaysia) and average (Russian Federation) PISA performers. Students who are most likely to blame teachers come from countries that earn the top PISA scores (Liechtenstein, Switzerland and Germany) and middle-level PISA scores (Norway, Sweden, Italy, Slovenia, France, Austria and the Czech Republic).

Self-condemnation as Result of Authoritarian Education

What's intriguing is that all the countries whose students are least likely to blame their teachers have a more authoritarian cultural tradition than the countries whose students are most likely to blame theirs. On the first list, Singapore, Korea, Chinese Taipei, Shanghai-China, Japan and Vietnam share the Confucian cultural tradition. And although Japan and Korea are now considered full democracies, the rest of the countries on the list are not.[2] In contrast, the list of countries with the highest percentage of students blaming their teachers for their failures ranked much higher in the democracy index. Norway ranked first, Sweden ranked second and Switzerland was at number seven. With the single exception of Italy, all 10 countries where students were most likely to blame their teachers ranked above 30 on the democracy index (and Italy ranked 32nd).

One conclusion to draw from this analysis: Students in more authoritarian education systems are more likely to blame themselves and less likely to question the authority—the teacher—than students in more democratic educational systems. An authoritarian educational system demands obedience and does not tolerate questioning of authority. Just like authoritarian parents (Baumrind, 1966), authoritarian education systems also have externally defined high expectations that are not necessarily accepted by students intrinsically but require mandatory conformity through rigid rules and severe punishment for non-compliance. More importantly, they work very hard to convince children to blame themselves for failing to meet the expectations. As a result, they produce students with low confidence and low self-esteem.

On the PISA survey of students' self-concept in math, students in Japan, Taipei, Korea, Vietnam, Macao-China, Hong Kong-China and Shanghai-China had the lowest self-concepts in the world, despite their high PISA math scores (OECD, 2013). A high proportion of students in these educational systems were worried that they 'will get poor grades in mathematics'. More than 70 per cent of students in Korea, Taipei, Singapore, Vietnam, Shanghai-China and Hong Kong-China—in contrast to less than 50 per cent in Austria, United States, Germany, Denmark, Sweden and the Netherlands— 'agreed' or 'strongly agreed' that they worry about getting poor grades in math (OECD, 2013).

Emperors' Ploy to Deny Responsibility

In other words, what Schleicher has been praising as Shanghai's secret to educational excellence is simply the outcome of an authoritarian education. In an authoritarian system, the ruler and the ruling class have much to gain when people believe it is their own effort, and nothing more, that makes them successful. No difference in innate abilities or social circumstances matters as long as they work hard. If they cannot succeed, they only have themselves to blame. This is an excellent and convenient way for the authorities to deny any responsibility for social equity and justice, and to avoid accommodating differently talented people. It is a great ploy that helped the emperors to convince people to accept the inequalities they were born into and obey the rules. It was also designed to give people a sense of hope, no matter how slim, that they can change their own fate by being indoctrinated with the exams.

PISA's glorification of educational authoritarianism goes beyond its romanticization of the misery that children suffer in authoritarian education. Because some authoritarian education systems seem to generate better PISA rankings, it has been concluded that systemic arrangements designed to enforce government-prescribed, uniform standards upon all children, should be emulated by the rest of the world. "High-performing school systems also share clear and ambitious standards across the board. Everyone knows what is required to get a given qualification," writes Schleicher (2013b). "This remains one of the most powerful system-level predictors in PISA."

In *Surpassing Shanghai: An Agenda for American Education Built on the World's Leading Systems*, Tucker (2011) explains what high-performing countries do and the USA does *not* do:

> Virtually all high performing countries have a system of gateways marking the key transition point from basic education to job training to the work force. The national examinations at the end of the upper-secondary school are generally—but not always—the same examinations that universities in that country use for admissions.

The advantages of such a system, Tucker notes, are numerous:

> In countries with gateway exam systems of this sort, every student has a very strong incentive to take tough courses and to work hard in school. A student who does not do that will not earn the credentials needed to achieve her dream, whether that dream is becoming a brain surgeon or an auto mechanic. Because the exams are scored externally, the student knows that the only way to move on is to meet the standard. Because they are national or provincial standards, the exams cannot be gamed. Because the exams are of a very high quality, they cannot be "test prepped"; the only way to succeed on them is to actually master the material. And because the right parties were involved in creating the exams, students know that the credentials they earn will be honoured; when their high school say they are "college and career ready," colleges and employees will agree. (Tucker, 2011)

But Tucker is wrong on all counts, at least in the case of China. Students may work hard, but they do not necessarily take tough courses. They take courses that prepare them for the exams or courses that only matter for the exams. Students do not move on to meet a high standard, but to prepare for the exams, which can be gamed, and have often been. Teachers guess possible items, companies sell answers and wireless cheating devices to students, and students engage in all sorts of elaborate cheating. In 2013, a riot broke because a group of students in the Hubei Province were stopped from executing the cheating scheme that their parents purchased to ease their college entrance exam (Moore, 2013).

Tucker's assertion, that "because the exams are of very high quality, they cannot be 'test prepped'," is completely untrue. Chinese schools *exist* to help students in test preparation. Every class, every teacher, every school is about preparing for the exams. In most schools, the last year of high school is reserved exclusively for test preparation. No new content is taught. All students do, the entire year, is take practice tests and learn test-taking skills. Good schools often help students exhaust all possible ways in which a specific content might show up in an exam. Schools that have earned a reputation for preparing students for college exams have published their practice test papers and made a fortune. A large proportion of publications for children in China are practice test papers.

Even if Tucker were right, the system he glorifies hinders the development of creative and entrepreneurial talents in a number of ways. First, national standards and national curriculum—enforced by high-stakes testing—can at best teach students what is prescribed by the curriculum and expected by the standards. This system fails to expose students to content and skills in other areas. As a result, students talented in other areas never have the opportunity to *discover* those talents. Students with broader interests are discouraged, not rewarded. The system results in a population with similar skills in a narrow spectrum of talents. But especially in today's society, innovation and creativity are needed in many areas, some as yet undiscovered. Innovation and creativity come from cross-fertilization across different disciplines. A narrow educational experience hardly provides children with opportunities to examine an issue from multiple disciplines.

Second, examinations such as the PISA assess cognitive skills. But creativity and entrepreneurship have a lot more to do with non-cognitive skills (Zhao, 2012). Confidence, resilience, grit, mindset, personality traits, social skills and motivation have been found to be at *least* as important as cognitive skills in the workplace (Levin, 2012; Brunello and Schlotter, 2010). The Chinese educational system motivates students to spend all their time preparing for the examinations and gives them almost no time to cultivate non-cognitive skills and traits. Meanwhile, the constant ranking and sorting continually put students in stressful situations that make them less confident.

Third, examinations reward one's abilities to find the correct answers and give those answers in expected ways. To obtain high scores, students need to learn to guess what the examiner wants and provide answers that will please him or her. This finding and delivering of predetermined answers is antithetical to creativity, which requires the ability to come up with new solutions and pose questions that have never been asked.

Chinese students are extremely good at well-defined problems. That is, as long as they know what they need to do to meet the expectations, and they have examples to follow, they do great. But in less defined situations, without routines and formulas to fall back on, they have great difficulty. In other words, they are good at solving existing problems in predictable ways, but not at coming up with radical new solutions or inventing new problems to solve.

Fourth, a gateway system such as China's educational system replaces students' intrinsic motivation with extrinsic, utilitarian motivation. Instead of caring about what they can learn, they care about what they can get by demonstrating to the authority that they have learned what the authority wants them to learn. Getting the credential is more important than actually learning—which explains why cheating at exams is rampant. Moreover, it is possible to impose basic skills and knowledge on students without them being the least bit interested or passionate about the subject. Thus, the Chinese system can successfully impose on students the skills and knowledge necessary for performing well in tests such as the PISA, which measures skills and content at the basic level. But no one can force those students to be creative or seek greatness if they have neither the interest nor the passion to do so.

In a nutshell, the Chinese education, a perfect incarnation of educational authoritarianism, is a powerful way to homogenize individuals by discouraging any pursuit that does not serve the emperor or government. This is one of the reasons China did not have the industrialists, naturalists, technologists, inventors and entrepreneurs it needed to start an industrial revolution. These professions were all disgraceful, compared to the scholar-official. Education, in the traditional Chinese perspective, should not be applied to help cultivate these less honourable professions. Education in China is, in essence, a process through which those willing to comply are homogenized, and those unwilling or unable to comply—but quite possibly talented or interested in other, non-scholarly pursuits— are eliminated.

Is This the End?

If I were a conspiracy theorist, I would suggest that PISA is a secret plan of Western powers to derail China's education reforms. China has been working hard to introduce numerous significant education reforms since the 1990s to overcome the apparent shortcomings of its education system in order to cultivate a more diverse, creative and entrepreneurial citizenry. Such a citizenry is urgently needed for China's successful transition from a labour-intensive economy to one that relies on innovation—a transition, China must make for its future development. The Chinese exam-oriented education has long been recognized as the culprit for limiting China's capacity for producing creative and diverse talents. Just as China's education reforms began to touch the core of its traditional education—the *Gaokao* or College Entrance Exam and the wide use of testing at all levels of education—PISA announced that the Chinese education is the best in the world. And the exam system, including the Gaokao, is glorified as a major contributor to China's success, making it difficult for the Chinese to continue the battle against testing. Even Marc Tucker, the President and CEO of the National Centre on Education and the Economy and one of the most prominent PISA proponents who has on many occasions expressed unequivocal admiration of China's education, admits:

> [M]any people in China are upset about the success of Shanghai on the PISA league tables, because they think that success will blunt the edge of their fight to dethrone the Gaokao from its premier position as the sole determinant of advancement in Chinese society. They see the Gaokao as enforcing an outdated ideal of education, one that rewards memorization and rote learning over understanding and the ability to apply mastery of complex skills to real world problems, particularly problems requiring innovation and creativity. (Tucker, 2014)

Putting someone on a pedestal is an effective way to ensure he or she does not veer far from his or her previous behaviours because any deviation could tarnish the bestowed honour. The Chinese call such actions *pengsha* or 'killing with flattery'. Pengsha derives from a story recorded almost 2,000 years ago: A nobleman rides on a beautiful horse and wins great praises from admiring onlookers. Enjoying the flattery, the nobleman keeps on riding till the horse dies from exhaustion.

But China, including Shanghai, refuses to be killed with flattery. 'Not interested in #1 on International Tests, Focusing on Reducing Academic Burden: Shanghai May Drop Out of PISA' is the headline of a popular newspaper in Shanghai (Wang, 2014). Published on 7 March 2014, the story reports that Shanghai "is considering to withdraw from the next round of PISA in 2015" because "Shanghai does not need so-called '#1 schools'," said Yi Houqin, a high-level official of Shanghai Education Commission. "What it needs are schools that follow sound educational principles, respect principles of students' physical and psychological development, and lay a solid foundation for students' lifelong development," says the article, quoting Mr Yi.

Shanghai has been developing and piloting its own system-level assessment, called 'green evaluation'. This assessment takes into consideration a much broader set of outcomes and indicators than PISA (Zhao, 2013). It includes student engagement, psychological and emotional well-being, physical fitness and academic performance in a variety of subjects beyond math, science and language. The Chinese Ministry of Education has been working with Shanghai to expand the experiment to the entire nation. Does this mean the end of PISA, at least in Shanghai?

References

Baumrind, D. (1966). Effects of authoritative parental control on child behavior. *Child Development*, *37*(4), 887–907.

Brunello, G. and Schlotter, M. (2010). *The effect of non cognitive skills and personality traits on labour market outcomes*. Analytical Report for the European Commission. European Expert Network on Economics of Education. Available at http://www.epis.pt/downloads/dest_15_10_2010.pdf

Hopmann, S. T., Brinek, G. and Retzl, M. (2007). *PISA zufolge PISA—PISA according to PISA*. Wiewn: Lit Verlag.

Kreiner, S. and Christensen, K. B. (2014). Analyses of model fit and robustness: A new look at the pisa scaling model underlying ranking of countries according to reading literacy. *Psychometrika*, *79*(2), 210–231.

Levin, H. M. (2012). More than just test scores. *Prospects*, *42*(3), 269–284.

Moore, M. (2013). Riot after Chinese teachers try to stop pupils cheating. *The Telegraph*. Retrieved from www.telegraph.co.uk. Accessed on 21 January 2014.

Morrison, H. (2013). *Pisa 2012 major flaw exposed, pace N. Ireland education weblog*. Retrieved from   https://paceni.wordpress.com/2013/12/01/pisa-2012-major-flaw-exposed/. Accessed on 13 May 2014.

OECD. (2013). *PISA 2012* results—*Ready to learn: Students engagement, drive, and self-beliefs* (Volume III). PISA: Paris.

Schleicher, A. (2013a). Are the Chinese cheating in PISA or are we cheating ourselves? *Education Today*. Retrieved from http://oecdeducationtoday.blogspot.com/2013/12/are-chinese-cheating-in-pisa-or-are-we.html. Accessed on 12 May 2014.

———. (2013b). What we learn from the PISA 2012 results, OECD. *Education Today*. Retrieved from oecdeducationtoday.blogspot.com/ Accessed on 13 May 2014.

Sjøberg, S. (2012). PISA: Politique, problèmes fondamentaux et résultats surprenants [PISA: Politics, fundamental problems and intriguing results]. *La Revue, Recherches en Education*, *14*, 1–21.

Stewart, W. (2013). *Is Pisa fundamentally flawed?* Retrieved from http://www.tes.co.uk/article.aspx?storycode=6344672. Accessed on 13 May 2014.

The Economist Intelligence Unit. (2013). *Democracy index 2012: Democracy at a standstill*. The Economist Intelligence Unit: London.

Tucker, M. (2011). *Surpassing Shanghai: An agenda for american education built on the world's leading systems*. Harvard Education Press: Cambridge.

———. (2014). *Chinese lessons: Shanghai's rise to the top of the PISA league tables*. National Center on Education and the Economy: Washington DC.

Wang, W. (2014). *Not interested in #1 on International Tests, Focusing on Reducing Academic Burden: Shanghai May Drop Out of PISA*. Retrieved from http://www.chinanews.com/edu/2014/03-07/5925215.shtml. Accessed on 1 February 2015.

Zhao, Y. (2012). *World class learners: Educating creative and entrepreneurial students*. Corwin Press: Thousand Oaks.

———. (2013). *Green evaluation: China's latest reform to deemphasize testing*, in *education in the age of globalization*. Retrieved from http://zhaolearning.com/2013/06/24/green-evaluation-china%E2%80%99s-latest-reform-to-deemphasize-testing/. Accessed on 15 March 2014.

2

Economic Development and Competitiveness: A Primary Driver of School Reform Policy in the USA

Janet H. Chrispeels

With globalization and shifting economic dynamics around the world, there is growing pressure on educational systems and individual schools within each system to enhance learning and achievement for all students. In today's flat world, governments recognize the need to ensure more students are able to assume the role of *knowledge workers* if their economies are to thrive, grow and remain competitive. To foster the development of today's learners, Spillane et al. (2002:387) have argued that 'reformers are using public policy to press for fundamental and complex changes in extant school and classroom behaviours' and to redefine what counts as teaching and learning practices. This redefinition requires educators at both the system and the school levels to understand that how well schools prosper in making these changes in large measure also depends on how well the system modifies its policies, practices and supports.

Public education policies are now judged by how well students perform not just against national but also international benchmarks, which unfortunately can diminish other important educational goals. Furthermore, the policy path needed to achieve economic as well as teaching and learning aims is not always straightforward. As the recent release of the Programme for International Student Assessment (PISA) data shows, even though the USA has invested heavily in school reforms—especially through the *No Child Left Behind* policy and the more recent *Race to the Top* initiative—the USA overall continues to perform relatively poorly in the PISA results compared to other OECD countries. Briefly exploring the policy-making process and the educational policies of several countries that have raised achievement may help to provide insights into how educational leaders and policy-makers might collaborate more effectively to achieve desired aims.

The Policy-making Process

Policy is the enactment of the values and beliefs, and the allocation of authority to some groups or practices over others. It is usually formulated to either prompt or constrain action in relation to a perceived problem. In democratic societies, there is usually open debate and tug and pull between different factions who hammer out the specific language of government policy until agreement is sufficiently reached to secure the passage of the policy by majority vote. Over time through the electoral process, the party that holds authority changes, which then leads to changes in the policy. These changes may be minor or substantial, welcomed or unwelcomed. In less democratic societies, policy negotiations within the ruling party can also be fractious, but the debate may not always be as visible, and citizens may not have opportunities to comment or influence the policy-making process. The important point is that changes in who has the authority to enact a policy brings changes in whose values and beliefs will dominate and shape the policy that must be implemented. The implementers, in the case of educational policy, are provincial, state and local educators—administrators and teachers—who may or may not fully agree with or understand the policy as policy-makers intended. This lack of agreement and/or misunderstanding can impede smooth policy implementation.

Policy Instruments

A critical area of interest in the educational policy arena is how a policy enacted at national, provincial or state levels influences school and classroom practices. Policy-makers work to influence the instructional and curricular practices of implementers (educators) through several important mechanisms: mandates, inducements, capacity building, system changing and symbolic levers (Honig, 2006; McDonnell, 2007; McDonnell and Elmore, 1987). These instruments are used in varying combinations and strengths and their effectiveness is closely connected to 'what must happen in practice to achieve policy aims' (Cohen and Hill, 2008:74).

In the past two decades, major educational reform legislation in countries around the world have incorporated all of these levers in hopes of securing changes in schools and in student achievements. Interestingly, even the title of legislation such as *No Child Left Behind* in the USA and *Thinking Schools, Learning Nation* in Singapore represent powerful examples of a symbolic lever. The most current legislation uses a combination of inducements and mandates. The initial focus of the *Thinking Schools* legislation, for example, used inducements for a few select schools to push the creativity, critical thinking and innovation agendas and a system-changing approach by granting these schools much greater autonomy. More recently, the Ministry of Education in Singapore is involving all schools. The critical linchpin of the policy will be the examination system—a mandate. The abolishment of the league tables, which publically ranked schools by performance levels, and the proposals to modify the national exams to include more holistic measures could begin to give meaning to the symbolic lever (Chua, 2013).

In contrast, the *No Child Left Behind* legislation was sweeping in its scope and focused more on mandates that needed to be met to receive the federal funding (inducement). The massive *Literacy and Numeracy* initiative in England, enacted in 1997–2005, used all these levers, but compared to it the US policy gave much more attention to the capacity-building lever. Ontario, Canada, similarly used capacity-building and system-changing levers to restore autonomy and professionalism of schools and teachers after a particularly contentious time between teachers' unions and a conservative government. In Ontario, the results have been a dramatic rise in student achievement and high school graduation rates (OECD, 2011). The OECD report 'Strong Performers, Successful Reforms' argues that the countries around the world that have high levels of student achievement on international benchmarks have all used capacity building and the development and treatment of teachers as professionals as the key to all successful school reforms.

Policy Interpretation

Because policies often result from intense negotiation, the final policy language can be very detailed in some aspects and vague in other areas, leaving considerable room for interpretation by those who are required to implement them. An excellent example is the US educational policy, *No Child Left Behind*, passed in 2001. The policy was very specific in setting the percentage of all subgroups of students (e.g., socio-economically disadvantaged, English learners and students with disabilities) who were to achieve proficiency each year if the school was to be considered as making *Adequate Yearly Progress* (AYP) for all. However, what was to count as proficient and how it would be measured was left to each of the 50 states to determine. This means that each school and district is given an AYP score, but the meaning of the score is not the same across the states since the measures are different. Thus, this federal policy pushed an important national issue to raise the overall achievement and address the achievement gap, and at the same time it also maintained the US tradition of state control of education by allowing states to set the measure of proficiency. This dialectic of pressing for change and allowing autonomy or local adaptation is not a new policy phenomenon and may often account for the problematic implementation of many policy reforms (Spillane et al., 2002).

Thus, a policy provides direction and a framework, but the many details are often filled in through regulations developed by the responsible government agency (Ministries of Education) and also through interpretation and the meaning-making by those 'on the ground', who must bring the policy to life (McLaughlin, 1987). Educators in provinces, states, school districts, schools and classrooms are the critical implementers who must translate the policy to action through the lenses of their own knowledge, experiences and current contexts, what McLaughlin (1990) referred to as mutual adaptation.

More recent studies of policy implementation have called the interaction of school reform policies with local educators as co-construction (Datnow et al., 1998). In other words, local educators play an active role in shaping what the policy looks like in districts and schools through their own sense-making of the policy (Spillane et al., 2002). These authors identified a number of key policy implementation issues where co-construction and sense-making most often occur in the following areas: (a) A school reform is not a linear, technical or a rational process and may encompass competing and even incompatible goals that require local sense-making. (b) Local educators have agency in terms of how they interpret and respond to the reform policy. (c) How educators respond depends on their cognitive structures (beliefs, knowledge and attitudes), the context and the impact of the policy instruments being used. (d) Within each setting there are differing perspectives regarding the reform, with some embracing the proposed change, others wanting to 'wait and see' and still others actively resisting. (e) The existing culture and experiences of the local educators mediate the reform process. (f) Local educators 'read the situation' and interpret what kind of response is needed based on how they view the consequences of acting or not acting to policy mandates. These factors help to explain why policies often do not achieve desired or predicted outcomes that policy-makers have in mind.

The distance between those who enact a policy and those who must implement it often creates considerable tension, especially as educators struggle to understand and make sense of broad, ambiguous and abstract educational goals (Spillane et al., 2002). These tensions can result in complaints that educators are resisting the policy, it is not entering the classroom door and thus, fails to improve student outcomes. On the other hand, educators frequently feel that the policy is either in conflict with their educational beliefs, knowledge and current educational practices or adds additional responsibilities to an already full curriculum plate. Even if policy-makers and the majority of educators are aligned to the policy in terms of values and beliefs, the policy demands may require substantial retooling, time and resources to be successfully implemented. The weakness of the capacity-building component in most pieces of national legislation frequently undermines policy implementation. Given the nature of policy-making and the challenges of implementation, important questions to ask are: What is the evidence of a strong policy–practice connection and what facilitates policy implementation?

Evidence of a Strong Policy or Practice Relationship

Countries vary considerably in the disbursement of educational authority with some systems being highly centralized and others allowing much more local authority. Regardless of the disbursement of authority, important policy drivers in education are financial resources, the curriculum and assessment. The power of assessment is particularly strong and effective in shaping teacher practices when the assessment determines important outcomes such as subsequent school placements and university admissions. When assessment, curriculum frameworks and professional development are aligned, the impact on practice is even greater (Chrispeels, 1997; Cohen, 1995; Cohen and Hill, 2008). A few examples of how a policy influences a practice illustrate the policy or practice relationship. Interestingly all initiatives were influenced by the idea that schools needed to play a larger role in preparing students to be able to be competitive in a global economy.

Ontario, Canada

In 2003, the newly elected Premier Dalton McGuinty launched a major reform of Canada's educational system with the guidance of Michael Fullan and other Canadian educational scholars.

A cornerstone of the policy was to rebuild relations with the teachers union, which had been very tense under the previous administration, with many strikes and work stoppages. The strategy was to increase school-level decision-making and engage teachers as partners in the reform process. Another key component was extensive professional development and capacity building. The government put in place structures for monitoring and integrating data so that it could identify the schools that were doing better, document successful practices that had positive outcomes and then share and scale up these successes. This approach also enhanced teachers' sense of professionalism as they saw their good work being recognized and embraced by the government. The government reallocated resources to schools most in need and put in place interventions for students not at mastery to ensure they would be proficient by the 6th grade.

The large-scale policy changes of Ontario, Canada, created the policy coherence and alignment of the curriculum, professional development and assessment systems, which research suggests are required to change teacher practices and achieve improved outcomes for students. More important, however, was the valuing of teachers and enhancing their professional status through messages of respect, building their capacity and engaging them in the process of reform (Edge, 2013; Levin, 2008). As teachers embraced the policy and put into practise many of the required reforms, the result for Ontario students has been that they now are ranked as one of the top achievers in the PISA comparisons.

Singapore

An important aspect of policy-driven reforms and changes in teachers' practices is to recognize that it does not occur once, but is often an ongoing process. Reforms can be pursued in steps or stages and appear relatively incremental in nature or they can appear as a major break with a previous policy if a dramatic electoral shift occurs. The Ontario example reflects a rather dramatic policy shift, whereas Singapore's educational reform can be portrayed as a series of reforms beginning in 1959 until the present. Each reform was designed to meet a rapidly changing economic environment (OECD, 2011). The OECD report divides Singapore's reform into three phases:

1. Survival Phase—1959 to 1978, designed to provide universal education and eliminate illiteracy, which was at 70 per cent. The goal was achieved, but the quality of teaching remained low.

2. Efficiency Phase—1979 to 1996, recognized the need to move away from the *one size fits all* policy and to create multiple pathways for students to reach their full potential and successfully complete their education. The policy stressed technical education as well as college preparedness and focused on enhancing the quality of teaching and providing schools with high-quality curriculum through a newly established Curriculum Development Institute.

3. Ability-based Aspiration Phase—1997 to present, acknowledged the rise of the global knowledge economy and a felt need for the educational system to focus on innovation, creativity and research if the country was to survive. This new focus was captured in the oratory policy title, *Thinking Schools, Learning Nation*. In this phase, attention has been given to an integrated approach and coordination of education with other key infrastructures such as manpower planning. A centralized, top-down approach was softened to grant schools considerable site-based autonomy, school goal setting and self-monitoring. Nevertheless, the certification and capacity building of teachers and leaders remains largely centralized to ensure high-quality professional development. Both hard skills—math, science and literacy—as well as soft skills are to be addressed in a holistic curriculum. However, the pace of change has been largely shaped by the degree of change in the assessment system. Only as universities and technical institutes have begun to modify their admission standards to include more holistic measures, have schools embraced newer approaches to student learning and engagement.

Singapore represents an important example again of the need for policy coherence and professional development to support the policy if educational policy is to influence practice. The latest initiative is also an interesting case of a somewhat paradoxical policy of pushing the site-level autonomy and divergent pathways for students and at the same time keeping centralized teachers' and leaders' professional development and assessment. It is uncertain, in what ways the centralized components facilitate or limit the autonomous components of the policy.

California: A Case Study from the USA

The previous two cases illustrate examples of fairly close policy or practice connection. There is a general perception that the outcome has been positive for students as measured by international benchmarks; therefore, there is an assumption that designing a policy that influences a practice is beneficial and should be pursued. The desirability of a close policy or practice relationship may depend on how the values embedded in the policy are perceived.

Beginning from mid-1980s to 1997, California initiated a large-scale, system-wide reform with the adoption of new Curriculum Frameworks and the implementation of an assessment system designed to assess students' problem-solving and thinking skills rather than factual recall. For educators who supported this as a needed change from the traditional textbook-driven curriculum approach, the policy was perceived positively. David Cohen and Heather Hill in *Learning Policy* (2008) present a persuasive case that this ambitious state policy impacted math practice, with teachers shifting their instruction from teaching algorithms to engaging students in problem-solving and conceptual understanding. Their longitudinal study of policy implementation, however, makes clear the critical relationship between high-quality, in-depth and sustained professional development if teachers are to alter instructional practices in alignment with a new policy. They found that if teachers did not have an opportunity to learn the new curriculum and needed pedagogical approaches, implementation would be problematic. While this is not a surprising finding, it is one frequently overlooked by policy-makers, who lament that educators are not implementing policies as intended. Frequently researchers point "to things such as bureaucratic difficulties, weak incentives to comply and differences in the preferences between policy-makers and implementers" (Cohen and Hill, 2008:6) rather than recognizing that teachers have had inadequate opportunities to learn the skills needed to make a change.

Related to this Californian policy, Chrispeels (1997) also found that teachers' practices were influenced by the changes in assessment and by the accompanying professional development. This study found that the cadre of teachers throughout the state who were recruited as part of the new state assessment system to score student work, learned new skills, gained insights into and understanding of the intent of the policy and, thus, embraced the changes more readily. A related and significant finding from both studies was that teachers were more likely to change their practices if they spent time in grade or department meetings reviewing student work that reflected new approaches to mathematics or language arts. In other words, student work provided a window into teacher practices, promoted collaborative professional development and allowed teachers to make sense of the policy and its implications for their practice. These new understandings increased teachers' level and depth of policy implementation. This review of student work may have been particularly helpful because the student assessment system at the time was aligned to the curriculum and required students to show their work and reasoning in the state exam. Although teachers were beginning to embrace this change in policy and shift their practice, the policy also met resistance among educators and other policy-makers.

By 1997, the governor and legislature overturned the policy, abandoned the new assessment system and returned to textbook-driven instruction and factual recall, and also standardized testing. This dramatic shift shows the close relationship between policy and politics. While initially there was some policy confusion, teachers rather quickly returned to or continued prior approaches to teaching that they saw aligned with the reinstated, standardized testing system. This case illustrates the close policy/practice connection, especially when assessment is involved. Interestingly, although California has rigorously followed a text-book driven and teacher-centred didactic approach to instruction for the past 15 years, in a recent comparison of students' achievement on the TIMMS and the National Assessment of Educational Progress, California ranked near the bottom among the 50 US states and other participating countries (National Center for Education Statistics, 2011). This finding raises the question: Is a close policy or practice relationship always the best for students if the policy does not reflect research-based educational practices?

How Do We Make Stronger Connections between Policy and Practice?

The lessons from these high-performing systems, if stronger connections between policy and practice are desired, are to enact policies that are coherent and create an infrastructure that addresses three major components for high-quality teaching and learning: curriculum, professional development and assessment. With the need for developing students to be critical thinkers, problem solvers and innovators, policy-makers and educational leaders must focus on the aspects of their system that are currently not contributing to those outcomes. What leadership or teacher practices need attention or revision? In many instances, inadequate attention has been given to teachers' opportunities for exploring their current practices and learning new ones. In addition, an assessment system may be out of alignment with the policy initiatives, which leaves teachers with few rational options but to continue as they have been doing in the past. Prime examples are USA and Singapore where current national curriculum changes calling for more problem-solving, critical thinking and creativity are in place, but assessment systems—especially for university admissions—have not been fully implemented to assess these skills. Consequently, many teachers are reluctant to change until assessment and curriculum policy expectations are aligned.

Another major stumbling block is the lack of professional development provisions in most policy proposals. For example, teachers and administrators in the USA have expressed the need for extensive professional development if they are to implement the newly adopted CCSS. The high-achieving systems discussed in the OECD report have achieved positive outcomes because professional development was made a priority. However, as the case of Brazil illustrates (OECD, 2011), raising the quality of teachers in a large country is a daunting task.

A third challenge is the university admission criteria. As long as entrance requirements to universities are not in alignment with new primary and secondary education policy initiatives, teachers, with parental support and pressure, will be reluctant to initiate changes in practices that previously ensured admission of student to institutes of higher education. A fourth factor is policy consistency. If there are frequent turnovers of those in power, educators may feel that 'this too will pass'. Japan is a good example of a country with a consistent policy focus, which has yielded a very strong educational system therein. Finland and Singapore also have demonstrated how important both consistency and coherence throughout the educational system are for sustained change and a close connection between policy and practice.

What Is the Role of School Leaders?

School leaders at all levels are critical to successful policy implementation. Earl et al. (2000) noted that high quality of leadership in place at regional levels was crucial to the launch of England's, Numeracy and Literacy Initiative (1997–2002). Several factors seem to be critical in determining how well educational leaders will be able to support policy implementation. First, leaders are likely to embrace the policy and work for successful implementation if they see it is generally in alignment with their values and beliefs about education. Second, leaders will be able to play an active role in policy implementation if they are provided sufficient professional development about the policy's purpose and expectations, especially if the policy represents a significant departure from current practices. Singapore, for example, has a centralized and intensive leadership development programme that enables the Ministry of Education to prepare and more closely monitor leadership actions in relationship to the policy. In addition, the deeper the leaders own curricular and pedagogical knowledge in regard to the policy requirements, the more likely leaders will be able to guide their staff in implementing the policy. In the words of Leithwood et al. (2004), they will be able to provide the needed intellectual stimulation and appropriate modeling for their staff.

A third factor influencing policy implementation is the degree to which leaders may feel overwhelmed with prior policy initiatives. Governments rarely revoke policy, but usually continue to layer one policy on another. Even if the new policy is to take precedence, frequently aspects of the old policy remain and have force, both through their continued existence and from habituated practice. Fourth, the more substantive the inducements and accountability sanctions, the more likely educational leaders are to implement the policy. Finally, and perhaps most importantly, if leaders see benefits for students emerging from the policy's implementation and it, in some way, aligns with their values and beliefs, the more likely they are to continue the press for implementation.

Concluding Thoughts

The use of international benchmarks such as PISA and TIMSS and the OECD reports on high-performing systems has accelerated policy-makers' efforts to enact educational reforms. These reforms often call for schools to redesign their systems and redefine what counts as teaching and learning in alignment with the 21st century learning skills such as critical thinking, problem-solving, innovation, entrepreneurialism, creativity and teamwork. To successfully implement these policy demands, educators at all levels of the system need to rethink and retool their knowledge and skills. Teacher-centred instruction will need to shift to more student-centred approaches. A review of policies of high-achieving countries on international benchmarks indicates that finding ways for teachers to actively engage in policy interpretation and sense making, if not in actual policy-making, is vitally important to meaningful and thoughtful policy implementation. Policy-making must be seen as a co-construction process, with educators playing an important role in shaping implementation. Furthermore, policy goals are unlikely to be achieved if infrastructures are not created which build educator capacity and provide adequate resources.

References

Chrispeels, J. H. (1997). Educational policy implementation in a shifting political climate: The California experience. *American Educational Research Journal*, *34*(3), 453–481.

Chua, P. (2013, October 24). Education reform in Singapore. *International Education News*. Retrieved from http://internationalednews.com/2013/10/24/education-reform-in-singapore/ Accessed on 2 February 2014.

Cohen, D. K. (1995). What is the system in system reform? *Educational Researcher*, *24*(9), 11–31.

Cohen, D. K. and Hill, H. C. (2008). *Learning policy: When state education reform works*. New Haven, CT: Yale University Press.

Datnow, A., Hubbard, L. and Mehan, H. (1998). *Educational reform implementation: A co-construction process* (Research Report No. 5). Santa Cruz, CA: Center for Research on Education, Diversity and Excellence (CREDE).

Earl, L., Fullan, M., Leithwood, K., and Watson, N. (2000). *OISE/UT Evaluation of the Implementation of the National Literacy and Numeracy Strategies. Summary: First Annual Report. Watching and Learning*. Toronto, Canada: Ontario Institute for Studies in Education, Toronto; and Department for Education and Employment, London. REPORT NO DfEE-0109/2000. Available at http://files.eric.ed.gov/fulltext/ED472211.pdf. Accessed on 20 February 2014.

Edge, K. (2013). Rethinking knowledge management: Strategies for enhancing district-level teacher and leader tacit knowledge sharing. *Leadership and Policy in Schools*, *12*(3), 227–255.

Honig, M. (2006). Complexity and policy implementation: Challenges and Opportunities for the Field. In M. Honig (Ed.), *New directions in education policy implementation: Confronting complexity* (pp. 1–25). State University of New York: Albany.

Levin, B. (2008). *How to Change 5000 Schools: A Practical and Positive Approach for Leading Change at Every Level*. Cambridge, MA: Harvard Education Press.

Leithwood, K., Jantzi, D., Earl, L., Watson, N., Levin, B. and Fullan, M. (2004). Strategic leadership for large-scale reform: The case of England's National Literacy and Numeracy Strategy. *School Leadership & Management*, *24*(1), 57–79.

McDonnell, L. M. (2007). The politics of education: Influencing policy and beyond. In S. H. Fuhrman, D. K. Cohen and F. Mosher (Eds.) *The state of education policy research*. 19–39. Mahwah, NJ: Erlbaum.

McDonnell, L. M. and Elmore, R. F. (1987). Getting the job done: Alternative policy instruments. *Educational Evaluation and Policy Analysis, 9*(2), 133–152.

McLaughlin, M. W. (1987). Learning from experience: Lessons from policy implementation. *Educational Evaluation and Policy Analysis, 9*(2), 171–178.

———. (1990). The Rand Change Agent Study revisited: Macro perspectives and micro realities. *Educational Researcher, 19*(9), 11–16.

National Center for Education Statistics. (2011). *U.S. States in a Global Context: Results from the 2011 NAEP-TIMSS Linking Study.* Available at http://nces.ed.gov/nationsreportcard/subject/publications/studies/pdf/2013460.pdf. Retrieved on 2 February 2014.

OECD. (2011). *Lessons from PISA for the United States,* Strong Performers and Successful Reformers in Education, OECD Publishing. Available at http://dx.doi.org/10.1787/9789264096660-en. Accessed on 10 February 2014.

Spillane, J. P., Reiser, B. J. and Reimer, T. (2002). Policy Implementation and cognition: Reframing and refocusing implementation research. *Review of Educational Research, 72*(3), 387–341.

Supovitz, J. A. (2006). *The Case for district-based reform: Leading, building and sustaining school improvement.* Cambridge, MA: Harvard University Press.

3

Innovative Schools and Their Role in the Education Policy Cycle in Russia

Isak Froumin and Anatoly Kasprzhak

Introduction

John Dewey visited Russia in 1928. He described this travel in a book *Impressions of Soviet Russia and the Revolutionary World* (Dewey, 1929). The American public and researchers did not pay much attention to this book. However, today this book can give us new insights into educational policy analysis. Unlike most experts in comparative education, Dewey did not analyse the amount of hours needed for teaching mathematics or language. Instead, the great philosopher concentrated his attention on school philosophy, the values of teachers and principals of school management. Dewey admired the intellectual courage of the early Soviet educators, who refused to work within the existing traditions and routines and developed innovative practices both in instruction and school organization.

Such innovations, Dewey noted, were actively supported by the Ministry (whom we call today as policy-makers). He was surprised to see that while guarding basic communist values, the policy-makers of that time looked at those innovative sites as a possible source of policy ideas. In his book, Dewey called for learning from

Soviet educators—not just their educational ideas but approaches for policy-making as well. He hoped that the innovative boldness of a Soviet school would help to overcome communist dogmatism and totalitarianism to bring about 'good society'. Unfortunately, it happened the other way round.

Majority of those innovations were stopped in the 1930s, which manifested a major shift in education policy-making. Instead of supporting a 'hundred flowers to bloom' and constructing policies based on the school experience, the government of the time decided that one centrally developed and top-down implemented policy would be enough.

This example shows two extremes in the relationship between policy and innovative practice.[1] Obviously, the second approach is the easiest for educational policy-makers to adopt and is still a feature of policy-making in different countries. One could call it linear or autocratic—to develop a detailed policy centrally (based on some political priorities) and to implement it throughout the system. The first way, that of ground-level innovation, is much more complex and risky. It requires nurturing action research, innovation and reflectivity. Plus the stages of the policy-making cycle are very different in these two approaches.

The linear approach requires strong leadership at the system level and specific leadership skills at the school level. School leaders in this context should work within the boundaries of the existing policy. They have to implement it to improve the quality and efficiency. They are asked for feedback and consultation (in more democratic forms of this policy-making and implementation processes) so that they are seen to influence the policy formation and evaluation to some degree. This is why we cannot say that this approach is strictly speaking 'top-down', as it could include significant degrees of participation. This approach has proved its effectiveness and efficiency in different settings. In this approach, the school system becomes a big corporation. Obviously, the intelligent 'headquarters' take into

---

[1] I have to stress that I am interested in the relationships between the policy and innovative or effective practice.

account particular contexts, thus school leaders are allowed and even encouraged to adapt policies as per the local circumstances.

The approach that Dewey advocated and supported is non-linear. On the one hand, they (policy-makers) are interested in effective ways to solve educational problems; on the other hand, they correctly see the innovators as a disruptive force. The policy implementation stage is also very different within the non-linear approach. Instead of scaling up the right 'exemplary' practices, the system leaders are there to help innovators to be reflective and to engage them and wider group of practitioners in the diffusion of the most effective innovations. Innovation is becoming a constant mode of education policy-making. This means that system leaders should be more reflective than charismatic, more thoughtful than decisive. They also need different school leaders than those that exist in a linear policy model.

Do we need innovation-driven education policy model today? This question requires further detailed analysis that compares the advantages and weaknesses of both approaches in the current context. For the purpose of this chapter, we assume that striving for innovation-based society requires flexible and adaptable education policy that constantly reinvents itself. This assumption has many supporters today (i.e., OECD project on innovations in education[2]). In this chapter, we argue that such a system cannot be created by traditional linear relationships between policy and practice. It requires new agents of change in the shape of innovative schools.

Our discussion below is based on the experience of the radical transformation of the Russian education system during the last 25 years and evidence from international research. We have to stress that there is a vast and growing literature on innovative schools that discusses them as specific institutions (e.g., Giles and Hargreaves, 2006; Raywid, 1995; Supovitz and Klein, 2003). However, we look at them from the perspective of education policy-makers within the system.

[2] http://www.oecd.org/edu/ceri/innovationineducationandtraining.htm

Challenges of Innovation-driven Policy Model

There are a number of challenges arising in the innovation-driven education policy model. First is the challenge of uncertainty. System leaders do not know what the next step will be. How can the system leaders choose the 'right' innovations and make the system transformation sustainable? Second is the challenge of diffusion. How to move innovations from small pockets of excellence and creativity to a wider system? In other words, how to scale up effectively? Third is the challenge of differentiation (heterogeneity). Should the system include both innovative schools that are doing risky experiments and 'normal' schools that just implement already piloted ideas? Or should all schools be innovative? The connections between policy and practice depend on the answers to these questions.

Early Soviet experience is not the only example of innovation-driven education policy. One can see some features of such an approach in different settings. Countries with high level of school autonomy, such as Hong Kong and Singapore, have innovative schools that drive rather than deliver policy. University laboratory schools in the USA played a critical role in the improvement of instructions in the US schools (De Pencier, 1967; Williams, 1992). Montessori schools in many countries became important players in the renewal of primary education. Networks such as *accelerated schools, free schools* and many others showed their capacity to influence all stages of the educational policy-making process. However, this experience still could be considered as marginal for the traditional linear educational policy-formation model. Turning to an innovation-driven educational policy model will require infusing this approach throughout the education system.

The Emergence of Innovative Schools in Post-Soviet Russia and Their Role in Education Policy Process

The first signs of the decay of the totalitarian ideology and the relaxation of the administrative control in schooling awakened hope and enthusiasm among thousands of educators in the early 1990s in Russia. Freedom opened unprecedented opportunities for implementing their original ideas. However, these ideas were not sufficiently operational. They were mostly formulated in the form of Perestroika slogans about democracy and respect for human rights (Eklof and Dneprov, 1993; Froumin, 2005). The teachers and schools that chose this option began to unite into clubs and associations. They received strong public support. Educational change was the central focus of the mass media. All these factors gradually undermined the rigid centralized system of Soviet education. Individual schools became the main drivers for change (Froumin, 1993). The educational reform process in Russia started from the bottom, where schools (we call them innovative) developed and implemented new ideas (Chapman et al., 1995; Kerr, 1994).

The main feature of innovative schools at that period was the courage to be different. Any deviation from the rigid, centralized guidelines and procedures looked like a brave innovation. Often those innovations were the reproductions of the well-known Western pedagogical approaches. They were based on original ideas of the Russian or Soviet origin. Some innovative schools used the 'whole-school innovation' approach; some made partial changes in the curriculum by introducing a few new subjects. Educational administrators at all levels initially supported the growth of the innovative sector because the general political climate was very favourable for non-traditional approaches. However, gradually educational administrators found themselves in a contradiction. The pluralism of the model put the policy-makers into a difficult situation.

Pluralism and freedom inside the Russian educational system are something more than a mere decentralization or school autonomy. They require not only the abandonment of the totalitarian administrative regime, but also going outside habitual democratic procedures. Pluralism means not just selecting one right viewpoint (even democratically) but rather striving not only to come to agreement, but also to mutually accept different viewpoints. School autonomy under these conditions brings a great complexity to policy implementation and management.

The experience of innovative schools is twofold; on one hand, were those which could not overcome the fear of such freedom to innovate. On the other hand, innovative schools showed all educators that much could be achieved under new conditions using new methods, textbooks and ideas. Even being in minority, the innovative schools became strong players in educational policy. Their leaders and representatives became members of the advisory bodies affiliated to the Ministry of Education and the regional (provincial) educational administrations. From 1987 to 2000, those advisory bodies lobbied such policy changes as:

1. replacing the government publishing house monopoly for textbook production by introducing a competitive market of different publishers and authors;
2. increasing school autonomy;
3. creating special government support programmes for school-based action research and curriculum innovations;
4. strengthening the flexibility of the curriculum to give more freedom to teachers and students.

The Evolution of Innovative Schools as Policy Players

Rapid changes in the post-Soviet education system slowed down in the mid-1990s, when a new regulatory framework for the Russian schools was developed, adopted and implemented. Most innovative schools legitimized and institutionalized their experiments. Their innovations became brand names. The list of such names includes well-known brands like Montessori and unique names as the 'School of adaptive pedagogy', 'Thinking development school' and 'School of the dialogue of cultures' (Kovaleva, 2003). The experiments and innovations became habitual ways of working. Eventually, the word 'alternative school' or 'school with a special curriculum' replaced the word 'innovative school'. The very existence of these schools manifested a new stage of the education development in Russia—diversity of schooling became a fact.

The proportion of such schools varied from 5 per cent to 20 per cent depending on the region in the early 2000s. The schools were led by energetic and charismatic leaders and became a part of the Russian education establishment. They remain an important part of an education policy. They continue to lobby for school autonomy, for new ways of teacher training and certification and for stronger voice of practitioners in education policy-making and implementation. It is important to stress that teacher unions in post-Soviet Russia have been weak. They have concentrated their efforts mainly on salaries and benefits. Professional associations of teachers of different subjects or school principals also either do not exist or are weak. So these alternative schools became the important voice of the professional community. They often tried to form their own professional sub-communities like associations of alternative schools of different kinds.

Raywid (1995) argues that the alternative schools often pioneered the reform of the whole system. However, he did not mention the divisions within the group of *alternative* schools; only a small part of them became truly reform-oriented. These innovative schools, however, made the process of experimenting and innovations permanent. Their search for better methods and content has not stopped. They have created a culture of reflective practice and continuing improvement. Such schools often became very popular and visible through media attention. They have also created a number of professional communities including the famous 'Eureka' network that meets twice a year for substantive dialogue with policy-makers (Adamsky, 2003).

Representatives of such schools appear as controversial but strong media figures. Their influence was strong at the national level of educational policy. In 2001, Anatoly Pinsky—a principal of a Moscow innovative school #1060—became an advisor to the Minister of Education and a co-chair of influential Ministry of Education Council for education reforms. He was a member of an informal network of innovative schools and promoted their views through the Ministry Council. At the same time the Ministry of Education used those school leaders to support the reform agenda. Their joint efforts resulted in a number of major initiatives such as introducing a flexible curriculum in upper secondary schools, establishing public governing councils in schools, and introducing transparent funding instruments and the unified country-wide school leaving external exam (Pinsky, 2007).

It is important to note that the relationship between the community of innovative schools and policy-makers has not always been harmonious and positive. The innovative school teachers and leaders were not the Ministry's puppets. Often they criticized policy proposals. Moreover, in some cases such schools became a headache for the local educational authorities because they questioned the regular and approved approaches, and argued for more flexibility against activities and rules imposed by educational authorities. Often the innovative school leaders found themselves in a conflict with local educational authorities. Annually one or two directors of such schools were fired because of such conflicts. These relatively independent public schools had difficulties in adapting to the ideology of stronger centralization that grew from the early 2000s in different sectors of the Russian state and society. Following Kirst's (1984) notion, one can say that during the last 10 years the education policy-making the pendulum has moved from freedom to control and from school autonomy to school accountability.

Current Role of Innovative Schools in the Russian Education Policy Process

Despite the controversies and complexities, innovative schools have established their place in the Russian educational policy process by the mid-2000s. The Ministry of Education created a number of mechanisms that allow involving these schools in the policy development and implementation. The Ministry has established such advisory groups for each significant innovation that it is going to develop and implement. Often the representatives of innovative schools chair such groups. One of the recent examples is the establishment of teachers' professional standards. An initial draft of the document was developed by the bureaucrats and faced severe criticism. The Ministry decided to establish an advisory group to develop a new draft and invited the principal of a famous innovative school (E. Yamburg) to chair the group. A new draft of the standards was radically different; it was more ambitious and forward-looking than the previous one. The advisory group launched a campaign to advocate for a new document through other innovative schools. As a result, the document received broad support and was adopted.

Another important role of the innovative schools is the *revision and evaluation of policy initiatives*. Often drafts of policy or regulatory documents are sent to the innovative schools for their feedback and practical recommendations. The main function of such feedback was not evaluation but getting practical recommendations for policy implementation. A good example of such interaction between policy-makers and innovative schools was the introduction of new accountability mechanisms. Such evaluation is often combined with *piloting major Ministry initiatives*. An interesting example of this activity is the participation of the innovative schools in piloting new national educational standards. A draft of standards was presented to the professional community in 2009. The Ministry asked those schools which wished to pilot these standards to volunteer. A network of such pilot sites (including mainly the innovative schools) was created. The experience of this pilot was invaluable for further elaboration of the standards and their wide dissemination.

The Ministry of Education is trying to support the innovative schools and their role in the education system. It established a special council for 'Innovations in Education' that gives special status to innovative schools. New Education Law (2013) has a special provision to protect the experiments in education and to allow deviations of experimental schools from 'normal' practices. At the same time, the risks for the innovators are still high. They often face difficulties being measured by 'universal' standards. The Federal Ministry did not invent effective approaches to protect these schools from local authorities.

Lessons for Education Policy Players

The experience of the evolution of the innovative schools in Russia allows us to draw some conclusions that could be important for the theory of interaction between education policy and practice as well as for education policy-makers in rapidly transforming societies.

A theoretical analysis of the phenomenon of innovative schools suggests that in exploring the links between policy and practice, we have to pay close attention to the notion of practice and practitioners. Education policy-makers and researchers often develop quite elaborate and complex policies. Practice is usually interpreted as relatively homogeneous across a large sector of schools and teachers. The case of innovative schools demonstrates that one has to consider the practice as a more complex phenomenon represented by a diverse group of interests. It questions the idea of 'whole system reform', suggesting that in the process of educational transformation, policy-makers face the necessity to interact with both conservative and innovative groups.

The main practical lesson is that innovative schools can be strong allies with the government in the process of the transformation of the system of education. They can be used as advocates for the reform. They also are able to demonstrate in practice, the success of new ideas and approaches. The best ways to engage these schools in the policy-making and policy implementation process are to delegate them the review and pilot educational improvements and initiatives, and to involve them in the public discussion process as 'critical friends'.

Another important lesson for policy-makers is that the innovative sector in the school system requires nurturing and respect. Being innovators, they can bring criticism and often threat for the status quo. It creates a risk of conflicts and alienation between policy-making and innovative practice. It also creates a risk for the very existence of the innovative schools as they depend on financing and regulatory environment, defined by the policy players. Giles and Hargreaves (2006) showed how the standardized reform pressure affected the innovative character of such schools. It meant that the status and conditions for their innovative work should have been secured within the regulatory framework. They also needed stable financing for the additional activities related to pedagogical experiments.

Finally, an important task of policy-makers and education administrators is to facilitate the interaction between innovative schools and the mainstream schools. The discussions on innovative ideas and the dissemination of innovative practices require a favourable regulatory framework and an institutionalized community of innovative schools, in order to make a difference.

References

Adamsky A. (2003). *Analitika innovatsionnykh proektov* [Analysis of innovative projects]. Moscow: Eureka.

Chapman, J., Froumin, I. and Aspin, D. (1995). Introduction. In J. Chapman, I. Froumin, D. Aspin, (Eds.), *Creation and managing the democratic school*. London: Falmer Press.

De Pencier, I. (1967). *The history of laboratory schools: The University of Chicago*. Chicago, IL: Quadrangle Books.

Dewey, J. (1929). Impressions of Soviet Russia and the revolutionary world. *New Republic*, 1–133, New York.

Eklof, B. and Dneprov, E. (Eds.). (1993). *Democracy in the Russian School: The reform movement in education since 1984*. Boulder, CO: Westview Press.

Froumin, I. (1993). The role of innovative schools in the educational reform in Russia. *Context*, 5(5), 14–16.

———. (1995) The child's road to democracy. In J. Chapman, I. Froumin, D. Aspin (Eds.), *Creating and managing the democratic school*. London: Falmer Press.

Froumin, I. D. (2005). Democratizing the Russian School: achievements and setbacks. In Eklof, Ben; Larry E. Holmes and Vera Kaplan (eds.) *Educational Reform in Post-Soviet Russia: Legacies and Prospects*. London: Routledge.

Giles C. and Hargreaves A. (2006, February). The sustainability of innovative schools as learning organizations and professional learning communities during standardized reform. *Educational Administration Quarterly*, 42(1), 124–156.

Kerr, S. (1994). Diversification in Russian education. In A. Jones (Ed.), *Education and society in the New Russia*. New York: M. Sharpe.

Kirst, M. (1984). *Who controls our schools? American values in conflict*. New York: Freemen.

Kovaleva, T. (2003). *Innovacionnay shkola: Aksiomy i gipotezy* [Innovation schools: axioms and assumptions]. Moscow: Moscow University Press.

Pinsky, A. A. (2007). *Liberalnya ideya I praktika obrazovaniya* [Liberal idea and education practice]. Moscow: HSE Press.

Raywid, M. A. (1995). Alternative schools: The state of the art. *Educational Leadership*, 52(1), 26–31.

Supovitz, J. A. and Klein, V. (2003). *Mapping a course for improved student learning: How innovative schools systematically use student performance data to guide improvement*. Paper presented at the Consortium for Policy Research in Education, University of Pennsylvania, Philadelphia.

Williams, R. (1992). Meeting the needs of an urban research university: The case of seeds UES. In B. Moller (Ed.), *The logics of education: Laboratory facilities as centres for educational practice and research*. Oldenburg University, Oldenburg.

4

School Leadership Development in Hong Kong: Taking a Retrospective and Prospective View on Policy and Practice*

Paula Kwan

Introduction

Schools in Hong Kong have been operating in a fast-changing external environment over the last two decades; not only do they have to follow the international trend of implementing various educational reform initiatives, but also have to adjust to the social changes brought about by the transfer of political governance. These changes have led to new expectations of the roles of school leaders and the ways in which potential leaders are prepared for these roles. This chapter discusses the changing expectations of school leaders in Hong Kong and explores the future leader's development opportunities, taking into consideration the unique nature of Chinese culture and the history of Hong Kong.

The resuming of sovereignty over Hong Kong by China in 1997 brought with it changes in education (Bray, 1998). The replacement

* This chapter is adapted and modified from an earlier article of the author, Kwan (2011).

of the three-year university curriculum by a four-year structure and the medium of instructional reforms were believed to be the measures aimed at aligning the Hong Kong educational system with that of Mainland China. Apart from implementing the local initiatives, Hong Kong schools had to adjust themselves to international educational reforms in the globalization era. The new demands on schools provoked new requirements for school leadership, which in turn, called for changes in the way school leaders were both selected and prepared.

The preparation of school leaders in Hong Kong has changed substantially in response to the reform; the emphasis has shifted from training to development, the process is now guided more by practitioners than policy-makers, the trainer-centric structure is giving way to a self-regulation mode and the approach is moving from being instructor-centred to peer-interactive learning. Although policies on leadership development have been established to help school leaders evolve, the actual exercise of leadership in schools remains susceptible to school-specific contexts. Therefore, it is believed that examining the evolution of these policies in tandem with changes in Hong Kong's external environment and internal school-specific contexts will be meaningful in deriving consensual directions for the future.

An understanding of school leadership cannot be developed without taking into consideration the contextual elements. Thus, a brief introduction of Hong Kong's educational system is given in the first section of this chapter. Discussions on the external reform environment, and on the internal school specific context, constitute the second and the third sections of this chapter, respectively. The fourth section reviews the development of leadership preparation in Hong Kong, and the fifth section explores future development opportunities. The last section concludes this chapter.

The Hong Kong Context

Hong Kong is located at the southeastern tip of China and covers a total area of only 1,103 km. It has a population of 7.2 million with approximately 98 per cent of which are ethnic Chinese (Hong Kong Special Administrative Region [HKSAR] Government, 2010). The Education Bureau (EDB) is the government department in charge of education and headed by the Secretary of Education.

The contemporary culture of the Hong Kong Chinese is a blend of the Western culture grafted on to an otherwise historically ingrained Chinese culture. Despite the powerful Western influences, the majority of Hong Kong Chinese share a Confucian cultural heritage that provides the basis for norms guiding Chinese interpersonal behaviours (Fang, 2000).

When compared to other cultures along the dimensions introduced by Hofstede (2001), the Chinese culture may be regarded as *collective* (group oriented) rather than individualistic. It stresses on a sense of belonging and group membership, and emphasizes the importance of harmony. Embedded in the collective orientation is a certain degree of *fatalism*; people are uncomfortable with uncertainty and seek to reduce this, while limiting risks by hanging on to traditions. Parallel with this fatalistic attitude is the likelihood of the Chinese being *replicative* instead of generative. In terms of power distribution, unlike in the Western societies where power is distributed more equally, people in Hong Kong are used to *large power distance*. Particularly in the Chinese culture, the unbalanced distribution of power is seen as ordinary and acceptable. Lastly, with regards to the aggression or consideration dimension, the Chinese culture is *both aggressive and considerate*, with both achievement and relationship being its core values (Fan, 2002).

Clearly, the Chinese culture is unique and differs significantly with the West. Its inherent characteristics can be influential to the concept and practice of school leadership. Extant research contains evidence showing that leaders in Chinese schools approach education in a way different from most Western leaders (Biggs, 1996).

The next section discusses the changes in the external environment that shape the requirements of school leadership.

The External School Context

The year 1997 marked not only the end of Hong Kong's colonial days but also a substantial change in its approach to the development of the educational system. It was the year in which the Education Commission Report No. 7 (ECR7) which laid the foundation for many subsequent reforms, was released.

As a British colony, Hong Kong did not have a clear vision of its educational development (Sweeting, 2004). Introduction of nine-year compulsory schooling in 1978 by the government was deemed more a response, rather than a planned strategy, to the criticism from the European Economic Community that prevalence of child labour in Hong Kong had kept commodity prices lower than its European competitors (Postiglione and Lee, 1997). Between the late 1970s and the early 1980s was a period described as the Quantitative Era of education development, with a focus on increasing the number of schools as well as their sizes (Cheng, 2002). During this period, Hong Kong saw remarkable economic growth, as it capitalized on China's closed-door foreign trade policy and its unique geographical location. Such an extraordinary economic growth implied greater demand for more skilled and knowledgeable manpower and, by extension, more schools. It was not until February 1984, however, that the government established the Education Commission (EC) to review the educational system's status and to advise on policies. The EC released its first report later that year and five more throughout the pre-1997 period, altogether proposing hundreds of policy recommendations such as the medium of instruction, teacher education and curriculum development.

The ECR7 differed sharply from the preceding reports in its business focus and market orientation; the business concepts, such as quality, accountability, efficiency and effectiveness, were introduced. Education was seen as a provision of service to satisfy multiple stakeholders, instead of being a learning process for students. A number of reform initiatives to hold schools accountable to students, parents and the public were introduced; among them were school self-evaluations, external reviews of schools and assessment of value addition achieved by schools. These quality assurance measures made available a common assessment framework for measuring school performance, and yet they created a platform for comparative purposes. Competition amongst schools (for students), for example, intensified with the declining student population in Hong Kong and the introduction of the 'Medium of Instruction' (MOI) policy. In 1998, all but 114 secondary schools in Hong Kong were instructed by the government to use Chinese as the medium of instruction. Although the particular directive was intended to help students gain knowledge in their mother language, it had led to a kind of labelling (or grading) whereby schools adopting English as the MOI became highly sought after by parents as they were the better performing schools that were allowed to use English as the MOI.

The pace of education reforms in Hong Kong maintained its momentum after the turn of the millennium; amongst the most prominent initiatives were the reactivation of the Direct Subsidy Scheme (DSS) in 2001, and the introduction of Incorporated Management Committee (IMC) and the New Senior Secondary Curriculum (NSSC) in 2007 and 2009, respectively. The DSS allowed grant-receiving schools the autonomy to redesign the curriculum, to recruit and select students themselves (being exempted from the central student allocation scheme) and to collect tuition fees. The IMC too altered the governance of schools to a certain extent by mandatorily requiring them to incorporate external members such as parents, teachers and alumni in their school management committees; the NSSC replaced a seven-year secondary school curriculum by a six-year structure and made general studies a mandatory subject.

Although the external educational landscape has changed rapidly in the last two decades, the corresponding school-specific internal changes have not quite followed the same pace. A brief discussion of this is in the following section.

The Internal School Context

School leaders saw the reforms as macro-level issues to be addressed by policy-makers and not as concerns that were under their prerogative. It was rare for them to be challenged by communities, as the demand for schools far exceeded the supply. Educational plans and initiatives had come and gone, leaving no permanent marks on the system (Lam, 2003).

The high power distance culture in which school leaders worked had earned them a great deal of respect from the community as well as parents and teachers. Decisions in schools could, thus, be made in an authoritarian and autocratic manner, without much consideration of staff participation and parental consultation (Dimmock and Walker, 1998). Consequently, schools were refrained from external interference.

Many initiatives that were introduced to help schools, turned out to be more of a burden than avenues for improvements in schools (Wong, 1995). For instance, the accountability system as introduced through the School Management Initiative, features of which resembled school-based management initiatives in other schooling systems, was designed to enhance schools' performances. Wong (1995) reported that the enormous paperwork required by the government in preparation for the restructuring had left school leaders and teachers doubting. Their reluctance and/or incapability to cope with the new set of requirements were, however, understandable because of the cultural context in which replication, rather than generation, was the norm. Principals who had been counting on previous experience and prior knowledge in managing schools found no precedents or ready solutions.

The lack of competency of Hong Kong principals to cope with uncertainties was further exacerbated by their lack of experience of working in different types of school settings. The career path through which most principals followed was largely stable, lifelong and punctuated infrequently by resignations due to various health reasons (Lam, 2003). It is not uncommon to find a principal who has worked in one school for his or her entire professional life. Such a commitment to a school, or to a school sponsoring (governing) body, is considered as patriarchy, a highly held value in the Chinese culture (Westwood, 1997). Its prevalence appears to reinforce the importance of affiliation, loyalty and long service in a particular school or school sponsoring body, and makes it difficult for principals wanting to change schools (Kwan, 2012). This practice implies a system that values continuity and uniformity more than change and innovation.

The career pattern of teachers in Hong Kong exhibits a mode of stability similar to that of school principals. Dismissal of teachers appointed on regular rather than temporary terms entails a very complicated and lengthy procedure. This has resulted in a high degree of tolerance for inadequate teacher performance in terms of school management. The reluctance of teachers to undertake additional responsibilities can also be attributed, in part, to the collectivist culture in Hong Kong schools. The 'face' concept, whereby detrimental actions to the respect, pride and dignity of an individual teacher are unacceptable, is so strongly upheld in the society that school leaders often avoid open and transparent assessment of teachers' performances (Leung and Chan, 2003). In this context of stability and tradition, there have been little incentives for teachers to take on additional responsibilities.

Working in a high power distance environment, school principals enjoy the kind of respect that is easily translated into the formation of a bureaucratic structure, as those who are lower in the hierarchy tend not to disagree with the views of their seniors for cultural reasons. This interacting effect of bureaucracy, as well as the collectivist orientation in Hong Kong schools, has been a clear division of responsibility between the ruler (school leader) and the ruled (teachers) and has had a significant impact on the implementation of reform initiatives. If the reform initiatives are seen as the endeavour of school principals striving to achieve personal objectives, teachers are less enthusiastic to embrace the proposals because they fail to see their own benefits from the changes.

The seemingly turbulent nature of the external reform has shaped the expectations of principals in Hong Kong schools, along with the continuing inertia of internal school-specific environments. The following section provides a brief review on the different leadership preparation programmes in Hong Kong.

Retrospect of the Development of School Leaders in Hong Kong

Leadership preparation and development in the 1980s was viewed as a measure serving administrative purposes, rather than educational objectives. New principals were required to attend a basic ten-day (for primary schools) or nine-day (for secondary schools) course. The design and delivery of the programmes were generally outsourced to universities, as a result of which they were usually designed and built around needs, deemed important by academics. The courses were conducted in a classroom setting with minimal involvement of practicing school principals (Walker and Dimmock, 2006). The importance of school leadership and leadership development in improving school performance was first acknowledged in ECR7, which stated that, "[T]o provide quality school education, we need quality principals and teachers... they should be provided with suitable support and development opportunities" (Education Commission, 1997:22). A policy for Continuing Professional Development for school leaders was introduced in 2002.

Under the new policy, differentiated leadership development programmes for aspiring, newly appointed principals (APs) and serving principals (SPs) were made mandatory with a time-regulated framework. APs were to attain, within a two-year period, a Certification for Principalship which required them to pass a 75-hour academic course, attend a one-day needs analysis workshop and submit a portfolio. Newly appointed principals (NAPs) were to undergo a needs assessment, an induction programme, a school leadership development programme and an extended programme. In addition, they were asked to present a professional portfolio to their school management committees every year. SPs, who were of diverse backgrounds in terms of their years of experience, educational level and professional knowledge, were expected to participate in a self-selected range of professional activities for a minimum of 150 hours over a three-year period (Education Department, 2002). The programme reflected a shift of focus from 'training' to 'development', from 'classroom' to 'multi-facet' and from 'off the job' to 'on the job'.

A specific feature of the one-year NAP programme was the incorporation of the 'mentoring' concept whereby three NAPs were assigned to one experienced principal who assumed the multiple roles of being the peer mentor, the principal coach as well as the professional counsel. The 'mentoring' arrangement has been a milestone in Hong Kong's school leadership development. It not only incorporates intensive involvement of practicing principals, but also creates (in the learning squares) a collegial environment in which participants can learn at their own pace and put emphasis upon topics they consider relevant to their respective schools.

Prospect of School Leader Development in Hong Kong

The discussion above shows that school leadership development in Hong Kong has undergone substantial policy changes in recent years, as a response to the turbulent changes and certain external factors. However, if these changes are considered in tandem with the still largely inert school-specific environments, it is clear that a number of areas are yet to be addressed by school sponsoring bodies and policymakers. What follows are some suggestions about the proposed areas that need to be addressed or strengthened.

Developing School Leadership Development Programmes for Vice Principals

In Hong Kong, the needs of vice principals (VPs) have been generally overlooked with no specific leadership development programmes

(Kwan and Walker, 2008). VPs working in a group-oriented culture with a high degree of power distance often find themselves incapable of striking a balance between being accountable to the principals for efficient implementation of changes in schools and simultaneously maintaining friendly relationships with teachers. Therefore, it is important that any development programme is oriented towards helping them effectively discharge the prevailing responsibilities of a VP rather than preparing them for role of the principal.

Encouraging Schools to Formulate Leader Succession Plan

Research evidence reports that Hong Kong VPs have rarely been involved in resource management (Kwan and Walker, 2009). This reflects a general absence of succession planning in schools, since VPs have not been given responsibilities pertaining to this area, which constitutes an essential duty of principals. Without the formulation of a leader succession plan that allows potential leaders to expose themselves to various leadership practices, the contribution of the NAP programme to enhance school management cannot be fully realized. In addition, the lack of experience in certain specific areas also hinders the NAPs from fully reflecting on and taking advantage of their mentors.

Creating a School Culture Conducive for Innovations

In a review of the NAP programme, Walker and Hu (2008) reported that participants value highly the shadowing arrangement and yet they find it difficult to take good practices back to their own schools despite valuing highly the shadowing arrangement. In part, the cultural resistance to change explains this, as innovations are often seen as the personal agendas of principals rather than an avenue to improve schools. Without the support of a team of like-minded and highly competent colleagues, the possibility of successful introduction of innovations always remains rather slim. Therefore, professional learning should not be confined to school leaders but should also be provided to all school members.

Developing in School Leaders the Commitment of Lifelong Learning

The basic concept underpinning the development of the NAP programme is networking. The professional networks can not only sustain professional learning and create opportunities for sharing of experiences with peers, but also provide emotional support (Walker and Hu, 2008). However, their purposes will not be fully served unless they are maintained and sustained beyond the official duration of the NAP programme.

Keeping a Group of Competent and Committed Experienced Principals

A critical factor in the success of networking and shadowing lies not only in the commitment of NAPs but also in the active involvement of experienced principals, whose roles range from mentors to coaches and counsellors. The commitment of experienced principals is linked to the sense of satisfaction that they obtain from receiving recognition from the NAPs while seeing that the practices they have followed (or even conceptualized in some cases) can be adopted in other schools (Daresh, 2004). The experienced principals have served the programme well, but at a price, especially when the school environment has become increasingly complex and the external factors awaiting individual school leaders have proliferated.

Strengthening Principals' Emotional Competency

In Hong Kong, internal candidates from the same school, or from schools of the same sponsoring body, are generally preferred over external candidates when hiring principals (Kwan and Walker, 2009). The promotion of a VP to the position of principal often triggers an abrupt change in the prevailing hierarchical structure of a school. The AP is no longer seen as a colleague but a supervisor who commands a high degree of respect in the high power distance Hong Kong culture. Teachers often choose to keep the principal at a distance and to maintain a minimum level of contact and interactions with them. The NAPs often find themselves alone, working without much support from their colleagues.

It is thus evident that only those who are not keen on social relations are more eager to assume the position of a principal (Walker and Kwan, 2009). As school leaders are promoted from positions that are collectively related to other teachers to positions and levels that are socially remote from the rest of the school, they need a certain level of emotional competency to adjust to the change. Therefore, leadership development needs to go beyond technical skills; leadership development must include the development of NAPs' emotional strengths.

Conclusion

Over the past two decades, Hong Kong has undergone changes against a unique politically transitional context as well as introducing a number of reform initiatives that mirror international trends. Its return to the sovereignty of China has complicated the issue as some of the initiatives are meant to serve political rather than educational purposes. Policies concerning leadership preparation, for example, are constrained by school-specific circumstances and context. The group-oriented and high power distance culture in

Hong Kong schools constitutes a considerable impediment to leadership practices.

In tracing the evolution of school leadership preparation and development programmes in Hong Kong, it is clear that a number of possible areas warrant further examination. Leadership preparation for one has shown to call for inclusion of emotional competency development as well as leadership and technical skills. Also, the development of VPs to assist principals in effectively discharging their current responsibilities is an issue that warrants policy-makers' consideration.

References

Biggs, J. B. (1996). Western misperceptions of the Confucian-heritage learning culture. In D. A. Watkins and J. B. Biggs (Eds.), *The Chinese learner: Cultural, psychological and contextual influence* (pp. 45–68). Hong Kong: University of Hong Kong, Comparative Education Research Centre.

Bray, M. (1998). Education and political transition in Hong Kong and Macau: A comparative analysis. In R. Ramos, J. R. Dinis, R. Wilson and D. Y. Yuan (Eds.), *Macau and its neighbors toward the 21st century* (pp. 199–209). Macau: University of Macau and Macau Foundation.

HKSAR Government. (2010). *Hong Kong key statistics.* Census and Statistics Department of HKSAR Government. Retrieved from http://www.censtatd.gov.hk/hong_kong_statistics/statistical_tables/index.jsp?tableID=001 (last accessed on 30 June 2014).

Cheng, K. M. (2002). The quest for quality education: The quality assurance movement in Hong Kong. In J. K. H. Mok and D. K. K. Chan (Eds.), *Globalization and education: The quest for quality education in Hong Kong* (pp. 41–66). Hong Kong: Hong Kong University Press.

Daresh, J. (2004). Mentoring school leaders: Professional promise or predictable problems? *Educational Administration Quarterly, 40*(4), 495–517.

Dimmock, C. and Walker, A. (1998). *Transforming Hong Kong's schools: A cross-cultural perspective.* New York: Falmer Press.

Education Commission. (1997). *Education commission report no. 7: Quality school education.* Hong Kong: Education Commission.

Education Department. (2002). *Continuing professional development for school excellence, consultation paper on continuing development of principals.* Hong Kong: Hong Kong Government.

Fan, Y. (2002). Questioning guanxi: Definition, classification and implications, *International Business Review, 11*(5), 543–561.

Fang, Y. (2000). The effect of distributive preferences on decisions: An empirical study of Chinese employees. *Cross Cultural Management—An International Journal, 7*(1), 3–11.

Hofstede, G. H. (2001), *Culture's consequences: Comparing values, behaviors, institutions, and organizations across nations* (2nd ed.). London: SAGE Publishing.

Kwan, P. (2011). Development of school leaders in Hong Kong: Contextual changes and future challenges. *School Leadership and Management, 31*(2), 165–177.

———. (2012). Assessing school principal candidates: Perspectives of the hiring superintendents. *International Journal of Leadership in Education: Theory and Practice, 15*(3), 331–349.

Kwan, P. and Walker, A. (2008). Vice-principalship in Hong Kong: Aspirations, competencies and satisfaction. *School Effectiveness and School Improvement, 19*(1), 73–97.

———. (2009). Are we looking through the same lens? Principal recruitment and selection. *International Journal of Educational Research, 48*(1), 51–61.

Lam, Y. L. J. (2003). Balancing stability and change: implications for professional preparation and development of principals in Hong Kong. In P. Hallinger (Ed.) *Reshaping the landscape of school leadership development: A global perspective* (pp.175–190). Lisse, the Netherlands: Swets & Zeitlinger.

Leung, T. K. P. and Chan, R. Y. K. (2003). Face, favour and positioning—A Chinese power game. *European Journal of Marketing, 37*(11/12), 1575–1598.

Postiglione, G. A. and Lee, W. O. (1997). Schooling and the changing socio-political setting: An introduction. In G. A. Postiglione and W. O. Lee (Eds.), *Schooling in Hong Kong: Organization, Teaching and Social Context* (pp. 1–22). Hong Kong: Hong Kong University Press.

Sweeting, A. (2004). *Education in Hong Kong, 1941 to 2001: Visions and revisions.* Hong Kong: Hong Kong University Press.

Walker, A. and Dimmock, C. (2006). Preparing leaders, preparing learners: the Hong Kong experience. *School Leadership and Management, 26*(2), 125–147.

Walker, A. and Hu, R. (2008, October 30–November 2). After the party: the impact of a principal learning programme on beginning principals. Paper presented at the 22nd annual conference of University Council for Educational Administration, Florida, USA.

Walker, A. and Kwan, P. (2009). Linking professional, school, demographic and motivational factors to desire for principalship. *Educational Administration Quarterly, 45*(4), 590–615.

Westwood, R. (1997). Harmony and patriarchy: the cultural basis of paternalistic headship among the overseas Chinese. *Organization Studies, 18*(3), 445–480.

Wong, K. C. (1995). Education accountability in Hong Kong: Lessons from the school management initiative. *International Journal of Educational Research, 23*(6), 519–529.

5

Movers and Shapers: Reframing System Leadership for the 21st Century*

Anthony Mackay and Albert Bertani

Introduction

Models of the 20th century system leadership encouraged and prepared individuals to lead to improvement in schools, systems and jurisdictions. Approaches and frameworks focused on the traits and behaviours of effective leaders, and leadership theories emphasized the role of individuals on system development. But the urgency and scale of the transformation facing today's leaders requires something more than incremental improvement. It requires leaders who:

1. build upon but move beyond the currently dominant leadership theories;

* This chapter draws significantly on Chapter 6 of *Redesigning Education: Shaping Learning Systems Around the Globe—Innovation Unit for the Global Education Leaders' Program* (2013), Booktrope Edition, which was written by a team of Innovation Unit consultants and researchers, including the authors of this chapter, who lead and learn from the Global Education Leaders' Programme (GELP) on behalf of its members and partners.

2. are geared to achieve more than incremental improvement;
3. lead through radical and swift innovation towards whole-system transformation;
4. reflect the possibilities enabled by changes in technology;
5. incorporate new models of learning; and
6. recognize the role of new providers in the field of education and training.

From where will the leaders come to address these demands? The 21st century system leaders might well be educators, or from the public service. However, they might also emerge from the ranks of new providers, be social entrepreneurs with an interest in the field (Hannon et al., 2013) or be learners within the system. Whatever is their backgrounds and experience, they need to be 'movers and shapers', whose task is 'reinvention' and management of the radical change that develops in this context, since

> '[R]einvention' is precisely the system transformation that is needed. Whilst the improvement model sees change happening along a determined and well-understood path ... the alternative is less predictable; more disruptive ... If the disruption theorists are right, then there is an inevitability about this process .... (Hannon, 2014)

Dominant Leadership Theories

During the early part of the 20th century, scholars began to take serious interest in leadership and understanding the work of leaders. With the dominant research base developed primarily in the USA, a number of theories began to emerge over several decades exploring different dimensions of what it meant to lead and to be a leader. All of these theories have been preoccupied with a focus on improvement—How can we make our current organizations and systems work better? Eight major leadership theories have dominated the leadership literature from the USA, and are summarized in Table 5.1

Table 5.1
Dominant Leadership Theories

Leadership Theory	*Major Component*
Great Man	Capacity for leadership is inherent
	Belief that great leaders are born and not made
	Leadership is heroic or mythic in concept
Trait	People inherit traits making them leaders
	Leaders possess certain personality characteristics
	Leaders have certain behavioural characteristics
Contingency	Variables dictate which leadership style is best
	No leadership style is best in all situations
	Success is dependent on a number of variables
Situational	Leadership actions are chosen based on situational variables
	Different styles are most appropriate for decision-making
	Authoritarian and democratic styles emerge as models
Behavioural	Belief that great leaders are made and not born
	Focus on the actions of leaders, not mental qualities
	Leaders learn to lead through teaching and observation
Participative	Ideal leadership style takes the input of others into account
	Leaders encourage participation and contributions
	Participation is used to increase commitment and relevancy
Management	Focuses on supervision, organization and group performance
	Uses rewards and punishments
	Maintains a transactional orientation to leadership
Relational	Focuses on relationships between leaders and followers
	Motivates and inspires others to a higher moral purpose
	Demonstrates a transformational approach to leadership

Source: Leadership-Central.com. (2015).

In addition to these theories or models that have dominated the field, there have also been efforts to describe what leaders actually do (Kotter, 1999). This research reflects leadership more broadly in contexts that include education, business, government and public leadership. However, once again the skills and competencies identified are focused on improving the existing systems.
Leaders…

Define the task—Set direction

Plan—Act as a change agent

Brief—Communicate

Control—Establish boundaries

Evaluate—Assess progress

Motivate—Bring out the best in people

Organize—Align peoples' actions

Set an example—Model

Handle uncertainty and crises

In the 1990s, common traits in key capabilities were identified by international longitudinal research as providing the foundation for effective leadership. The traits were particularly apparent when leaders motivated people towards a clear goal, on the basis of established knowledge and a fixed paradigm, and while operating within effective structures and policy frameworks. These capabilities included:

1. Charismatic or value-based leadership.
2. Team orientation.
3. A humane and participative approach (Grove, 1995).

These remain valuable attributes. Such leaders tended to be successful in the 20th century. They aimed for improvement through the definition of tasks within their set context—and the planning, control, evaluation and motivation associated with those tasks. In terms of the 21st century demands, however, there is an increasing awareness that this is no longer enough and that there is

[A]n emerging sense of the inadequacy of a paradigm built for a different age, with different purposes. The schooling system created in the context of the 19th century industrial revolution ... left little room for autonomy, creativity, collaborative capacity or the development of personal values or purpose. Employers and civil society in general, cry out for these attributes. (Hannon, 2014)

In a rapidly changing environment, with very different demands, leaders are increasingly required to help shape the future of education, not just react—either to how things have been previously or to what emerges with the passage of time. Doing what we have always done, or making incremental change to that practice, is no longer enough. Up to now, relatively limited attention has tended to be given to proactive exploration of more flexible alternatives—encouraging leaders to discover practical and actionable differences between policies that aim at system improvement (endogenous) and those that aim at inviting experiments for systemic transformation (exogenous). Miller (2013) frames leading innovation as experimentalist strategic leadership. His reframing serves as a model for the 21st century leadership helping leaders learn to *walk on two leadership legs*—advancing the conventional improvement of the existing systems while simultaneously making sense of innovation experiments outside these systems.

Of course, in a time of transition, it is important to maintain improvements within the existing paradigm. However, at the same time, the new leaders must create the conditions for radical transformation to meet the changing needs of the society they serve and deliver on an improved present and prepare for the transformed future of learning. For that, a pervasive culture of innovation is needed. Since systems tend not to encourage radical innovation, part of the educational leaders' role must now be to advocate for policies, teaching practices and styles of learning, assessment and evaluation that address the changing demands being made upon them, their institutions and their staff.

Achieving More than Incremental Improvement and Leading Transformation

In the past, innovative work in education has tended to be carried out in discrete institutions, in parts of institutions or even by individuals in an institutional setting. Where this work has been perceived to be successful and has wider possible application that system leaders value, it may have been 'rolled out' across the system. Improvement has tended to be incremental and has still emphasized matching the existing paradigm. In a complex and hyper-connected world, a more embedded culture of innovation is more appropriate, transcending boundaries in much the same way as the social media to which we have so quickly become accustomed to in our everyday lives. New qualities and behaviours will be required by innovation leaders to create and sustain environments where such a culture can develop and system-level transformation can result.

Who Are the New System Leaders?

Individuals can be inspirational but system-level transformation cannot be sustained by individual effort alone. System leaders in the 21st century will succeed by engaging others and distributing leadership (see, e.g., Harris, 2014, and Spillane, 2006) with the mandate to explore innovation throughout the system. Leaders heading a system, and those working within that system, will still need the attributes and skills that they now exhibit. As noted earlier, on one hand they still have to work for improvement in the existing context. On the other hand, if they are to work for transformational change, they will require additional skills and qualities. Working in collaborative leadership teams will provide one way of ensuring that the required skills are available across a number of settings.

Internationally, over the last five years, the GELP[1] provided a space for systems leaders to reflect upon what education innovation looks like at the system level, and what is entailed in its leadership (Hannon, 2014). This work has led to the identification of a range of skills and qualities that characterize effective system leadership. These include being:

1. systems oriented, which is a given, in the context;
2. inclusive, acknowledging that contributors to the work may come from a wide range of backgrounds and will bring a commensurate range of skills;

[1] For further details about the organization and its work, see www. *gelponline.org/*

For an additional profile, see The Innovation Unit's 2013 publication *Redesigning Education: Shaping Learning Systems Around the Globe.*

3. design thinkers, who can conceive and model new change processes;
4. entrepreneurial, combining and disseminating new ideas in creative ways;
5. strategic and able to keep their eye on the big picture rather than becoming lost in the detail and
6. grounded, in the realities of what is needed and what is done.

In addition, it has been observed that the 'movers and shapers' in the 21st century system leadership show behaviours that are not customarily associated with conventional education leaders, and which reflect their more challenging role to help shape the future of education. These dimensions include:

1. Knowledge Diffusion—where the leaders are outward looking, both in terms of their own intellectual curiosity and in promulgating new ideas.
2. Social Networking—across sectors and geographical boundaries, building relationships, partnerships and circles of support, to pursue system transformation and seek out sources of different ideas, expertise and experience.
3. Cultural Competence—moving easily beyond their own comfort zones, sharing and learning across contexts, developing cross-cultural literacy and building their range of resources, world view and skills.
4. Technology Brokerage—where the leaders apply their own skills in the new learning and communications technologies, but also bring together and access the additional skills of innovators and use the full range of social media to gather, disseminate and share their vision and experience;
5. Political Activism—recognizing the need to be active in 'movement making', and to create and argue a case for change in ways that will be effective and
6. Experimentalism[2]—being willing to engage in their vision of an education system not yet in existence and to help develop

---

[2] See Riel Miller's discussion of this concept in his 2013 *Evaluating GELP: Towards Making Experimentalist Leadership Practical*, Global Education Leaders' Program, London.

the conditions where it will grow, while managing the risks of experimenting outside the existing paradigm.

Hannon (2014) noted that the extent to which such characteristics and behaviours can be developed in leaders is unclear, but that knowledge of how to create innovative capacity is growing and already some processes seem to hold particular potential. These processes include:

1. deliberate creation of diverse cadre groupings, widening the ideas pool and breadth or depth of knowledge;
2. coaching and the development of leaders who can coach others;
3. participants acting as co-designers of powerful learning opportunities;
4. designing and implementing programmes that embody progressive group action enquiry;
5. creation and development of a new paradigm in the uses of technologies and
6. exploring the uses of tools and frameworks to make sense of participant experience in a variety of ways.

As Hannon (2014) remarked, "... such leaders are working with the grain of change: coming, ready or not."

We recognize that leaders can emerge from almost anywhere—in different sectors, across different age groups and at different speeds. Having a diversity of innovators across a diversity of contexts innovating on different scales could potentially be exactly what is needed to ensure equity and excellence in education and learning environments across the world. We should at least be willing to learn from innovators beyond traditional educational organizations and understand what it takes to actually grow an innovation to impact existing educational institutions (Hannon et al., 2013).

Modelling the Change

Leadership in the 21st century faces the challenges of being adaptive and experimental, while continuing to work in a time of transition, from a long-established existing paradigm to a more uncertain future. Leaders have to preserve both the valued aspects of the old and introduce and demonstrate the benefits of new ideas and practice. A significant part of their role is to clarify and balance the tensions, focusing on the positives that emerge from the associated debate.

The new leaders, with their new visions, can model what they try to achieve and can share the new ideas and habits and ways of thinking. The degree to which they are successful depends on how that modelling is perceived and the capacity of those in their systems, institutions and teams to adopt, embed and diffuse the transformation that is demonstrated. This means overcoming entrenched positions taken by government agencies, groups and individuals, which tend to cling to institutionalized or familiar practices and behaviour. It means recognizing and taking risks. This enterprise is vitally important if the education that we offer to our young people is to adapt appropriately and rapidly enough and to match the changing demands of the society in which we live.

References

Grove, C. N. (1995). *Introduction to the globe research project on leadership worldwide.* Retrieved from http://www.grovewell.com/pub-GLOBE-intro.html. Accessed on 15 March 2014.

Hannon, V. (2014, February). *Can transforming education systems be led?* CSE Seminar Series (Paper No. 231). Melbourne: Centre for Strategic Education. Accessed on 15 March 2014.

Hannon, V., Gillinson, S. and Shanks, L. (2013). *Learning a living: Radical innovation in education for work.* A & C Black Music, Bloomsbury. Retrieved from http://www.wise-qatar.org/2012-wise-book. Accessed on 15 March 2014.

Kotter, J. P. (1999). *What leaders really do.* Harvard Business Review Book. Retrieved from https://hbr.org/product/john-p-kotter-on-what-leaders-really-do/8974-HBK-ENG. Accessed on 15 March 2014.

Leadership-Central.com. (2015). *Leadership Theories*. Retrieved from http://www.leadership-central.com/leadership-theories.html#axzz3erkhRe8y. Accessed on 15 March 2014.

Miller, R. (2013). *Evaluating GELP: Towards making experimentalist leadership practical*. London: Global Education Leaders' Program.

Spillane, J. (2006) *Distributed leadership*. San Francisco: Jossey-Bass.

6

Leading System-wide Educational Improvement in Ontario

Carol Campbell

Introduction

During 2003, a new government was elected in Ontario, Canada, with a priority commitment to improvement in education. There continues to be a consistent and sustained focus on developing leadership and professional capacity at all levels of the education system within government, for school district and school leaders, and for teacher leaders to develop, adapt and implement changes in leadership and teaching practices to support improvements in student outcomes. Locating the Ontario case within the larger context of whole system reform and system leadership to achieve both excellence and equity in educational outcomes, this chapter discusses the context of Ontario, the results achieved to date, the theory of action informing the educational change strategies and the development of a culture, infrastructure and capacities for leading improvements throughout the education system.

Whole System Reform and System Leadership

The existence and persistence of inequalities in educational experiences within schooling and in outcomes for students is a long-standing concern. Low levels of educational achievement, not graduating from high school and/or large gaps in the performance of different student groups have serious consequences for individuals' life chances and for wider economic, social and community development. There are compelling arguments about the importance of educational change for moral (Fullan, 2010), social justice (Hargreaves and Shirley, 2009) and economic (OECD, 2010a) imperatives. The rising use and profile of national and international assessments (e.g., OECD, 2010a), debate about international benchmarking (Schleicher, 2009), and research on the educational strategies, practices and outcomes in different national contexts (e.g., Barber and Mourshed, 2007; Darling-Hammond, 2010; Fullan, 2010; Jensen et al., 2012; Mourshed et al., 2010) have contributed to rising interest in the content and processes of 'whole system' educational change at national and/or state/province levels. The quest of whole system reform is to support all students to learn, all teachers to teach, all education leaders to lead and all schools (and systems) to improve. Both educational quality (high standards of achievement) and equity (low differences in achievement for different students and schools) are the priority goals.

Discussions of whole system reform generally combine an overarching theory of action with attention to change processes (Fullan, 2009, 2010). There is no one-size-fits-all approach to educational improvement and there are considerable variations between, among and within countries. While authors vary in details (e.g., Barber and Mourshed, 2007; Fullan, 2009, 2010; Jensen et al., 2012; Mourshed et al., 2010), I identify whole system reform as including the following features:

1. A central focus on improving teaching and learning, including supporting conditions such as leadership development, attention to equity, curriculum and assessments.

2. A small number of ambitious but relevant and realistic goals, widely communicated, understood and acted upon.
3. Effective allocation of resources aligned to the priority goals and strategies.
4. A sustained focus on key goals and linked priority strategies while managing potential distractions from the main reform agenda.
5. Capable key senior leaders committed to sustained prioritization of educational improvement plus engagement and development of leaders and leadership throughout the education system.
6. High standards and expectations for all students and schools to achieve combined with use of data to identify current performance, monitor improvements and target where further improvement is required.
7. A combination of valuing and being transparent about the existing professional practice while also holding high expectations for further improvements in professional practice and student learning.
8. An emphasis on, and support for, respecting, valuing and developing professional capacity (individual and collective) through a system of recruitment, training, development, recognition, working conditions and career progression for educators.
9. A commitment to continuous improvement and use of evidence to identify and spread effective practices and to innovate next practices.
10. Strong attention to the implementation processes of delivering the strategies and improvements in practices and outcomes.

Nevertheless, the ideals informing whole system reform and the realization in the details of policies and practices are contentious. A main area of debate is the nature and balance of 'top-down' reforms from government combined with 'bottom-up' professional initiatives and/or with lateral collaboration across peers for learning and innovation. Hargreaves and Shirley (2009, 2012) suggest that while the designers and deliverers of whole system reform are well intentioned, the approach to implementation is too autocratic and the detail of implementation is too data driven, contrasted with alternative approaches valuing distributed leadership, shared ownership and professional judgment. A crucial issue is that the nature of whole system reform in practice is influenced by leadership decisions and actions. There is a need, therefore, for further detailed consideration of the leadership practices of system leaders for an educationally appropriate, ethical, socially inclusive and just whole system reform.

Harris (2010) proposes that whole system reform requires a new model of change, new capacities and new ways of working: "To change an entire system undoubtedly requires leadership of a different nature, order and scale ... the importance of developing leadership at all levels in the system in order to be successful" (Harris, 2010:204). Conceptualizations of 'system leadership' emphasize the importance of developing and distributing leadership throughout the education system and the need for interaction, linkages and networks among and between leaders at all levels of the system. Furthermore, 'system leaders' involve an expanding range of leaders, as Fullan (2010:xv) proposes, "All systems must encompass all leaders." In this expansive, yet distributive, conception of system leadership, the majority of attention has been focused on developing the professional capacities and educational leadership practices of teachers and administrators at school and district or network levels. These are vital and important developments and must continue as central to educational change. Nevertheless, if we are serious about system leadership as encompassing change, competence, capability and capacity "at all levels of the system" (Harris, 2010:197), then we also need to examine, understand and develop leadership capacities and practices at the government level. This chapter examines the theory of action and approaches to developing leadership capacities for educational improvement within government, for formal district and school leaders, and for cultivating and valuing teachers' leadership in Ontario.

Context of Ontario

The province of Ontario spans over one million square kilometres with a population of over 13.5 million people. Ninety five per cent (over two million students) of school-age children in Ontario attend Ontario's publicly funded education system. Twenty seven per cent of students in Ontario were born outside Canada, with 20 per cent self-identifying themselves as members of a visible minority; 4.5 per cent of Ontario students are French speaking. Ontario's publicly funded education system is overseen and funded by the provincial government through the Ontario Ministry of Education. There are almost 5,000 schools in Ontario governed through four pub-licly funded education systems—English Public, English Catholic, French Public and French Catholic—and administered through 72 school districts and 11 smaller school authorities.

Elected in 2003, the new Liberal government committed to make significant improvement in education. Three priority goals were identified and became the focus for the work of the Ministry of Education, the education system and partners in a whole system reform approach for:

1. increased student achievement;
2. reduced gaps in student achievement;
3. increased public confidence in publicly funded education.

Related to these goals, targets were established to have 75 per cent of students achieve at the provincial standard (70%, or a B grade) in reading, writing and mathematics in the sixth grade (at the age of 12) and secondary school graduation rate of 85 per cent of students. Targets to reduce primary class sizes (grades 1–3) to an average of 20 students with flexibility of up to 23 students if required for practical reasons, were also established.

In spring 2014, a renewed vision for Ontario education was announced— *Achieving Excellence*—with updated goals for achieve-ment, equity and public confidence, plus a new goal for well-being, specifically:

1. *Achieving excellence.* Children and students of all ages will achieve high levels of academic performance, acquire valuable skills and demonstrate good citizenship. Educators will be supported in learning continuously and will be recognized as among the best in the world.
2. *Ensuring equity.* All children and students will be inspired to reach their full potential, with access to rich learning experiences that begin at birth and continue into adulthood.
3. *Promoting well-being.* All children and students will develop enhanced mental and physical health, a positive sense of self and belonging and the skills to make positive choices.
4. *Enhancing public confidence.* Ontarians will continue to have confidence in a publicly funded education system that helps develop new generations of confident, capable and caring citizens. (Ontario Ministry of Education, 2014)

Results Achieved

Ontario is recognized as a province that has high levels of both academic achievement and equity, with a lower-than-average impact of socio-economic status on educational outcomes compared to countries across the Organisation for Economic Co-operation and Development (OECD, 2013). In the Programme for International Student Assessment (PISA), 2012, from a total of 65 participating jurisdictions, Canada ranked 7th in reading, 9th in science and 13th in mathematics. Ontario's scores are at a similar level to the Canadian average.

Considerable progress on the Ontario government's education goals and related targets has been achieved.

1. *Increased student achievement.* From the starting point in 2002–2003, 54 per cent of elementary students achieved or exceeded the provincial standard in reading, writing and mathematics, whereas by 2013–2014, 72 per cent of students met or exceeded the provincial standard. The high school graduation rate also improved considerably. Based on the

analysis of students who graduated from Ontario's publicly funded schools within five years, Ontario's graduation rate has increased from 68 per cent in 2003–2004 to 83 per cent in 2012–2013.

2. *Reduced gaps in performance.* Alongside an overall increase in student achievement, the Ontario government is committed to reducing gaps in performance. At the school level, this has focused on supporting all schools to improve, with additional support for schools identified as lower achieving or struggling to improve. Over the period from 2005–2006 to 2012–2013, the proportion of elementary schools identified as low performing (defined as fewer than 50% of their students meeting or exceeding the provincial standard on more than half of the assessments in the school) has more than halved from 13 per cent in 2005–2006 to six per cent in 2012–2013. At the same time, there has been an increase in the proportion of 'high-performing' schools (identified as schools where 75 per cent of students achieve the provincial standard on at least half of the provincial assessments administered in the school) from 29 per cent in 2005–2006 to 51 per cent in 2012–2013. At the student level, the most substantial improvements in 'reducing gaps' have been for English Language Learners (ELL). In 2002–2003, the performance gap for ELL students ranged from 32 to 17 percentage points in provincial assessments for reading, writing and mathematics in grades 3 and 6, whereas in 2013–2014, the gap narrowed to between nine and three percentage points. Although not as substantial, there have also been reductions in performance gaps for students identified as having special educational needs.

3. *Increased public confidence in publicly funded education.* Public opinion survey data indicates increasing satisfaction levels with the Ontario education system. According to Hart (2012):

   i. In 2012, 65 per cent of the public was satisfied with schools, compared to 44 per cent of in 1998.

ii. In 2012, 70 per cent of the public was satisfied with the kind of job that teachers were doing, compared to 62 per cent in 1998.

Satisfaction rates are higher for parents than for the general public. In 2012, 77 per cent of parents were satisfied with schools and 76 per cent were satisfied with the jobs that teachers were doing.

Leading Educational Improvement: Ontario's Theory of Action and Leadership Capacities for Implementation

In the OECD's study of Ontario as part of their *Strong Performers and Successful Reformers in Education* series, the OECD concluded:

> The Ontario strategy is perhaps the world's leading example of professionally-driven system change. Through consistent application of centrally-driven pressure for higher results, combined with extensive capacity building, in a climate of relative trust and mutual respect, the Ontario system was able to achieve progress on key indicators, while maintaining labour peace and morale throughout the system. (2010b:75)

Let's now discuss how Ontario led educational improvements through a thoughtful theory of action applied to developing leadership capacities and practices throughout the education system so as to contribute to the improved student outcomes.

Ontario's Theory of Action for Educational Improvement

Five key elements of Ontario's theory of action (Campbell et al., 2015b) for educational improvement can be identified as:

1. **Focus: Identification of Key Priorities for Improvement**. Three goals have informed the focus of Ontario's educational improvements for over a decade: increasing student

achievement, reducing gaps in performance and increasing public confidence in publicly funded education. In 2014, these goals were revised and renewed with the introduction of a fourth priority focus on enhancing well-being. These goals have provided a consistent focus for action throughout the education system.

2. **Tri-level Reform: System-wide Coherence and Alignment**. A vast array of policies, strategies, initiatives and actions have been undertaken over the past decade. However, all actions are intended to be aligned with the core goals outlined above and have involved coordinated attention at provincial, school district, school and classroom levels. To support systemic action and coherence, a central feature has been laying emphasis on developing professional partnerships, trust and respect between the provincial government, all provincial stakeholders, the teaching profession and wider public.

3. **Support and Positive Pressure: Capacity Building with a Focus on Results**. A key element of the Ontario strategies is 'capacity building with a focus on results' involving the development of educators' knowledge, skills and practices with a particular focus on instructional improvements to support students' learning and achievements. Where student achievement is identified as being lower, for example, for a particular groups of students and/or schools, additional attention, resources and support is provided to target and improve educational practices. The Ontario approach emphasizes developing the capacity of all people involved through fostering collective commitment and collaborative action for educational improvement.

4. **Shared Leadership: Respect for Professional Knowledge and Practice**. The Ontario approach to educational change places emphasis on developing professional capacity and leadership throughout the education system. The existing professional knowledge is valued and respected. A combination of professional knowledge, identification and sharing of successful or promising practices plus the use of data and research

locally and from international leading practice is combined to inform the Ontario strategies and actions.

5. **Professional Accountability: Results without Rancor or Ranking.** Educators are considered to be professionals with responsibility for self- and peer-improvement. The government does not label 'failing' schools requiring firing of staff or takeover models. Rather, where underperformance in students' achievement is identified, the view of the Ministry of Education is to develop the 'will and skill' of educators to improve programmes and instructional practices, plus supporting conditions, to enable students to learn, achieve and thrive at school and beyond.

Ontario's Improvement Strategies and Initiatives

Informed by this theory of action, Ontario's Ministry of Education and education partners have developed a culture and infrastructure for the implementation of policies and actions to develop professional capacity, leadership and teaching practices to support improved student outcomes. In summary form, key elements of provincial initiatives include:

1. Focus on transforming professional capacity to improve classroom teaching and learning for 'elementary school' strategy.
2. Focus on transforming programmes, pathways and support for students to succeed in high school, transition to post-secondary education and career in 'secondary or high school' strategy.

A focus across all schools on:

1. Whole system supports for all schools combined with intervention partnerships with schools at different performance levels;
2. Targeted supports and interventions for students and schools that are struggling to improve;

3. Support for professional collaboration, teams and collective capacity within schools and districts with focus on evidence about student learning;
4. Provision of a range of professional learning, development and resources for specific education priority areas and to foster teaching quality and leadership;
5. Facilitation of networks to share and support improved practices across schools and districts;
6. Development of culture, value and practice of using research, evaluation and data to inform, monitor and adapt strategies and practices;
7. Substantial resources and infrastructure for system capacity;
8. Creating an enabling policy environment and partnerships with the profession, stakeholders and public.

Approaches for Implementation of Educational Improvement

Deliberate attention has been paid to turn the theory of action for 'building capacity with a focus on results' and 'shared leadership' into actual implementation of improvements in professional capacities and practices for government leaders, district and school administrators, and teachers.

Creating a Government Culture and Structure Focused on Leadership of Educational Improvement

Debates about whole system reform and lessons from international assessments of higher and lower performing education systems tend to prioritize the need for reforms affecting teachers and teaching, and school leaders and their leadership practices. However, the focus cannot simply be on government's demanding or supporting educators to improve. Governments also need to look internally at their own capacities and practices to contribute appropriately to educational improvement. Put simply, it requires leadership and capacity to develop leadership and capacity.

Political Leadership with Sustained Priority Commitment to Education

In 2003, Dalton McGuinty was elected as the Premier (political government leader) of Ontario with a commitment to being the 'education premier'. In 2011, Dalton McGuinty stepped down and Kathleen Wynne—a former Minister of Education in McGuinty's Cabinet with a long career connected to education—became the Premier of Ontario. Both Premiers were proactive in advancing a priority focus on educational improvement. While there were differences in leadership styles and there have been differing details in the emphasis on educational priorities, there has been a consistent focus and political commitment from the key political leaders for a sustained period of time.

Guiding coalition: Capable Political and Official Leadership for Strategy and Action

The term 'guiding coalition' has been used to describe a strategy group of the most senior political (prime ministers or premier and minister of education or equivalents) and official (permanent secretary or deputy minister and head or chief of the educational change strategies) leaders, with support from advisors and assistants. The purpose of the 'guiding coalition' is to develop, deliver, oversee and adapt the educational change strategy (Barber, 2010).

They are to lead 'from the top': "There is no getting around it. For the entire system to be on the go, one needs relentless, resolute leadership from the top leadership that focuses on the right things and that above all, promotes collective capacity and ownership" (Fullan, 2010:13).

In Ontario, the concepts of a 'guiding coalition' became adapted to an Education Results Team involving the political leaders (premier and minister of education) and advisors, plus senior government officials (deputy minister and assistant deputy ministers) and relevant staff. A central element has been the careful appointment of senior government officials committed to the government's student achievement and educational improvement agenda and with the 'know how' to lead both the Ministry and the wider education sector to improve educational outcomes. Nevertheless, while an executive team of senior leaders with capable government and educational leadership is required; the approach cannot be exclusively a handful of handpicked leaders 'from the top'. Rather leadership needs also to be distributed and shared throughout the Ministry of Education and with the education system.

Developing the Culture, Infrastructure and Educational Leadership of the Ministry of Education

In Ontario's case, the equivalent of a 'guiding coalition' involves approximately 10 people, whereas the Ministry of Education (equivalent of national or state education department) employs almost 2,000 people. The commitment and capacity of *all* officials in the Ministry of Education is vital for developing, leading, supporting and contributing to effective educational improvements.

Restructuring government bureaucracies can be time consuming and energy absorbing; at the same time the status quo may not be best organized or equipped if the intention is innovative educational transformation. In Ontario, the Ministry of Education has become organized and staffed to increase the priority focus on contributing to educational improvement in partnership with the education system. Bureaucratic operations for legislation, regulation and the traditional work of government still have an important function, but they are not foreground in the Ministry's culture and mode of operation. Broadly conceived, the Ministry has become supportive of *instructional leadership* whereby educational expertise is valued and, for those in non-education specific roles, the emphasis is laid on how all Ministry's officials' work can provide the enabling conditions— legal, financial, human resources, audit and so on—to support the focus on improving instruction, student achievement and outcomes.

At the start of the government's priority focus on educational improvement, a new organization was established (in 2004)—The Literacy and Numeracy Secretariat (LNS)—with a mandate "to drive change and achieve results with a sense of urgency" (Glaze et al., 2013:15). The LNS is part of the government but operates differently from a traditional Ministry branch in the following ways. According to the LNS (2012:5):

1. It plays a unique role within a larger strategy—the province's literacy and numeracy strategy, charged with developing, coordinating and delivering the government's literacy and numeracy strategy in elementary schools.
2. It is also responsible for ensuring that programmes and initiatives result in greater instructional effectiveness at the classroom level leading to improvement in student learning and achievement.
3. Its strategic implementation work is drawn from research related to school improvement efforts which reflect that successful education systems provide opportunities for teachers and school leaders to learn, develop and own strategies through practice. Also, sustained continuous improvement is built and developed in partnership with classroom, school and district leaders.

The LNS, organized on the basis of seven regional and one French-language teams, works across the province directly with district school boards and schools. Each team consists of educational leaders, Student Achievement Officers (SAOs), who have recent experience as teachers, principals, school consultants/coaches/ coordinators or senior district school board leaders. The teams allow the LNS to support schools and district school boards' improvement efforts in a way that respond to diverse contexts and needs, while further establishing collaborative partnerships focused on student learning and achievement.

The LNS continues to work on building partnerships with district school boards and fostering a climate of trust and collaboration and continues to work with districts and schools to construct and support precise instructional and assessment practices at the school and classroom levels.

LNS is organized on the basis of Regional Teams of SAOs that work with districts and schools plus central strategic teams in the ministries for Leadership and Implementation, Capacity Building and Research, Evaluation and Data Management and central operations teams to support the running of LNS. A lesson may be that if governments seek to transform educational leadership 'in the field' (districts, schools and classrooms), they may also need to transform their own infrastructure and leadership capacity to support transformation within itself and across the education system.

An important way of bringing together both government or policy knowledge and educational leadership to develop educational strategies with the potential for implementation and impact has been through the deliberate hiring of both civil servants with extensive government experience and also hiring or temporarily seconding educators with relevant practical educational expertise. For example, Mary Jean Gallagher (the Chief SAO and Assistant Deputy Minister of the Student Achievement Division [SAD], Ontario Ministry of Education) explains that this combination of expertise is considered to be particularly important.

> I would say the LNS has been designed as a particularly effective infrastructure for implementation. The staffing itself is a combination of school system staff and government staff. OPS [Ontario Public Service] people bring the public policy piece forward; they bring a deep understanding of how policy can affect action and structure, what are the strategic levers that might work and how you build these logic models that actually are thorough and careful. On its own, that gives you policies or programmes that can be implemented, not necessarily policies that are implemented. Because the reality is, in a school everybody is running down the hallway, so busy dealing with day to day issues that too often, really good documents, research, concepts and programmes sit on a shelf and never become implemented in a way that the system owns them. So the other side of LNS staff is a collection of exceptional educators. Whether they have come into our research staff, whether they've come into our field staff or our leadership staff, they are embedded at every level of our organization. It's a combination of both of those kinds of staff, because you have to design the programme's policies and documents with implementation and an understanding of how schools and Boards function in mind and then you have to continue to be nimble and modify as you go along (Campbell et al., 2015b).

The benefit of this blended staffing model is both for building capacity for educational improvement within the Ministry and for those educators who return to working in the education system, to enhance understanding, ownership and collective leadership for the educational strategies within and across the education sector.

It is important that educational improvement priorities—and a linked change in culture and capacity—become owned, integrated and embedded throughout the government. In Ontario, after the initial urgency of activity requiring a different approach through the

LNS, the next phase of leading change required an emphasis on aligning and integrating work within and across the Ministry. In 2008, LNS became part of a newly established SAD within the Ministry, bringing together the elementary-school-focused LNS with the high-school-focused student success/learning, to 18 branches for a new K-12 student achievement focus. The emphasis is on collaboration throughout the Ministry for shared leadership on achieving the government's priority educational goals.

In summary, creating a government culture and structure focused on the leadership of educational improvement requires attention to political leadership with a sustained priority commitment to, and understanding of education, developing a senior team with political and official leadership for strategy and action, and most importantly developing the culture, infrastructure and educational leadership capacities throughout the entire Ministry of Education to support transformation internally and in partnership with the education system.

Developing the Leadership Capacities and Practices of System and School Administrators to Initiate, Adapt and Implement Improvement

Ontario has placed a priority emphasis also on developing the capacities and practices of school district leaders and school administrators to fulfil their formal leadership role to oversee, promote and support their organizations and the staff, students, communities and partners involved.

Developing Formal Leadership

Through the Ontario Leadership Strategy (OLS), Ontario has focused on recruiting and developing district and school leaders. Each school district in Ontario is provided with funding and support to develop and implement a Board Leadership Development Strategy (BLDS) to focus on four key areas. These are:

1. *Recruiting and selecting leaders* through structured and innovative succession planning.

2. *Placing and transferring leaders* in ways that sustain school and system improvement.
3. *Developing leaders* through mentoring, performance appraisal and differentiated learning opportunities that meet the needs of leaders in diverse contexts and at various stages of their careers.
4. *Coordinating support for leaders* to buffer them from distractions, make information easily accessible and assist them in building coherence across different initiatives (Ontario Ministry of Education, 2012).

Within the overarching expectations of the BLDS, school districts vary in their approach to identify and recruit people into formal leadership positions. As part of their succession planning, many school districts offer a leadership development programme as the first step for aspiring leaders, which may include topics such as developing positive relations with parents, the link between leadership and student achievement and work-life balance. Some programmes also include a job-shadowing component where prospective administers are placed with a practicing principal or vice principal. As part of the OLS, newly recruited principals and vice principals are offered mentoring for their first two years in each role. Throughout their career, principals and vice principals are appraised every five years through a Principal Performance Appraisal process. Therefore, there are formalized requirements, resources and approaches for the training, recruitment and development of district and school leaders with the goal of enhancing leadership capacities and practices (Campbell et al., 2015b; Pervin and Campbell, 2015).

Furthermore, approaches to leadership development and practice are intended to be informed by the Ontario Leadership Framework (OLF). Consistent with the main findings of the research of Leithwood et al. (2004) on educational leadership to influence student learning, the OLF contains five priority areas of leadership practices (Leithwood, 2012). These are:

1. Setting directions.
2. Building relationships and developing people.

3. Developing the organization to support desired practices.
4. Improving the instructional programme.
5. Securing accountability.

A revised and updated version of the OLF now also contains personal leadership resources for the following domains (Leithwood, 2012):

1. *Cognitive resources*: Problem-solving expertise and knowledge about school and classroom conditions with direct effects on student learning.
2. *Social resources*: Perceiving and managing emotions, and acting in emotionally appropriate ways.
3. *Psychological resources*: Optimism, self-efficacy and resilience.

The OLF is intended to promote a common language to foster an understanding of leadership and what it means to be school and district leaders, and to guide the design and implementation of professional learning and development of school and district leaders. Therefore, Ontario's approach to develop people in administrative positions includes attention to the identification of aspiring leaders and succession planning, recruitment and career development, plus supports for professional and personal leadership capacities.

Leading through Tri-level Partnerships for Improvement

Along with developing the formal leadership capacities of individuals holding administrative responsibilities, the Ontario approach to develop districts and school leaderships emphasizes shared leadership and ownership for educational improvements. There is a focus on aligning and developing capacity across K-12 with an emphasis on instructional leadership and teaching practices. A K-12 School Effectiveness Framework (SEF) (see Figure 6.1) is intended to inform and provide a focus for identification of goals, priorities and actions at the school district level through the Board Improvement Plan for Student Achievement (BIPSA) and for schools through School Improvement Plans.

Figure 6.1
K-12 School Effectiveness Framework

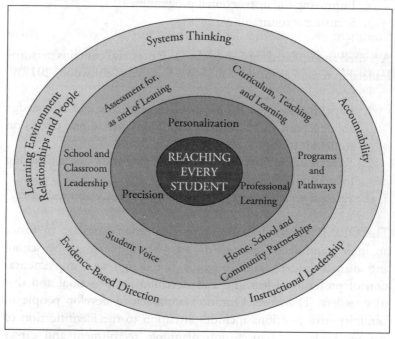

Source: Ontario Ministry of Education, 2013.

Relatedly, the K-12 System Implementation and Monitoring (SIM) initiative provides funding to support school districts to identify a SIM Team to work with School Improvement Teams within and across networks of schools to improve pedagogy and instructional leadership. According to LNS (2013), through professional dialogue and study, teams will further develop their capacity to:

- observe, describe, and analyze student work
- set specific goals and targets for student learning
- plan and implement specific teaching and learning strategies
- monitor student achievement results and adjust strategies as needed
- support the professional learning required to raise achievement

- align resources to meet achievement goals
- engage students and parents in school improvement.

Consistent with Ontario's theory of action for 'tri-level reform', there is attention to developing capacities at classroom, school, board and provincial levels. However, the emphasis is not simply on each level of the education sector, but also on developing a coherent approach to system-wide reforms.

> Things like BIPSA [Board Improvement Plans for Student Achievement], the School Effectiveness Framework, school improvement planning structures and board improvement planning structures fit into what I would refer to as the systematization of reform. It's how you take it from happening in some isolated schools or one Board and try to build it as a comprehensive activity for everyone. It can't simply be done by saying, "Oh, we're going to have a policy that says Boards have to have an improvement plan or schools have to have an improvement plan". What we were building was an infrastructure to engage reflective thinking, and also to deliver reforms, but the reforms we were delivering were not just the reforms of the government's making or the Ministry's making, these were the reforms of the schools' making and the school boards' making and building that partnership. So it became about a structured way of systematizing the de-privatization of teaching and leading. (Mary Jean Gallagher, Student Achievement Division, Ontario Ministry of Education; quoted in Campbell et al., 2015b)

While 'systematizing' approaches to improvement, the emphasis is not on standardization of top-down directives. Rather, the goal is to identify the value and develop professional capacity linked to professional accountability.

> When we're working with Boards or schools or teachers, it's a treasure hunt not a witch hunt, and all of our processes are founded on a deep respect and regard for the work of teaching and learning and a deep respect and regard for our educators. We would never go in and deliver to them "look, here is 'the' strategy for how you teach maths, or 'the' strategy for how you teach literacy and if you would just do it this way results will improve," because that is not how kids learn. Kids learn when you have a dedicated teacher who understands deeply where kids are and has a whole backpack full of teaching strategies. The professional capacity, the professional judgement comes in deciding how you are going to do that. (Mary Jean Gallagher, Student

Achievement Division, Ontario Ministry of Education; quoted in Campbell
et al., 2015b)

The intent is fostering a 'collaborative professionalism' throughout
the education system.

Leading from the Middle

Alongside developing the leadership capacities of district and school
leaders to support tri-level reforms aligned with provincial directions, the Ontario approach also values and supports the development of local leadership within and across schools and districts to
innovate new practices and to share existing promising practices.
One of the earliest actions of the LNS (Glaze and Campbell, 2007)
was to research the existing effective or promising practices in schools
(Campbell et al., 2007) and in districts (Campbell and Fullan, 2006).
We identified four strategic areas, encompassing 12 components, of
the existing effective district-wide strategies to raise student achievement in literacy and numeracy (Campbell and Fullan, 2006):

1. Leading with purpose and focusing direction

   i. Leadership for learning
   ii. Vision and shared focus on student achievement as the priority
   iii. Moral purpose informing practices to unlock potential for system,
   school and student development

2. Designing a coherent strategy, co-ordinating implementation and reviewing outcomes

   i. Overarching strategy
   ii. Resources prioritized to focus on improved student achievement
   iii. Effective district organization
   iv. System and school-level monitoring, review, feedback and
   accountability

3. Developing precision in knowledge, skills and daily practices for
   improving

    i. Capacity building and professional learning for teachers and principals

    ii. Curriculum development, instruction and interventions to improve teaching and learning for all students

    iii. Use of data and development of assessment literacy

4. Sharing responsibility through building partnerships

    i. Positive and purposeful partnerships

    ii. Communication

After observing the existing practices in Ontario's districts and schools, we emphasized the importance of leadership for learning.

We refer here to *leadership for learning* to emphasize that the leadership was purposeful and focused on supporting learning. This focus on learning includes leadership both to support professional learning and to direct strategies and actions for improved student learning and achievement. The educators we met with—directors, supervisory officers, coaches, principals, teachers—were instructional leaders demonstrating deep knowledge of teaching and learning, which they discussed, modelled, and encouraged throughout the district. We use the broader term leadership for learning, however, to indicate that the district leaders we met who were not directly educators, for example supervisory officers with business qualifications, also shared a strong commitment to, and understanding of, the importance of their role in supporting student learning at the system level.

Across the districts, there was strong evidence of individual and collective leadership being exercised and fostered. This combination of both individual and collective leadership is important. Individuals demonstrated strong leadership skills both in the processes of supporting system change and in their individual educational expertise. By working collaboratively through teams, collective leadership was also developed and encouraged to ensure that shared leadership was drawn on the range of individual expertise to produce best thinking to inform strategies and actions. This is part of developing the two-way street between individual expertise and system transformation through shared leadership.

The districts demonstrated leadership for learning at all levels of the system. This leadership provided clear strategic direction, focusing on raising student achievement in literacy and numeracy. Trustees supported board and school leaders to focus on building the capacity of the system to raise student achievement. The director consistently provided leadership focused on raising student achievement at the system level. The senior administrative team and board staff demonstrated leadership in promoting and developing capacity for literacy and numeracy. Principals were trained as instructional leaders and this reflected in their daily practices. At the school level, the principal's leadership was very important to support school improvement and successful practices for improving teaching and learning. Teacher leaders were developed, for example, to lead literacy and numeracy teachers, to support system, school and classroom improvement in literacy and numeracy instructions and to build the professional capacity of colleagues. (Campbell and Fullan, 2006:17–18)

Developing individual and collective leadership to support both professional learning and student learning is critical to achieving system-wide improvements. This requires not only 'leadership from the top' (Fullan, 2010:13) but also, vitally, 'leadership from the middle' (Hargreaves and Braun, 2012:15) from district leaders and/or networks of education professionals.

Hargreaves and Braun (2012) coined the phrase 'leading from the middle' in their study of school districts implementing Ontario's special education policy. Instead of the Ministry of Education mandating how implementation would work in a top-down way, the government provided $25 million (CND) to the Council of Ontario Directors of Education (CODE)—the organization representing the professional leaders of school districts—to develop and support the implementation of professional development for the new policy. CODE worked with a steering group of educational leaders (recently retired and reputable former school district leaders) and in partnership with districts, as well as the Ministry of Education, to effectively support professional development and implementation of locally developed district plans and projects to advance support for students identified as having special educational needs. Hargreaves and Braun (2012:15) conclude that leading from the middle took three forms, namely:

1. The high-level stakeholder representation that also applied to other provincial reforms in education
2. Collective commitment and advocacy of all or most leaders, and
3. Development and steering by a team of middle-level leaders.

The practice of supporting both individual and collective leadership development of educators has been the central feature of Ontario's approach to educational improvement.

In summary, Ontario's approach to the development of leadership in districts and schools includes attention to the recruitment and development of people appointed to formal leadership positions, providing a K-12 emphasis and supports for shared leadership through tri-level reform aligning provincial priorities and local implementation, plus also enabling leadership 'from the middle' for local initiative, innovation and action.

Fostering Teacher Leadership for Innovation, Inquiry and Improvement in Teaching and Learning

Consistent with Ontario's theory of action prioritizing professional capacity, Ontario has an extensive range of professional development and learning opportunities connected to teachers' career stages, to implementation of new initiatives, aligned with provincial, district and school priorities, and also with opportunities for teachers' self-selected professional learning needs and activities. Figure 6.2 provides a schematic representation of the overall approach to teachers' growth and development (see also Campbell et al., 2015b).

Teachers' Learning and Leadership With, By and For Teachers

Of particular importance, there has been attention to developing the (informal) teacher leadership of classroom teachers. Coming out of a Working Table on Teacher Education—importantly involving the teacher unions partnering with the government—it was recognized that there was a need to support the professional development of experienced classroom teachers, particularly those who select to continue as classroom teachers rather than move into administrative positions. In contrast to Ministry- or district- or school-directed professional developments, the need for teacher-led professional

Figure 6.2
Teacher Growth and Development

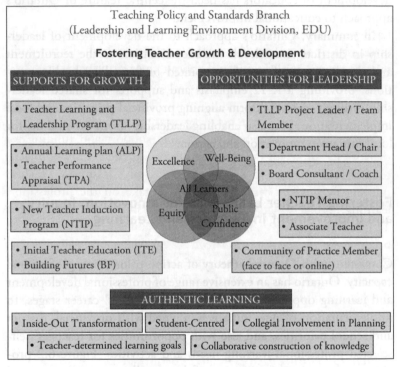

Source: Teaching Policy and Standards Branch, Ontario Ministry of Education.

learning opportunities was also identified as important. In 2007, the Teacher Learning and Leadership Programme (TLLP) was launched to support professional learning 'with, by and for teachers'. A vital feature of the TLLP is that it is developed and delivered in partnership between the Ministry of Education and the Ontario Teachers' Federation (OTF) with shared goals to:

1. support experienced teachers undertake self-directed advanced professional development;
2. develop teachers' leadership skills for sharing their professional learning and exemplary practices and

3. facilitate knowledge exchange for spread and sustainability of practices.

Each year, experienced teachers—individually or more commonly in teams—apply to conduct a TLLP project. School district committees review applications and submit their priority choices to a provincial committee comprising of teacher union and government representatives, who select projects for funding. An average of 78 projects per year have been funded over the past seven years.

Successful applicants receive training, support and funding for their TLLP projects. Prior to embarking on their TLLP projects, teacher leaders attend a Leadership Skills for Classroom Teachers training to support their preparation to take on the professional learning, project management and leadership expectations of a TLLP. Throughout their TLLP project, and beyond, participants become part of *Mentoring Moments*—an online community to share resources, learning and discussions—and, at the end of their TLLP project, TLLP teams attend the Sharing the Learning Summit to showcase completed projects and to strengthen the spread and sustainability of practices.

Teachers Leading Professional Learning

Teachers self-identify topics that they are passionate about investigating and improving to form the basis of their TLLP project. Hence, a wide range of project themes exist. The most prevalent TLLP project topics include: technology, differentiated instruction, literacy, math, student assessment and students identified as having special educational needs (Campbell et al., 2013, 2015a). The 'TLLP approach' is grounded in a commitment to 'authentic learner led learning ... by teachers, for teachers' (Campbell et al., 2014). The teacher-led, self-directed nature of TLLP is considered to be unique and vital, particularly for experienced teachers looking for new ways of developing their professional learning. In our survey of the current and former TLLP teacher leaders (Campbell et al., 2015a), the majority of professional learning activities undertaken through TLLP projects included: teacher collaborative learning groups (68.7% of respondents), engaging in professional dialogue (67.5% of respondents), opportunities for self-reflection (63.8% of respondents), analysis of student data and/or work (58% of respondents), engaging in a literature/research review (56.8% of respondents) and time and opportunity for planning purposes (53.9% of respondents). Other forms of professional learning activities included: conducting action research, providing or participating in workshops and courses, professional networking (including online), co-teaching, attending conferences and/or seminars and working with an external specialist and/or with other organizations. The majority of TLLP participants responding to our survey identified benefits for improvements in their knowledge and understanding, instructional practices, collaboration and communication between teachers, energy and inspiration, and sense of self-efficacy.

The combination of creating or accessing new resources and materials with highly collaborative professional learning interactions is a common theme of the TLLP approach, indicating that effective professional learning combines high-quality content with attention to opportunities for professional collaboration, networking and co-learning. The approach of TLLP involving both individual and collective learning with, by and for teachers embodies the features of professional capital envisaged by Hargreaves and Fullan (2012)—combining the human capital of individual teachers' knowledge and skills with the social capital of groups of teachers collaborating, communicating, networking and improving practices together with the decisional capital of experienced and informed professional judgment.

Developing Teachers' Leadership Practices

While the concept of 'teacher leadership' has become an "umbrella phrase", often meaning different things in different settings (Harris, 2005:204–205), the form of teacher leadership developed and experienced by TLLP teacher leaders involves an instructional component, a relational component and an enabling component, as suggested by

Murphy (2005) and summarized by Harris (2005:205): "Teacher leaders are chiefly concerned with securing enhanced instructional outcomes, generating positive relationship with staff and students, and creating the enabling conditions for others to learn."

TLLP teacher leaders do not learn leadership primarily by studying or conceptualizing it in the abstract, rather they learn, innovate, adapt and develop their leadership 'by doing'. As one TLLP interviewee commented: "This is grassroots leadership at its finest .... This has been some of the best and most rewarding work in my career" (Campbell et al., 2013). In vignettes written by TLLP teacher leaders (Campbell et al., 2014), various themes emerged about their leadership practices including: collaboration, building relationships, creating a vision and sharing leadership, planning a project, implementing a project, going public with their teaching and learning technology. Relatedly, TLLP survey respondents indicated a host of practical leadership skills and practices being developed, including facilitation, presentation, project management, communication, interpersonal or relationship building, problem-solving, change leadership and conflict resolution skills.

Participating teachers strongly valued the development of their leadership through the TLLP in the following ways:

> Leading this project was the most useful leadership based professional learning that I have been involved with in my teaching career (TLLP teacher leader, vignette).
>
> With respect to what our project was to me, it was more than just helping students. It was an opportunity for me as team leader to become a better leader. Our TLLP project was a way to heighten our professionalism and do something that really mattered. The project is proof that teachers can learn and lead when they are provided the support or conditions they require to do good work (TLLP teacher leader, vignette).

While TLLP teacher leaders faced, and mostly overcame, challenges of time, resources, logistics and change management, the overall experience was rewarding and enriching for experienced teachers to develop as leaders. As one TLLP teacher commented:

> Professionally, I don't have a leadership position within my school community. I'm not a chairperson, I'm not a vice principal; I'm a teacher. I felt that

it was a way for me to become a specialist in a particular area in a short period of time .... It was rewarding, enriching, inspiring, invigorating, captivating, so that the three of us on the core team would just sort of feed off one another and just dream big thoughts that normally we would never have the time to do, nor offered the opportunity (Campbell et al., 2013).

The combination of leading their own and other teachers' professional learning to support improvements for students' learning was a powerful leadership development.

Sharing Professional Knowledge and Spreading Changes in Practice

The third goal of TLLP to support knowledge exchange supported teachers to de-privatize their practice and share their learning across classrooms, schools, districts, provincially and, in some cases, internationally. In our analysis of recent TLLP projects (Campbell et al., 2014, 2015a), the majority of projects shared their learning through developing and providing professional learning sessions, through staff meetings, and also through the use of online media, including Twitter, blogs and websites. Other major forms of sharing included: professional learning communities or groups, conference presentations, modelling and classroom visits, mentoring, communications or publications (school newsletter, local newspapers and journal articles) and engaging in or with community events. To support sharing and spread of practices, a majority of TLLP projects develop actionable materials that can be used in classrooms, for example, lesson plans, resource lists, assessment tools and instructional materials. The development of professional learning resources and online materials is also important. The twin strategies of developing professional collaboration and practical resources for teachers' use appear to be the most impactful and prevalent approaches for sharing professional learning and spreading practices.

In summary, developing teachers' professional learning and leadership with, by and for teachers is powerful and important. Teachers' value the opportunity to identify a topic or practice of particular concern to them, to engage in their own professional learning, to contribute and collaborate for professional learning of/and with other teachers, to learn leadership by doing and to develop approaches for sharing their learning and for developing and providing tangible resources that can be applied in other classrooms and schools.

Conclusions

It takes leadership and professional capacity to develop leadership and professional capacity. While attention can be focused on each level of the education system—'leadership from the top' (Fullan, 2010), 'leadership from the middle' (Hargreaves and Braun, 2012), school leadership (Leithwood et al., 2004) or teacher leadership (Harris, 2005)—the reality is that education systems, serious about improving their capacities in order to achieve the larger goals of advancing equity and excellence in educational outcomes, need to pay serious attention to develop leadership and professional capacities throughout the education system.

The Ontario case demonstrates the importance of having a thoughtful theory of action to guide the whole system's reforms and educational changes. The following five key principles inform the Ontario theory of action:

1. Focus: Identification of key priorities for improvement.
2. Tri-level reform: System-wide coherence and alignment.
3. Support and positive pressure: Capacity building with a focus on results.
4. Shared leadership: Respect for professional knowledge and practice.
5. Professional accountability: Results without rancour or ranking.

Delivering this theory of action requires sustained attention over more than a decade with a range of improvement strategies and actions being initiated and adapted as appropriate over time, linked to an emphasis on the implementation of educational improvement within, across and among the government, school districts, schools and classrooms. Consistent with a tri-level notion of governance of educational change (Fullan, 2010), in this chapter I (Carol Campbell) discuss the priorities for leadership capacity and implementation action. First, creating a government culture and structure focused on leadership of educational improvement, including the benefits of political leadership with a sustained priority commitment to, and understanding of, education; a guiding coalition of capable political and official leadership for strategy and action; and developing the culture, infrastructure and educational leadership capacities throughout the Ministry of Education. Second, developing the leadership capacities and practices of district leaders and school administrators to initiate, adapt and implement improvement, including developing formal leadership through the recruitment and development of leaders; leading through tri-level partnerships for improvement and leading from the middle. Third, fostering teacher leadership for innovation, inquiry and improvement in teaching and learning, including the value of teachers' learning and leadership with, by and for teachers; teachers leading professional learning; developing teachers' leadership practices; sharing professional knowledge and spreading changes in practice.

While the governance of education may function in a tri-level manner (government, district/network and school), the nature, influence and practices of professionals should not be confined to, or constrained by, structural notions of 'top', 'middle' or 'bottom' in leadership of educational change. Rather the lessons from Ontario are that professional knowledge, innovation, practices and improvement flow through networks of peer-to-peer interactions, professional collaboration and team work, sharing of practical professional resources and increasing use of social media and virtual networks. Leading system improvement involves leadership through both formal governance structures and through more organic professional networks connecting individuals and collective leadership throughout the education system. In conclusion, leading whole system educational improvement requires cultivating and valuing leadership from, for, by and with all involved in influencing and contributing to improvements in practices and outcomes.

References

Barber, M. (2010). How government, professions and citizens combine to drive successful educational change. In A. Hargreaves, A. Lieberman, M. Fullan and D. Hopkins (Eds.), *Second international handbook of educational change* (pp. 261–278). Dordrecht: Springer.

Barber, M. and Mourshed, M. (2007). *How the world's best performing school systems come out on top.* New York, NY: McKinsey & Company.

Campbell, C. and Fullan, M. (2006). Unlocking potential for learning: Effective district-wide strategies to raise student achievement in literacy and numeracy—Project report. In C. Campbell, M. Fullan, and A. Glaze (series editors), *Unlocking potential for learning: Effective district-wide strategies to raise student achievement in literacy and numeracy.* Toronto, ON: Queen's Printer for Ontario.

Campbell, C., Comper, J. and Winton, S. (2007, February). Successful and sustainable practices for raising student achievement in literacy and numeracy. *Changing Perspectives*, 31–36.

Campbell, C., Lieberman, A. and Yashkina, A. (2013). *The teacher leadership and learning program: A research report.* Toronto, ON: Ontario Teachers' Federation.

Campbell, C., Lieberman, A., Yashkina, A., Carrier, N., Malik, S. and Sohn, J. (2014). *The teacher learning and leadership program: Research report 2013-14.* Toronto, ON: Ontario Teachers' Federation.

Campbell, C., Lieberman, A. and Yashkina, A. (2015a). *The teacher learning and leadership program: Research report 2014-15.* Toronto, ON: Ontario Teachers' Federation.

Campbell, C., Osmond-Johnson, P., Lieberman, A. and Sohn, J. (2015b). *International teacher policy study: Ontario case report.* Toronto, ON: Ontario Institute for Studies in Education, University of Toronto.

Darling-Hammond, L. (2010). *The flat world and education: How America's commitment to equity will determine our future.* New York, NY: Teachers College Press.

Fullan, M. (2009). Large scale reform comes of age. *Journal of Educational Change, 10*(2–3), 101–113.

———. (2010). *All systems go: The change imperative for whole system reform.* Thousand Oaks, CA: Corwin Press.

Glaze, A. and Campbell, C. (2007). *Putting literacy and numeracy first: Using research and evidence to support improved student achievement.* Paper presented to American Educational Research Annual Meeting, Chicago, Illinois.

Glaze, A., Mattingley, R. and Andrews, R. (2013). *High school graduation: K-12 strategies that work.* Thousand Oaks, CA: Corwin Press and Toronto, ON: Ontario Principals' Council.

Hargreaves, A. and Braun, H. (2012). *Leading for all: The CODE special education project.* Toronto, ON: Council of Ontario Directors of Education.

Hargreaves, A. and Fullan, M. (2012). *Professional capital: Transforming teaching in every school.* New York, NY/Toronto, ON: Teachers College Press/Ontario Principals' Council.

Hargreaves, A. and Shirley, D. (2009). *The fourth way: The inspiring future for educational change.* Thousand Oaks, CA: Corwin Press.

———. (2012). *The global fourth way: The quest for educational excellence.* Thousand Oaks, CA: Corwin Press.

Harris, A. (2005). Teacher leadership: More than just a feel-good factor? *Leadership and Policy in Schools*, *4*(3), 201–219.

———. (2010). Leading system transformation. *School Leadership and Management*, *30*(3), 197–207.

Hart, D. (2012). *The 18th OISE survey of educational issues: Public attitudes towards education in Ontario 2012*. Toronto, ON: Ontario Institute for Studies in Education, University of Toronto.

Jensen, B., Hunter, A., Sonnemann, J. and Burns, T. (2012). *Catching up: Learning from the best school systems in East Asia*. Victoria: Grattan Institute.

Leithwood, K. (2012). *Ontario Leadership Framework 2012: With a discussion of the research foundations*. Ontario: The Institute for Education Leadership.

Leithwood, K., Seashore Louis, K., Anderson, S. and Wahlstrom, K. (2004). Review of research: How leadership influences student learning. New York, NY: The Wallace Foundation.

Literacy and Numeracy Secretariat (LNS). (2012). *Moving towards coherence—LNS 2011–12 year in review*. Ontario: Literacy and Numeracy Secretariat.

———. (2013). *K-12 system implementation and monitoring (SIM)*. Retrieved from http://www.edu.gov.on.ca/eng/policyfunding/memos/nov2013/SIMkto12.pdf. Accessed on 3 July 2015.

Mourshed, M., Chijioke, C. and Barber, M. (2010). *How the world's most improved school systems keep getting better*. New York, NY: McKinsey & Co.

Murphy, J. (2005). *Connecting teachers leadership and school improvement*. Thousand Oaks, CA: Corwin Press.

Ontario Ministry of Education. (2012). *Board leadership development strategy manual*. Retrieved from http://www.edu.gov.on.ca/eng/policyfunding/leadership/BLDS2012Manual.pdf. Accessed on 3 July 2015.

———. (2013). *School effectiveness framework: A support for school improvement and student success*. Retrieved from: http://www.edu.gov.on.ca/eng/literacynumeracy/SEF2013.pdf. Accessed on 14 August 2015.

Ontario Ministry of Education. (2014). *Achieving excellence: A renewed vision for education in Ontario*. Toronto, ON: Queen's Printer for Ontario.

Organisation for Economic Cooperation and Development (OECD). (2010a). *PISA 2009 results: What makes a school successful? Resources, policies and practices* (Vol. IV). Paris: OECD.

———. (2010b). *Strong performers and successful reformers in education: Lessons from PISA for the United States: Ontario, Canada: Reform to support high achievement in a diverse context*. Paris: OECD.

———. (2013) *PISA 2012 results in focus: What 15-year-olds know and what they can do with what they know*. Paris: OECD.

Pervin, B. and Campbell, C. (2015). Systems for teacher and leader effectiveness and quality: Ontario, Canada. In L. Darling-Hammond and R. Rothman (Eds.), *Teaching in the flat world: Learning from high performing systems*. New York City, NY: Teachers' College Press.

Schleicher, A. (2009). International benchmarking as a lever for policy reform. In A. Hargreaves and D. Shirley (Eds.), *Change wars* (pp. 177–133). Bloomington: Solution Tree.

SECTION 2

Professional Level

Leading Futures: Leading Professional Learning

Moving from the whole system level to the level of professional practice and learning, this section looks at effective leadership development from a range of perspectives and countries. In particular, the chapters in this section, in their various ways and from their different contextual vantage points, probe how highly effective leaders are developed, providing a commentary on how far collaborative professional learning processes are part of an effective professional learning for emerging educational leaders.

In Chapter 7, Nicholas Pang and Zoe Leung focus on professional learning communities (PLCs) in Hong Kong. PLCs are a central part of the system reform process and an integral part of professional development for all leaders and teachers in Hong Kong. This chapter outlines findings from a small-scale qualitative study which explored how far the features of PLCs could be located in a sample of schools in Hong Kong. The findings show that further work and support is required in some schools to build the professional capacity for teachers to authentically engage in this collaborative way of working.

Chapter 8 by Corinne Jacqueline Perera, Donnie Adams and Vasu Muniandy looks at professional learning in another part of Asia. It concentrates specifically upon the preparation and professional learning of principals in Malaysia. This chapter highlights the policy imperatives and empirical findings that reinforce the centrality of the principal in securing better school and system performances. It charts how the new 'National Professional Educational Leadership Qualification' (NPQEL) has been introduced and made mandatory for all aspiring principals. Chapter 9 by Louisa Rennie focuses on principal certification. It highlights the importance of principals taking charge of their own learning.

The next two chapters both look at the challenges of improving schools in challenging or disadvantaged communities and describe how professional collaboration within and between schools can bring significant benefits. These chapters emanate from very different cultural contexts but interestingly reach largely similar conclusions. In Chapter 10, Christopher Chapman focuses on the power of professional collaboration to secure better outcomes in schools within the Greater Manchester Challenge in England. In Chapter 11, Serge Kosaretsky, Irina Grunicheva, Marina Pinskaya, Alma Harris and Michelle Jones outline the initial stages in a project (supported by the World Bank and the Moscow Higher School of Economics) to improve schools in acutely disadvantaged circumstances in three regions in Russia.

In Chapter 10, Chris Chapman outlines the benefits of moving beyond an individual school to look between and beyond the school boundaries. The author outlines the concrete benefits of doing so and the future possibilities of putting in place collaboration with impact. Chapter 11 discusses how in Russia, until relatively recently, certain schools have not been identified as failing or in need of any additional support or resource. This chapter outlines several features of effective leadership in these contexts and argues that through professional collaboration and much greater sharing between schools, significant gains can be made.

In the last chapter of this section, Pak Tee Ng traces a unique partnership between the Ministry, universities and schools in Singapore. The author describes in detail how they have worked together to deliver leadership training of an exceptionally high quality. This chapter describes three core strategies that are used to ensure high-quality outcomes on these programmes. These strategies are: emphasizing the development of leaders' ability to deal with complexity, strengthening the theory–practice nexus through authentic school-based projects and enhancing university–schools–government partnership. This chapter describes a leadership development program for middle leaders also and concludes with the view that in order to build leadership capacity for even higher improvement in Singapore, schools require highly skilled leaders at all levels in the system.

7

Exploring the Practice of Professional Learning Communities: Case of Hong Kong Primary Schools

Nicholas Sun-keung Pang and Zoe Lai-mei Leung

Introduction

Although professional learning communities (PLCs) have gained intense attention in teacher professional development for the past years in the Western world (DuFour and Eaker, 1998; Hord and Sommers, 2008; Servage, 2009), there is comparatively less literature regarding the development of PLCs in Hong Kong. This chapter attempts to explore the present status of PLCs in the Hong Kong education field through examining five cases in the primary school sector.

Literature Review

Generally, there are two main theoretical tracks in the development of the concept of PLCs. One is Senge's work on the learning organization, which evolved from the corporate business sector. Another track is the concept of community of practice put forward by Wenger (1998). It focuses on values of social interactions through which people share information, insight and advice, and help each other solve problems. These two tracks of ideas evolved into the field of education and formed the term 'PLC'.

Until now, there is still no universal definition about what is a PLC, as a PLC is interpreted differently in various educational contexts (Stoll et al., 2006). But some consensuses on its basic ideas have been reached based on Western settings. Dufour and Eaker (1998:xi) expounded that a professional is 'someone with expertise in a specialized field', learning means 'an ongoing action and perpetual curiosity' and community refers to 'a group of people linked by common interests'.

Hord (1997) conceptualized and argued that PLCs should have the following five characteristics: shared and supportive leadership, shared values and vision, collective learning and application, shared personal practice and supportive conditions. Such conceptualization has been widely accepted and has received extensive applications. In addition, another important construct of a PLC is supportive leadership (Dufour, 1999; Huffman and Jacobson, 2003; Lindahl, 2011). There are still some other characteristics of PLCs, including result orientation (Dufour and Eaker, 1998), inclusive membership and networks and partnerships with outside (Stoll et al., 2006), focus on learning assessment (Lindahl, 2011) as well as data-based decision-making (Thompson et al., 2004).

The PLC Concepts

PLC is 'an ongoing process, in which educators works collaboratively in recurring cycles of collective inquiry and action research to achieve better results for the students they serve' (DuFour et al., 2010:11). In other words, PLC is a continuous job-embedded learning for teachers with the core mission to improve students' learning. Being guided by a shared vision of what the schools must become in order to ensure that each student learns, staff members in schools make collective commitments, clarifying what they will do to create such an organization. The effectiveness of the PLC is assessed on the basis of students' intended learning outcomes.

Members of the PLC work collaboratively in teams that engage in collective enquiry to identify any discrepancies between the best practices in learning and teaching, and the current condition of their school. This stage includes collecting and analysing data and information regarding learning and teaching, thus identifying weaknesses and areas of concern. This collective enquiry process facilitates PLC members to come to a consensus in developing strategies and competencies to build on strengths and address the specific weaknesses and concerns in learning or teaching (Harris and Jones, 2010). In general, there are three crucial questions, which need to be explored by the PLC members at this particular stage (DuFour, 2004:8). These are:

1. What do we want each student to learn?
2. How will we know when each student has learned it?
3. How will we respond when a student experiences difficulties in learning?

Shared knowledge is then built by discussions, sharing of personal practices and even organizing staff development programme(s) for teachers to acquire new skills and capabilities in order to address the issues concerned with the PLC (Hord and Sommers, 2008).

Members of PLC are also action orientated. They realize the importance of learning by doing. They understand that unless members in their school act differently, there will not be any differences in their students' learning outcomes. Hence, after implementing the new knowledge and strategies, the team members analyse the changes and explore what is effective in improving their students' learning. An ongoing improvement cycle is then formed by applying continuously the new findings and knowledge in school practices through the PLC (DuFour et al., 2010).

Evidences from different educational contexts seem to have reached a consensus that developing PLCs significantly contribute to the implementation and sustainability of school reforms (Harris, 2010). Educational reforms are increasingly linked to the practice of PLCs. After years of exploration, there is consensus that the practice of PLCs holds promise for teacher development (Wong, 2010), school reform (Harris and Jones, 2010), thus enhancing student learning (Hord, 1997; Stoll et al., 2006).

Most of the existing pieces of literature on PLCs focus on Western settings which mainly discuss the nature of PLCs with limited empirical research (Hairon and Dimmock, 2012); the concept and practice of PLCs in Asian contexts have been largely ignored and relevant research is particularly lacking. Under these circumstances, the study outlined in this chapter aims to examine the form and processes of PLCs in Hong Kong schools. Based on the literature reviewed and our understandings about PLCs in the Western context, we attempt to explore the structures, processes and practices of PLCs in Hong Kong schools.

Professional Learning Communities in Hong Kong

In Hong Kong, the Advisory Committee on School-based Management launched a consultation document, 'Transforming Schools into Dynamic and Accountable Professional Learning Communities' highlighting PLCs for enhancing the effectiveness of learning and teaching and for improving students' learning outcomes (Advisory Committee on School-based Management, 2000:1).

The Advisory Committee on Teacher Education and Qualifications (ACTEQ, 2009:25) also recommends that schools should adopt 'a collaborative approach to teachers' professional learning to enhance school quality'. Through engaging in interactions, dialogues, feedback and reflections, each PLC member views his or her colleagues as learning partners and is willing to contribute to other's professional learning. According to ACTEQ (2009:29), "... the notion of 'teachers as co-learners' should be actively promoted to exert a good influence on other teachers, cultivate a collective learning culture and atmosphere, and help activate the process of change."

Pang's (2006) study on 890 primary and secondary school teachers showed that school administrators in Hong Kong were generally weak in communicating their missions and goals clearly to their staff, whereas teachers were also reluctant to contribute to the establishment of the school mission. Hence, there is an urgent need for schools to transform themselves into learning organizations by means of PLCs, so that they are more competent to cope with the challenges created by the current educational reforms and to provide quality education for their students.

The Present Study

The present study was an initial attempt to investigate the development status of PLCs in Hong Kong primary school settings by using a naturalistic inquiry approach and thematic analysis of data collected in 25 interviews with principals and panel chairs of five primary schools in Hong Kong. It is hoped that the study can shed light to the following research question: What is the development status of the professional learning community in Hong Kong's primary schools?

As convenience sampling was adopted in the present research, the findings of the present study cannot be generalized to a wider population or make bold claims about them.

Background of Schools in the Sample

All five schools in the study were whole-day primary schools in Hong Kong. A brief description of each school (with a fictitious name) is as follows:

Sunshine Primary School

This was an aided whole-day school with a history of more than 40 years. It was located at a public housing estate in an old residential area in Hong Kong. There were 18 classes in total, with three classes at each level from Primary 1 to 6 (A, B, C). Sunshine Primary had an enrolment of 460 at the time when this research was undertaken. There were 35 teachers in the school with teacher–student ratio of 1:13.1. Its linked secondary school, Sunshine Secondary School was a CMI (Chinese as Medium of Instruction) school in the same district. The major challenge faced by Sunshine Primary was that there was a drop in enrolment of Primary 1 students.

Kornhill Primary School

This was a government whole-day school established in the 1950s. There were 24 classes in total, with four classes at each level from Primary 1 to 6 (A, B, C, D) at the time of study. It had an enrolment of 738 at the time when this study was undertaken. There were 39 teachers in Kornhill Primary School with teacher–student ratio of 1:18.9. Kornhill had three linked secondary schools and one of them was an EMI (English as Medium of Instruction) school in Hong Kong. Kornhill was one of the most popular primary schools in the same district of Sunshine Primary.

Goodwill Primary School

This was an aided whole-day school founded in the 1980s. There were 30 classes, with five classes in each grade from Primary 1 to 6. There were 53 teachers and 485 students in the 2011–2012 academic year. The teacher–student ratio in Goodwill Primary was 1:9.2. There were no linked secondary schools for their Primary 6 graduates. Goodwill Primary had once been one of the most popular schools in the area despite its inconvenient location (i.e., half-way up the hill). Recently, two new primary schools opened in its neighbourhood, which might have created keen competitions for Goodwill Primary as both of them were located near the main road at the bottom of the hill.

Morningside Primary School

This was located at the northern part of Hong Kong near the border where many of their students were 'Newly Arrived Children

(NAC)' from China. It was an aided whole-day school founded in 2009. There were 25 classes, with four classes at each level except that five classes were at the Primary 5 level. The number of enrolments in Morningside was 645 students. There were 47 teachers in Morningside Primary, with teacher–student ratio of 1:13.7. In 2012–2013 academic year, about 40 per cent of their Primary 6 graduates were students of Territory Band-1[1] in the 'Secondary School Places Allocation' (SSPA) System. As there had been a continuous influx of NAC across the border, Morningside Primary was not affected by the declining birth rate in Hong Kong, which often led to enrolment problems.

Franklin Primary School

This was an aided whole-day school with a history of more than 140 years. The school was supposed to be one of the most prestigious primary schools in Hong Kong. There were 24 classes in total, with four classes at each level from Primary 1 to 6 (A, B, C, D). The number of enrolments was 750 at the time this study was undertaken. There were 46 teachers in Franklin Primary School, with teacher–student ratio of 1:16.3. Its feeder secondary school, Franklin High School (with a 5-minutes walking distance from the primary school) was one of the 114 EMI schools in Hong Kong. Moreover, 70 per cent of their Primary 6 graduates entered the feeder secondary school at the central allocation stage through SSPA in the 2011–2012 academic year.

Data Collection

In each school, the principal and the panel chairs of Chinese, English, Mathematics and General Studies attended a 30-minute

---

[1] All students in the SSPA are put into an order of merit according to their scaled internal assessment results in their primary schools. There were altogether three territory bands. The top one-third of the territory students are called students of 'Territory Band 1' whereas the bottom one-third are called students of 'Territory Band 3'.

semi-structured interview with the researcher individually. The interviews were conducted in Cantonese. With informants' consents, all interviews were audio-recorded by a recording pen. The recording not only allowed the researcher to concentrate on the informants during the interviews, but also served as a record of the events, which could be replayed for transcription or translation and data analysis. The audio files were transcribed and then translated into word documents for later coding and analysis by using the NVivo 10 qualitative analysis software.

Discussion and Findings

Before exploring the development status of PLC in Hong Kong, we first investigated whether any other forms of PLCs existed in the subject schools. With reference to the definition of PLCs, it seemed that the 'lesson study' found in the sampling schools resembled the construct of PLCs (DuFour et al., 2010). However, only two out of five primary schools (i.e., Franklin and Kornhill) had this in their key subjects (see Table 7.1).

Table 7.1
Lesson Study per School Year

Subjects	Sunshine	Kornhill	Goodwill	Morningside	Franklin
Chinese	0	1	0	0	2
English	0	1	0	0	2
Math	0	1	0	0	2
General Studies	0	1	0	0	2

Note: In Franklin Primary, two lesson studies were conducted in the four key subjects in a school year; Chinese Panel Chair of Franklin: Each lesson study lasted for one to two months depending on the unit chosen for the Chinese panel.

Whereas in Kornhill only one lesson study was administered per year, the duration of the lesson study was much shorter than that of Franklin Primary, as the form subject teachers only needed to choose one period for the lesson study.

Collective Enquiry

In both Kornhill and Franklin Primary schools, subject meetings were organized for the lesson studies. In the meetings, topic(s) were chosen for conducting lesson studies according to the teaching schedule and all teachers teaching in the same form prepared the learning or teaching materials together.

Maths Panel Chair of Kornhill: "We have at least one teacher, so called the 'Seed Teacher', who taught the same grade last year. This means he/she has got experience in teaching that grade... In the first lesson preparation meeting, he/she will share with us the learning difficulties which students encountered in the previous year...this information is really useful for planning the lessons."

Chinese Panel Chair of Kornhill: "Let say, we are teaching expository writing. All the form subject teachers will discuss what kinds of skills students need before they can write the composition. Then, we divide the learning goals into different implementation stages and the learning goals are further divided into several learning objectives for each lesson."

The above dialogues indicate that teachers in these schools designed their learning or teaching strategies and materials through collective inquiries and decisions in the lesson studies. It is worth noting that in Kornhill Primary, experienced teachers in various subjects would share the learning problems of students in the previous year with their colleagues, which could be rather useful in planning the lessons.

Student-centred, Learning-focused and Data-driven Lesson Study

During the lesson study, each subject teacher took turns to teach the planned lesson while his or her fellow teachers would be the peer observers. A post-observation meeting was held both in Franklin and Kornhill Primary in which the teacher being observed would have his or her self-reflection about the lesson, while his or her peers shared their comments with regard to his or her teaching strategies and skills as well as the students' performance. The suggestions made in the post-observation meetings were used immediately for revising the teaching activities in the following lessons.

Chinese Panel Chair of Kornhill: "In the post-observation session, we made reflections on the lesson observed to see if any amendments needed to be made... for example, when we found that students had difficulties in the lesson, we included some more activities in the lesson plan, which meant that the other fellow teacher needed to follow the revised lesson plan in the lesson being observed the next day."

Chinese Panel Chair of Franklin: "The lesson study includes a class observation session. Suppose we have designed a 4-classes lesson study. Teacher B, C and D will observe Teacher A implementing the plan in her class. Then, we have post-observation meeting on that day to see if the activity designed has worked well with the teaching objectives. If her students failed to catch up with their teacher at a certain point; which probably implied that the activity guidelines were unclear; we immediately made amendments in the lesson plan that would be carried out by Teacher B in her lesson next day."

In Franklin's case, a common assessment task would also be administered after each lesson in order to evaluate students' learning. Remedial actions would be initiated right away whenever students' difficulties were identified during the lessons.

Chinese Panel Chair of Franklin: "We discuss and design the teaching flow and activities for the lessons together. We anticipate students' responses, including what they need if the lessons work well with them. We also come up with remedies if our students cannot follow the lessons... We try to come up with a number of remedies or follow-up strategies. Whenever we design a teaching activity, we devise a common assessment (for all classes of the same grade). If students do fail in the assessment, we make reflections on that lesson and then carry out appropriate follow-up actions."

The above dialogues show that teachers in both schools were rather confident in designing their learning or teaching strategies and materials through collective enquiries and decisions at the early stage of the lesson studies. Additionally, they appeared to feel empowered in modifying their teaching practice based on the evidences they collected and by observing students' performance during the lessons. It is important to note that teachers in Franklin Primary seemed capable of utilizing the data collected in the common formative assessments, to inform their teaching practice.

Monitoring Process of PLCs

Although neither the principal nor the 'Primary School Master Curriculum Development' (PSMCD) attended the lesson study meetings, teacher representatives of the four key subjects in both schools were invited to conduct sharing sessions about their lesson studies in front of the principal, head teachers as well as other teaching staff.

English Panel Chair of Franklin: "In the sharing session, we are asked to present the planning, implementation and the findings from the lesson study of one chosen grade."

Principal of Kornhill: "Each period is video-taped. In one of the staff meetings, teachers are invited to share their experience and comments in the lesson study; particularly concerning his or her classroom routines and teaching practice. I believe that it is some kind of reflection or feedback for their teaching practice."

Although there was no formal monitoring or assessing by the principals or PSMCDs, the sharing sessions mentioned above appeared to be some kind of evaluation to provide an oversight or to monitor the PLC practices in these schools.

Leadership Support

Regarding the support offered by the principals for teachers' professional development, the principal of Franklin Primary School mentioned that she had initiated the lesson studies since 2006, which aimed at improving students' learning.

Principal of Franklin: "I asked our teachers to examine the way our students learnt, and discussed our curriculum carefully bit by bit.

We tried to review the teaching objectives one by one and started our lesson preparation based on students' difficulties in learning."

Furthermore, the PSMCD in Franklin devised a number of reflection forms for teachers, which probably encouraged teachers to make self-evaluation about their teaching.

For Kornhill Primary, the principal indicated that she had implemented two professional development programmes in her school, that is, the 'learning module' and the 'practice module'.

Principal of Kornhill: "The learning module includes three staff development days and a number of school-based support programmes organized by different professional bodies, such as CDI (Curriculum Development Institute) and the Chinese University of Hong Kong... All of these are inputs for teachers... In the collaborative lesson planning (CLP) and peer observations, teachers are asked to put the knowledge gained in these learning modules into practice... That is, they need to apply the knowledge for their students' benefits."

The above dialogues appeared to indicate that the school leaders at both schools played an important role in initiating PLCs, by implementing the lesson studies in their schools.

Organizational Support and Incentives

With regard to the structures and resources that facilitate the establishment of PLCs, one of the teachers in Kornhill commented:

Maths Panel Chair of Kornhill : "The 'Seed Teacher' allocated to each form really helps in lesson planning as he or she has a clearer understanding about the curriculum."

For Franklin, the school leaders facilitate the peer observations of the lesson study by allowing teachers to swap their lessons with their colleagues teaching the same classes.

English Panel Chair of Franklin: "We need to fill in a form about the swapping of lessons and submit to the vice-principal. She then notifies the rest of the teaching staff about the swapping."

In addition, it is rather surprising to note that teachers in both schools did not expect their school administers to spare a few lessons for their CLPs, since most of the teacher informants understood that it would create a lot of difficulties in the timetabling.

Concerning the incentives or rewards for those teachers participating in the lesson studies, the principal of Kornhill explained:

"After teachers' sharing of their video-clips in the staff meeting, a small gift will be presented to them... I think it is some kind of recognition."

However, Franklin's principal had a rather different view in terms of incentives for teachers participating in the lesson studies.

Principal of Franklin: "Our teachers have high expectations from themselves... They don't bother about the material stuffs but rather the spiritual stuffs, that is, job satisfaction. I asked my colleagues in the academic committee whether we needed to present any gifts to teachers; however, they told me that it was time-wasting to think about the actual rewards to their colleagues. They believed that the things which their fellow teachers would most treasure would be seeing that their students had improvement in their learning and showed appreciation on their efforts made in their daily teaching."

The above responses seemed to show that teachers in both schools respected their own profession. They valued respect and appreciation from their students and their colleagues, much more than any actual rewards or gifts granted to them.

Community of Practice

Teachers in Kornhill commented that the school leaders listened to their suggestions and ideas for curriculum development in general.

English Panel Chair of Kornhill: "As for subject development, I think that the leadership model is more or less 'bottom up'. For example, when some teachers voiced out their opinions that the textbooks from Hong Kong Council of Early Childhood Education and Services (HKCECES) were not so suitable for our students, the school allowed us to swap to another publisher...I think our colleagues did a good job in voicing out their opinions."

Similarly, teachers in Franklin also expressed a view that distributed leadership was practiced in their school.

Maths Panel Chair of Franklin: "It's a 'bottom-up approach'. For preparing a three-year development plan in Maths, all teachers in my subject panel sit together and discuss the SWOT table. Then as the panel chairperson, I summarize their suggestions in compiling the development plan ...that's why I think the plan is more acceptable by my colleagues."

It appears that these 'bottom-up' approaches were helpful for nurturing a sense of community in these schools. As teachers generally felt that their suggestions would be listened to by the school leaders, they became more eager to voice out their opinions, no matter whether at the school level or at the subject level. Most importantly, such attitudes are particularly important in collective enquiries, one of the essential elements in establishing PLCs.

Conclusion

After examining the sampling schools, it seemed that only two out of five of the sampled schools possessed certain essential constructs of PLCs. The development and practice of PLCs in the Hong Kong primary schools are only at their infancy stage. According to DuFour and associates' (2010) definition in which PLCs are an 'ongoing improvement cycle' formed by continuously applying the new findings and knowledge in school practices, it appears that only a weak version of PLCs was implemented in both the schools owing to the fact that the action-research lesson studies were conducted only once or twice in a school year and not continuously throughout the academic year.

The findings of this small-scale qualitative study show that the practice of PLCs is not commonplace in Hong Kong primary schools. It is also worthy to explore further what are the forms, structures and processes of PLCs in most of Hong Kong secondary schools. As Hong Kong students have been consistently performing very well in the international league tables (Programme for International Student Assessment [PISA], the Progress in International Reading Literacy [PIRLS] and the Trends in International Mathematics and

Science Study [TIMSS]), it is interesting to pursue further and to explore the relationship between PLCs (or other mechanisms) and school improvement in Hong Kong.

References

Advisory Committee on School-based Management. (2000). *Transforming schools into dynamic and accountable professional learning communities school-based management consultation document.* Hong Kong: Hong Kong Government.

Advisory Committee of Teacher Education and Qualifications. (2009). *Third report on teachers' continuing professional development (2009).* Hong Kong: ACTEQ.

DuFour, R. (1999). Help wanted: Principals who can lead professional learning communities. *NASSP Bulletin, 83*(614), 12–17.

———. (2004). Schools as learning communities. *Educational Leadership, 61*(8), 6–11.

Dufour, R. and Eaker, R. (1998). *Professional learning communities at work: Best practices for enhancing student achievement.* Bloomington, IN/Alexandria, VA: National Education Service/ASCD.

DuFour, R., DuFour, R., Eaker, R. and Many, T. (2010). Learning by doing: A handbook for professional learning communities at work (book and CD-Rom) (2nd ed.). Bloomington, IN: Solution Tree.

Elliott, J. (2001). *Action research for educational change.* Buckingham: Open University Press.

Harris, A. (2010). Leading system transformation. *School Leadership and Management, 30*(30), 197–207.

Hairon, S. and Dimmock, C. (2012). Singapore schools and professional learning communities: teacher professional development and school leadership in an Asian hierarchical system. *Educational Review, 64*(4), 405–424.

Harris, A. and Jones, M. (2010). Professional learning communities and system improvement. *Improving Schools, 13*(2), 172–181.

Hord, S. M. (1997). Professional learning communities: What are they and why are they important? *Issues About Change, 6*(1), 1–8.

Hord, S. M. and Sommers, W. A. (2008). *Leading professional learning communities.* CA: Corwin Press.

Huffman, J. B. and Jacobson, A. L. (2003). Perceptions of professional learning communities. *International Journal of Leadership in Education: Theory and Practice, 6*(3), 239–250.

Lindahl, R. A. (2011). Professional learning communities: A feasible reality or a chimera? In J. Alford, G. Perreault, L. Zellner and W. Ballenger (Eds.), *Blazing new trails: Preparing leaders to improve access and equity in today's schools. The 2011 yearbook of the national council of professors of educational administration.* (pp. 47–58, ERIC: ED523595). Lancaster: DEStech Publications Inc.

Pang, N. S. K. (2006). *Transforming schools into learning organizations* (School Education Reform Series No.31). Hong Kong: Faculty of Education, The Chinese University of Hong Kong and The Hong Kong Institute of Educational Research.

Servage, L. (2009). Who is the 'professional' in a professional learning community? An exploration of teacher professionalism in collaborative professional development settings. *Canadian Journal of Education, 32*(1), 149–171.

Stoll, L., Bolam, R., McMahon, A., Wallace, M. and Thomas, S. (2006). Professional learning communities: A review of the literature. *Journal of Educational Change, 7*(4), 221–258.

Thompson, S. C., Gregg, L. and Niska, J. M. (2004). Professional learning communities, leadership, and student learning. *Research in Middle Level Education Online, 28*(1), 1–15.

Wenger, E. (1998). *Communities of practice: learning, meaning, and identity.* Cambridge/New York: Cambridge University Press.

Wong, J. L. N. (2010). What makes a professional learning community to be possible? A case study of a Mathematics department in a junior secondary school of China. *Asia Pacific Education Review, 11*(2), 131–139.

8

Principal Preparation and Professional Development in Malaysia: Exploring Key Influences and Current Practice

Corinne Jacqueline Perera, Donnie Adams and
Vasu Muniandy

> I have never seen a good school with a poor principal, or a poor school with a
> good principal. I have seen unsuccessful schools turn around into successful
> schools and regrettably outstanding schools slide rapidly into decline. In each
> case, the rise or fall could be readily traced to the quality of the principal.
> **Fred M. Hechinger,** Former Education Editor of *The New York Times*

Malaysian Education

The national education system in Malaysia has undergone
extreme changes and development in response to its evolving
education policies and national aspirations that have grown over
time. Educational priorities are focused on improving the quality of
education, to attain the objective of the nation in becoming a fully
developed country by the year 2020, as envisaged by Vision 2020
(United Nations Report, 2005). As such, schools have to move in
tandem with these changes and raise their performance.

In 1999, when Malaysia first participated in Trends in International Mathematics and Science Study (TIMSS), the average student score exceeded the international average score, placing Malaysia in the forefront (Malaysian Education Blueprint, 2012). However, in Programme for International Student Assessment (PISA) 2009 Malaysia stood at the bottom one-third of the average student score (NST, 2012; World Bank Report, 2013). Given the cleft in this international assessment, the Malaysian Ministry of Education (MoE) is looking into improving the future scores of TIMSS and PISA, within the next 15 years, with the aim of achieving the top-three placing in these international assessments. As such, the Malaysian educational system is under enormous pressure to raise the quality of learning, teaching and academic achievements in schools (Jantan and Khuan, 2004)

One of the prime concerns of the MOE is to realize the goals of Vision 2020 in making Malaysia the centre of educational excellence in the region (Ahmad, 2004). To this end, the MOE has established the National Education Blueprint 2013–2025, (referred to thereafter as 'NEB') as a means of monitoring the progress of the education system against international benchmarks (MOE, 2008).

National Education Blueprint 2013–2025

The NEB represents the government's initiatives to formulate a comprehensive transformational plan, identified by its '11 shifts' to elevate the country's education system (Malaysian Education Blueprint, 2012; The STAR, 2013). It is an agenda that outlines policy initiatives for implementation over a span of 13 years, sequencing its transformation process to occur in three strategic 'waves' of change.

The NEB has mapped out a priority list of commitments for nationwide educational reforms, with reform efforts being directed towards reconstructing educational conceptions to suit local capacity. According to the NEB, principal leadership ranks high on the list of priorities for school reforms and the role of principal leadership has become all the more essential. The NEB defines an extended meaning of what leaders have to do in the future:

> School leaders will be asked to perform to the high expectations set and agreed to for their school. They will need to stay open to new ways of working, to involve the community in school improvement, and to serve as coaches and trainers to build capabilities in their staff as well as for other schools. (Malaysian Education Blueprint, 2012)

Among the major impacts envisioned by the NEB, 'Shift 5' elaborates on enriching the quality of principal leadership in schools. It highlights the strategic approaches aimed at equipping all schools with high-performing principals who will adopt sharper accountability for improving student outcomes. Outstanding principals will be selected to serve at low-performing schools where their expertise can be leveraged on. They are also encouraged to take up these positions in lieu of faster career progression opportunities and attractive revised incentives provisioned for them through a New Principal Career Package designed to assist principals achieve their full potential towards delivering higher student outcomes (Malaysian Education Blueprint, 2012).

Taking the lead from (Barker, 2008; Bush, 2008; Fullan, 2004; Hallinger and Heck, 2011; Hopkins and Reynolds, 2001; Teddlie and Reynolds, 2000), large-scale reforms are adaptive challenges that require leaders to understand the critical role they play, as well as become more efficient in leading their organizations towards continuous sustainability. Likewise, as professional leaders, Malaysian school principals are supposed to understand the nation's philosophy of education surrounding the NEB and communicate the philosophy, goals and strategies aimed at stepping up the quality of education.

Evidence shows that school leaders, particularly the principals, do play a significant role in improving their school outcomes, supporting the premise that principals are responsible for promoting the learning environment in their schools (Ghani et al., 2011; Jainabee and Jamelaa, 2011; Karim, 1989; Khuan et al., 2004; Marzuki,

1997; Marzuki and Ghani, 2007; Ahmad et al., 1999; Sharma, 2010; Tahir and Kaman, 2011; Tee et al., 2010). These studies place the principal in the highest order of priority and regard a principal's practices as the main contributing factor in creating effective schools.

Principal Leadership

In the Malaysian school setting, those in formal leadership positions include the school principal, the senior assistants, senior subject teachers, members of the Parent–Teacher Association Board, administrative staff holding positions of responsibility and other people of influential authority (Bajunid et al., 1996). Although a range of leadership roles exist in many schools, the principal remains at the apex of leadership in a school's social system (Tee et al., 2010). In Malaysian public schools, 'headmaster or headmistress' refers to the heads of primary schools, while 'principal' refers to the head of secondary schools (Ibrahim Ahmad Bajunid, 2000). However, in the scope of this chapter, the term 'school leader' refers specifically to the heads and principals of both primary and secondary public schools in Malaysia.

There is an overall concern that Malaysian principals need to reskill and deploy effective strategies that can drive student outcomes. However, there is also a growing emphasis and general consensus among policy-makers that a school's outcome is the responsibility of the school principal. Increasingly, therefore, initiatives aimed at attaining educational excellence are locating the prime responsibility of the principal leadership.

This changing role of the principal strongly emphasizes the importance of effective principal leadership in bringing about greater achievement in students' academic performances (Leithwood and Mascall, 2008; Sim, 2011). 'Key Performance Indicators' and the 'School Improvement Performance Index' are used to measure academic results such as the number of 'As' obtained and the 'passing rate percentage' (Tee et al., 2010). With academic measures being the prime concern, schools in Malaysia are now reinforcing the principal's role in stimulating academic success (Tee et al., 2010).

In the local context, however, some findings reinforce that an effective principal leadership is the most important role that determines students' academic excellence and that schools with a positive learning environment can enhance academic excellence (Mahmood, 1993; Suraya and Yunus, 2012). In the context of attaining excellence in education, active support and endorsement of school leadership is required for the implementation of planned change. Essentially, a principal has always been looked upon invariably as the school's leader, whose role in school leadership is to steer the school towards achieving excellence (Nor et al., 2008; Suraya and Yunus, 2012).

Roles and Responsibilities of Malaysian Principals

The "Competency Standards for Malaysian School Principals" (IAB, 2010) outlines the general duties and responsibilities of Malaysian school principals. Their main job includes the implementation of educational programmes stipulated by the MoE, supervision of the teaching–learning processes, monitoring of discipline, supervision of co-curricular activities and their supportive involvement in the Parent–Teacher Association (PTA) and with the Board of Governors.

A study that examined 221 Malaysian principals on their level of leadership and management competency discovered that these principals possessed relatively low leadership and management competencies (Fook, 2008). The competencies of principals' skills in recognizing individual and cultural differences and appreciating staff contributions were at the lowest mean level. The co-curriculum management competencies were comparatively lower than the competencies in curriculum planning and implementation. This indicates an imbalance in the focus on co-curriculum activities in schools.

Overall, the principals were discovered to possess a moderate level of competencies in curriculum and co-curriculum management.

In another study (Sharma, 2010), 30 principals from Malaysian national schools were rated by 300 teachers who were reported to have at least six years of experience with their respective principals. Findings from this study revealed that the teachers' perception of their principals' leadership was positive and that their leadership competencies were perceived as moderate.

In June 2013, a pilot study was conducted at three of Malaysia's best-performing schools in the town of Kuching, Sarawak. Three principals were interviewed to find out what their daily leadership practices were, what influenced these practices and what their views were on effective school leadership. These principals also shared their leadership training experiences and the impact of this training on their professional learning. The interim findings from this pilot study indicate that the leadership styles of these performing principals were largely influenced by their years of practical experience as teachers and then as principals. As for training courses, these principals had not undergone any formal training in preparation for principalship like the National Professional Qualifications for Headship (NPQH) or National Professional Qualification for Educational Leaders (NPQEL) but had participated in workshops and short professional development courses.

It was interesting to note that despite having undergone fairly rudimentary training courses in principalship, these principals spoke of the various leadership styles—a combination of transformational, instructional and distributed styles. The findings from this research suggests that these are outstanding principals who are forward-thinking and have a considerable impact on their school's academic outcomes and that their practices have not been influenced directly by any training courses.

Similarly, another study (Amin and Abdul Razak, 2008) conducted in Malaysia showed that leadership training had no direct relationship on the quality of school leadership and management. However, others argue strongly in support of the benefits gained by school leaders in acquiring improved knowledge, skills and attitude (Nur Anuar et al., 2006; Ruhaya et al., 2006).

Principals' Leadership Development

In Malaysia, until recently, formal training was not a prerequisite to be appointed as a principal. The appointment of principals used to be based on their seniority and job performance as teachers (Jamilah Ahmad and Yusof Boon, 2011). Most principals held a teaching certificate at the onset of their appointment and it was customary that principals underwent a leadership course only *after* they held office as a principal (Jamilah Ahmad and Yusof Boon, 2011).

In 1999, the NPQH was introduced by the MoE to prepare principals to face the challenges of running a school (Singh, 2009). This was the first professional qualification (Ibrahim Ahmad Bajunid, 2000) designed as a principal's preparation programme specifically for aspiring school principals who wanted to be appointed to headship (Anthony and Hamdan, 2010). The NPQH was then regarded as an entry-level qualification for newly appointed principals. *Institut Aminuddin Baki* (IAB), or in english the National Institute of Educational Management and Leadership (NIEML), played an influential role in developing the curriculum for NPQH, which was adapted from the UK model (Singh, 2009).

In 2009, the NPQH was changed to NPQEL and was offered as a specialized school leadership course for teachers who aspired to be principals. The NPQEL began as a five-month in-service training programme, tailored to equip 'next-in-line' principals with the knowledge, skills and abilities to meet educational challenges and perform their expected roles (Anthony and Hamdan, 2010).

In July 2013, the MoE announced that as of 2014, only teachers with NPQEL qualifications could be appointed as principals in Malaysian public schools (IAB Report, 2013). As England dropped the mandatory nature of the NPQH, Malaysia did the opposite. It has now become mandatory for a new, first-time principal to acquire the NPQEL certification before assuming his or her position as a public school principal.

In line with the MoE's initiatives to raise the quality of education through school leadership, the IAB has also been commissioned to develop high-impact training programmes that can give rise to a generation of highly professional school leaders in Malaysia. Through professional leadership trainings, school leaders can gain more insight into and understand the complexities of school leadership in new and more meaningful ways.

'Managing Educational Leadership Talent' (MELT), framework, introduced by IAB is an initiative to refine leadership skills, attitude and practices to become more effective and respected school leaders (Anthony and Hamdan, 2010). In their effort to improve the assessment of training needs for school leaders, IAB developed a competency needs assessment tool, called the KOMPAS that was developed through the 'High Impact School Leaders Competency' research conducted in 2008 to determine the competencies required by school leaders for their training and development needs. The national 'Competency Needs Index' is published annually to provide the level of training needs required by school leaders, so that they can plan their training ahead of time, and to build a professional learning community (Harris and Jones, 2010, 2011; Khair Mohamad Yusof, 2011).

In 2007, the MoE signed a memorandum of understanding with King's College, London, and appointed 30 excellent principals to undergo leadership training at the College for two months (EPRD, 2007). These courses were designed specifically to cater to the training needs of Malaysian school leaders, as they were challenged with increasing educational accountabilities and had to keep pace with various emerging phenomena in the teaching and learning arenas (Ibrahim Ahmad Bajunid, 2000; Jainabee and Jamelaa, 2011; Rosnarizah Abdul Halim, 2008).

Recognition and Awards for Principals

In line with the nation's aspirations to be a knowledge-based economy through the pursuit of educational excellence by the year 2020, the MoE has introduced a number of awards (Khuan et al., 2004; Nur Ain Wong Abdullah, 2009; Rahimah Haji Ahmad, 1998). Since 1991, the 'National Aspiring School Award' has been introduced and presented to schools that exhibit overall excellent quality management. This award was a form of recognition and a token of appreciation to schools for their achievement towards the development of education (Wan Chik Rahman Wan Din, 2002).

Beginning 1998, the 'National Excellent Principal Award' was introduced to reward deserving school principals who displayed excellent leadership qualities as a result of their achievement in attaining 'Aspiring School Awards' (Chan and Gurnam, 2009) and for their added compliance to the established quality standards (Ibrahim Ahmad Bajunid, 2000). Recipients of School Awards are generally passionate about achieving these awards and are thus driven with increased team spirit to stay competitive and maintain their school's rankings (Tee et al., 2010).

In 2005, in an effort to sustain school excellence and exceptionally outstanding school leadership, excellent principals were reappointed for further promotion and were awarded the designation of a 'super principal' (Chan and Gurnam, 2009). Principals with effective leadership and management competencies were awarded this achievement to enhance their professional self-confidence and to continue leading their schools efficiently.

Effective Leadership: Leading Change in the 21st Century

Findings from various studies also show that preparation does make a difference to the leadership quality and school outcomes (Bush, 2009; Bush and Oduro, 2006; Lumby et al., 2008). Although the need for effective leadership preparation is widely accepted, the kind of leader ideal for the 21st century schools needs to be well rounded, confident and able to engage all stakeholders for the benefit of learners (Bush, 2011).

The 21st century principals will be challenged and expected to lead schools that are far different from those today. Therefore, in preparation for tomorrow's challenges, the role of a principal needs to be redefined with central priority being given to improving student learning. Recognizing the raised expectations for principals and acknowledging the centrality of leadership for student learning, principals should learn how to enrich their experiences while mobilizing their skills and competencies to creatively resolve school-based conflicts. With the right combination of knowledge and experience, principals should also strive to improve their personality and attitude, and persevere towards developing new knowledge and refining their behaviour to be more effective and respected leaders. In that way, the aspiration of the Malaysian Blueprint to produce high-quality leaders would be fulfilled.

References

Ahmad, R. H. (2004). Malaysian school principal: Predicament of leadership and management. Paper presented at the International Conference on Principalship and School Management Practices in the Era of Globalisation: Issues and Challenges. Kuala Lumpur, Malaysia.

Amin, S. and Abdul Razak, M. (2008). *Competency based training and development.* Paper presented at the Oman-Malaysia Educational Seminar, Muscat, Oman.

Anthony, Santhanamary R. and Hamdan Said. (2010). Educational Leadership Preparation Program for Aspiring Principals in Malaysia. Edu Press: Universiti Teknologi Malaysia.

Bajunid, I. A., Ghani, A. W. B. A., Bakhtiar, M., Kandasamy, M., Haddad. Y. A., Kim, L. O. and Mac, R. J. S. (1996). Malaysian educative leadership: interim research findings. *International Journal of Educational Management, 10*(2), 21–26.

Barker, B. (2008). School reform policy in England since 1988: Relentless pursuit of the unattainable. *Journal of Education Policy, 23*(6), 669–683. doi 10.1080/02680930802212887

Bush, T. (2008). *Leadership and management development in education.* London: SAGE Publications.

———. (2009). Leadership development and school improvement: contemporary issues in leadership development. *Educational Review, 61*(4), 375–389. doi: 10.1080/00131910903403956

———. (2011). Succession planning and leadership development for school principals: Comparing English and South African approaches. *Compare-a Journal of Comparative and International Education, 41*(6), 785–800. doi: 10.1080/03057925.2011.595968

Bush, T. and Oduro, G. K. (2006). New principals in Africa: Preparation, induction and practice. *Journal of Educational Administration, 44*(4), 359–375.

Chan, Y. F. and Sidhu, G. K. (2009). Leadership characteristics of an excellent principal in Malaysia. *International Education Studies, 2*(4), 106.

EPRD, M. M. (2007). Report Card: Education Development Master Plan (PIPP) 2006–2010. Educational Planning and Research Division. Information Management Division, Ministry of Education, Malaysia.

Fook, C. Y. (2008). *Effective training for school improvement: A case study in Malaysia.* Paper presented at the 3rd International Conference on Principalship and School Management, Institute of Principalship Studies, University of Malaya.

Fullan, M. (2004). *Leadership and sustainability: System Thinkers in Action.* Thousand Oaks: Corwin Press.

Ghani, M. F. A., Siraj, S., Radzi, N. M. and Elham, F. (2011). School effectiveness and improvement practices in excellent schools in Malaysia and Brunei. *Procedia - Social and Behavioral Sciences, 15*(0), 1705–1712. doi: http://dx.doi.org/10.1016/j.sbspro.2011.03.355

Gurcharan Singh, B. S. (2009). *The national professional qualification for headship (NPQH) programme for secondary school headteachers in Malaysia: An evaluative case study.* The University of Birmingham: United Kingdom.

Hallinger, P. and Heck, R. H. (2011). Exploring the journey of school improvement: Classifying and analyzing patterns of change in school improvement processes and learning outcomes. *School Effectiveness and School Improvement, 22*(1), 1–27. doi: 10.1080/09243453.2010.536322

Harris, A. and Jones, M. (2010). Professional learning communities and system improvement. *Improving Schools, 13*(2), 172–181.

———. (2011). *Professional learning communities in action.* Leannta Publishing: London.

Hopkins, D. and Reynolds, D. (2001). The past, present and future of school improvement towards the third age. *British Educational Research Journal, 27*(4), 459–475.

IAB Report. (2010). Competency Standards for Malaysian School Principals. Institute of Aminuddin Baki: Malaysia.

———. (2013). *Laporan Tahunan IAB 2012* (R. I. b. R. Midin, Ed.).Institute of Aminuddin Baki, Ministry of Education: Malaysia.

Ibrahim Ahmad Bajunid. (2000). Educational management and leadership in Malaysia: The training and professional development of school principals. *Asia-Pacific Journal of Teacher Education and Development, 3*(2), 49–75.

Jainabee, M. K. and Jamelaa, B. A. (2011). Promoting learning environment and attitude towards change among secondary school principals in Pahang Malaysia: Teachers' perceptions. *Procedia-Social and Behavioral Sciences, 28*, 45–49.

Jamilah Ahmad and Yusof Boon. (2011). Amalan Kepimpinan Sekolah Berprestasi Tinggi (SBT) Di Malaysia [Leadership Practices in Malaysian High Performing Schools (HPS)]. *Journal of Edupres, 1*(September),323–335.

Jantan, A. H. and Khuan, W. B. (2004). Malaysian windows to leadership excellence. *Principalship and school management.* In Rahimah Haji Ahmad & Tie Fatt Hie (Eds.). University of Malaya: Kuala Lumpur.

Karim, M. N. (1989). *Characteristics of effective rural secondary schools in Malaysia* (PhD thesis). University of Wisconsin, Madison, USA.

Khair Mohamad Yusof. (2011). *Branding higher education: Institute Aminuddin Baki as a center of distinction for educational leadership.* Retrieved from https://www.google.com/#q=premier+center+of+Institute+of+Aminuddin+Baki. Accessed on 7 March 2015.

Khuan, W. B., Chua, H. T. and Manaf, A. R. (2004). *Aspiring for school excellence: A Malaysia case.* Paper presented at the Proceding Seminar Nasional Pengurusan dan Kepimpinan ke-12, Institut Aminuddin Baki, Genting Highlands, Malaysia.

Leithwood, K. and Mascall, B. (2008). Collective leadership effects on student achievement. *Educational Administration Quarterly, 44*(4), 529–561. doi: 10.1177/0013161x08321221

Lumby, J., Walker, A., Bryant, M., Bush, T. and Björk, L. (2008). Research on leadership in a global context. In Young, M. D., Crow, G., Murphy, J. and Ogawa, R. (eds.). *Handbook of research on the education of school leaders.* NewYork/London: Routledge.

Mahmood, H. (1993). *Kepimpinan dan Keberkesanan Sekolah [Leadership and School Effectiveness].* Kuala Lumpur: Dewan Bahasa dan Pustaka.

Malaysian Education Blueprint. (2012). *Malaysia Education Blueprint: 2013–2025.* Ministry of Education: Malaysia.

Marzuki. (1997). Kajian sekolah berkesan di Malaysia: Model Lima Faktor [Effective Schools Studies in Malaysia: 5-Factor Model]. Universiti Kebangsaan, Malaysia.

Marzuki S. and Ghani, M. F. A. (2007). Pembentukan Model Sekolah Berkesan Malaysia: Satu Kajian Delphi [The Formation of Malaysia's Effective School's Model: A Delphi Study]. *Jurnal Pendidikan, 27*(1), 179–199.

MoE. (2008). *Malaysia education for all—Mid decade assessment report 2000–2007.* Malaysia: Malaysian Ministry of Education.

Nor, S. M., Pihie, Z. A. L. and Ali, S. (2008). Instructional leadership practices of rural school principals. *International Journal of Learning, 15*(7), 231–238.

NST. (2012, September 9). *Improving quality in all areas of education.* Retrieved from http://www.nst.com.my/nation/general/improving-quality-in-all-areas-of-education-1.140797. Accessed on 7 March 2015.

Nur Ain Wong Abdullah. (2009). "Leading school improvement in a secondary school in Kuala Lumpur." (unpublished thesis), University of Malaya: Kuala Lumpur.

Nur Anuar, A., Faridah, A., Rohana, Z., Monoto, M. and Nur Fakhriyyah, E. (2006). *Kajian penilaian graduan NPQH [NPQH Graduates Evaluation Study].* Paper presented at the 13th National Management and Educational Leadership Seminar. Institute of Aminuddin Baki. Genting Highlands, Malaysia.

Rahimah Ahmad, Manaf, Z. A. and Marzuki, S. (1999). School effectiveness and school improvement in Malaysia. *Third milliiennium schools: A world of difference in effectiveness and improvement.* Amsterdam: Swets and Zeitlinger.

Rahimah Haji Ahmad. (1998). Educational development and reformation in Malaysia: Past, present and future. *Journal of Educational Administration, 36*(5), 462–475. doi: 10.1108/09578239810238456

Rosnarizah Abdul Halim. (2008). *Assessing the needs of competencies for training and development: Case of two states in Malaysia.* Paper presented at the Educational Research Conference 2009, Bangkok.

Ruhaya, H., Rosnarizah, A. and Shariffah, S. (2006). *Penilaian program latihan IAB: Satu tinjauan terhadap program NPQH Kohort 9/2005* [Evaluation of Training Programme (IAB): An Overview of NPQH, Kohort 9/2005]. Paper presented at the 13th National Management and Educational Leadership Seminar. Institute of Aminuddin Baki. Genting Highlands, Malaysia.

Sharma, S. (2010). *Attributes of school principals-leadership qualities and capacities.* Kuala Lumpur, Malaysia: Institute of Principals Studies, University of Malaya.

Sim, Q. C. (2011). Instructional leadership among principals of secondary schools in Msia. *International Research Journals, 2*(12), 1784–1800.

Suraya, W. H. and Yunus, J. N. (2012). Principal leadership styles in high-academic performance of selected secondary schools in Kelantan Darulnaim. *International Journal of Independent Research and Studies*, 1(2), 57–67.

Tahir, M. and Kaman, A. (2011). Kepimpinan Situasi Dalam Kalangan Guru Besar Daerah Johor Bahru [Situational Leadership among Headmasters in Johor Bahru District]. *Journal of Educational Management*, 1(8), 1–24.

Teddlie, C. and D. Reynolds. (2000). *The international handbook of school effectiveness research*. London: Falmer.

Tee, O. P., Hoon, O. P., Liu, O. P., Ting, H. and Porodong, P. (2010). Investigating the role of school principals in creating a harmonious 3r+1r learning environment. In Z. M. Jelas, A. Salleh and N. Azman (Eds.), *International conference on learner diversity 2010* (Vol. 7, pp. 181–190). Amsterdam: Elsevier Science Bv.

The STAR (2013, September 2). Raising the bar of education, *STAR*.

United Nations Report. (2005). Malaysia achieving the millennium development goals (Department, E. P. U. P. M. s., Trans.). Malaysia: United Nations.

Wan Chik Rahman Wan Din. (2002). *Malaysia: Overview of evaluation system of schools*. Paper presented at the International Seminar on School Evaluation for Quality Improvement, Vistana Hotel, Kuala Lumpur.

World Bank Report. (2013, December). Malaysia Economic Monitor: High Performing Education. Bangkok: The World Bank.

9

Designing and Developing Australian Principal Certification: With the Profession, For the Profession

Louisa Rennie

Introduction

Effective school leadership has long been the source of discussion, research and inquiry. This chapter investigates the influence of educational leadership on teaching and learning outcomes. It also explores the knowledge, understanding and actions exhibited by exemplary school leaders. This chapter sets out some preliminary implications for the implementation of the Australian Principal Certification Program. For the purpose of this chapter, the following definition of leadership has been adopted (Northouse, 2007): "Leadership is a process whereby an individual influences a group of individuals to achieve a common goal."

"Education research shows that most school variables, considered separately, have at most small effects on learning. The real payoff comes when individual variables combine to reach critical mass. Creating the conditions under which that can occur is the job of the principal" (Wallace Foundation, 2012:2).

This statement from the Wallace Foundation leads us part-way to understand the complexity of measuring school leader effectiveness. An international corpus of research has determined that there is a link between school leadership and student achievement. It has shown that school leaders can implement their knowledge and understanding to positively impact the quality of student learning outcomes (Leithwood et al., 2004). The indirect nature of the leadership influence, however, makes it difficult to measure, as inevitably social processes are reciprocal and interdependent.

Despite such difficulties, the research literature on educational leadership places a strong focus on the leadership of teaching and learning. Instructional leaders display an ability to articulate values and vision around student learning and achievement, and to make the connections to behaviours and 'the necessary structures to promote and sustain them' (Hopkins, 2011:5). Effective leaders place an emphasis on whole school improvement and understanding exactly how students learn. They make informed decisions that shape organizational culture and engage in the appropriate distribution of resources (Hopkins, 2011). The most effective principals 'create an organizational structure that reflects the school's values, and enables the management systems, structures and processes to work effectively' (AITSL, 2011: 10).

As stated in the Australian Principal Standard, the best school leaders 'model effective leadership and they are committed to their own ongoing professional development' (AITSL, 2011:9). This chapter focuses particularly on the literature relating to the impact and influence of educational leadership, in order to contextualize and outline the design, development and implementation of the Australian Principal Certification Program.

The Context

So what is Principal Certification? In the Australian context, Principals Australia Institute, in consultation with Australian principals and their respective principal associations, is designing a Principal

Certification *for* principals, *by* principals. Principal Certification is the active demonstration of the Australian Principal Standard, based on clear evidence of high-quality and sustained effective leadership. Principal Certification recognizes the central importance of school leadership and its impact on student learning, the work of teachers and school performance. In short, Principal Certification is professional and public recognition of the Australian Principal Standard in action.

The aim of the Australian Principal Certification Program is to drive continuous improvement in practice, through a publicly credible, quality assured certification system. Unlike other qualifications or designations, here the profession creates its own programme and takes the responsibility for building its own professional learning system. By determining its own standards, the implication is that the profession gains greater control over the purpose and direction of its own professional learning. Inevitably, programmes provided by universities, leadership institutes and other professional learning organizations will continue to be important, but the key question for school leaders will be, "How does this professional learning course help me move towards meeting the standards for professional certification?"

Despite a large volume and variety of leadership preparation and development programmes available in Australia, a four-year teaching qualification and registration remain the only 'formal requirements for school leaders' (Anderson et al., 2007:64). Unlike other education systems, there is no qualification at the national level in order to be a principal. The Australian Principal Certification Program will complement, not replace, the registration, qualification and performance management arrangements within particular Australian education systems. Most certification systems are run independent of particularly employing authorities, whereas performance management systems are the responsibility of particular employing authorities (Ingvarson, 2014:5).

The Australian Principal Certification Program recognizes that leadership development is longitudinal, ongoing, responsive to context, developed within relationships and, ultimately, lifelong. Principals will seek certification to:

1. gain *professional recognition* for exemplary leadership,
2. affirm that principals are integral to *student success,*
3. make formal contribution to *leadership research,*
4. elevate the *status* of the profession,
5. *build and sustain expertise* within the profession,
6. demonstrate the achievement of the *Australian Principal Standard,*
7. address the *National Declaration* on the Educational Goals for Young Australians (MCEETYA, 2008),
8. participate in a national network of *leading learners.*

As highlighted earlier, the research evidence validates that principals are integral to a school's success and to shaping the teaching and learning culture in the school. However, it has been consistently difficult to measure the effectiveness of a principal and the relative impact that he or she has on student learning because of the complexity of a school as a social system. Therefore, the fundamental challenge, in gauging the impact of school leaders, is separating out their contributions from the many other factors that drive student achievement (Branch et al., 2013). Finding practical ways to appropriately assess the contribution of school leaders is an important component of improving practice and improving outcomes (Goldring et al., 2007).

Without the inclusion of the expertise of principals, school and instructional leaders, evaluation systems may neither be improved nor attain the desired results, and principals may not view feedback as informative for improvement of their practice (NAESP and NASSP, 2013:1). Developing principal evaluation as a strategy for strengthening leadership and improving schools requires systemic change. Therefore, the Principals Australia Institute, in collaboration with the profession, will develop an assessment and evaluation framework to underpin the Australian Principal Certification Program. While the Australian Principal Standard sets out what principals know, understand and do to achieve in their work (AITSL, 2011), the Australian Principal Standard itself cannot capture or recognize effective professional practice. The Australian Principal Certification Program presents a unique opportunity for all Australian principals to demonstrate the Australian Principal Standard in practice.

While there is no hierarchy implied in the Australian Principal Standard, it is important to note the prominence of leading teaching and learning in the integrated model. Principals have a key responsibility for developing a culture of effective teaching—for leading, designing and managing the quality of teaching and learning—and for students' achievement in all aspects of their development (AITSL, 2011:9) as shown in Figure 9.1.

Figure 9.1
Australian Principal Standard Integrated Model

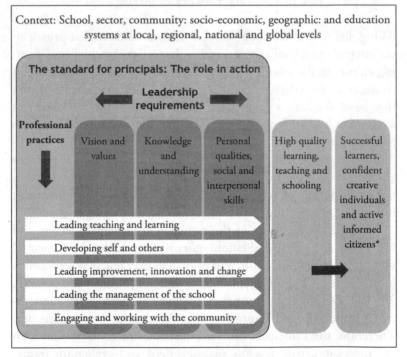

Source: www.aitsl.edu.au

For this to be realized in practice, it is imperative that principals have a high level of understanding about how students learn and a belief in the capacity of all students to learn, achieve and succeed. Principals must also know and understand the many factors that impact on student learning and achievement. The major challenge in improving teaching lies not so much in identifying and describing quality teaching but in developing structures and approaches that ensure widespread use of successful teaching practices: To make best practice, common practice (Dinham et al., 2008:14). Principals should, therefore, set a benchmark of high expectations for self and others and focus on creating a learning environment where all members of the community are challenged and engaged in the learning process.

Conclusion

Earlier in this chapter, I reflected on the literature that examines the linkage between school leadership and student learning. Much can be drawn from this research to guide the design, development and implementation of the Australian Principal Certification Program. Early implications for its design and some key questions that will need to be addressed are set out below:

1. **Implication 1:** Leadership for learning is not the dramatic flourish or grand announcement of a new innovation. Rather, it is the persistent focus on improving the conditions for learning and creating coherence in values and actions across classrooms day in and day out in the school (Hallinger,2010:137). How will the Australian Principal Certification Program allow for a principal to demonstrate how they have created the conditions for learning?
2. **Implication 2:** If the practices and capabilities of leaders evolve as leaders move through their careers (AITSL, 2011:2), how will the Australian Principal Certification Program allow principals to demonstrate the learning that occurs across their career trajectory and the impact of that professional learning?
3. **Implication 3:** Identifying the leadership mediators (Leithwood et al., 2004) does not necessarily help principals to determine where to focus their attention or indeed, how to maximize student learning culture. So, the question

is (Hallinger, 2010): Where should principals put their focus in order to develop the school's capacity to produce a positive impact on student learning? A principal's ability to respond to this question will be a key element in the design of the Australian Principal Certification Program. The Program will need to ensure that principals can show, discuss and reflect upon how they, first, assess their schools capacity for improvement and, second, put their learning, knowledge and understanding into practice.

4. **Implication 4:** If principal engagement and the promotion of teacher professional learning has such a positive impact, then the challenge is to design the Australian Principal Certification Program in a way to allow principals who engage in certification to demonstrate how they have supported teacher learning and the impact it has had on the teaching and learning cultures within their school.

5. **Implication 5:** Leadership is commonly viewed as a driver for exceptional organizational performance and change (Hargreaves et al., 2014). Consequently, this reinforces the imperative for the Australian Principal Certification Program to focus on the leader and the *practices* they exhibit rather than their role and responsibilities, thus, creating an opportunity for principals to reflect, change, improve and be recognized for the accomplished practice of leadership.

6. **Implication 6:** Leadership is a process of mutual influence. Effective leadership for learning is adaptive and responsive to the changing conditions of the school over time (Hallinger, 2010). The Australian Principal Certification Program must recognize that principal professional learning has to be responsive to the context and the needs of the school, the students and the community. It has to be developed through relationships that provide a platform for principals to positively influence others with a mutually beneficial effect.

7. **Implication 7:** It is not sufficient for principals to have knowledge and understanding of leadership, they must be able to *do* and *act*. Accomplished principals know how to

make the right things happen and take appropriate action when the need arises. Among the central purposes of Principal Certification is to 'gain professional recognition for exemplary leadership practice'. It cannot be emphasized too strongly that this particular purpose is of paramount importance. We need to know much more about outstanding school leaders and be able to exemplify that practice to others. We need to identify them, connect them and illuminate their work (Caldwell, 2013). In the design and delivery of the Australian Principal Certification Program, attention will be paid to recognition but also the possibility of gaining system wide knowledge about accomplished leadership practice.

8. **Implication 8:** The future is not some place we are going to but one we are creating. The paths are not to be found, but made, and the activity of making them changes both the maker and the destination (Shaar, 2000). We know that the very nature of designing the Australian Principal Certification Program will bring challenges. Work of any consequence always does. The opportunity to recognize principals throughout Australia for the amazing work they do each day is a central driver.

Accomplished principals will always ensure that student learning, the quality of teaching and whole school improvement are the key focus areas of their schools. These principals strive to improve student outcomes by setting the learning standards and creating the organizational culture where effective learning takes place. They play a critical role in supporting and fostering quality teaching through coaching and mentoring, and by promoting a culture of high expectation in schools. The Australian Principal Certification Program is fundamentally about reward, recognition and reciprocal acknowledgement of accomplished leadership practice by principals, for principals.

The Australian Principal Certification Program is not about producing detail without substance. Evidence against clear criteria will be an important component of its design. Essentially, Principal Certification is about creating an infrastructure where effective and accomplished leadership practice is duly rewarded and recognized. For this to happen, Principal Certification will need to have 'extrinsic' and 'intrinsic' values. It will need to be inherently useful to other principals as well as those seeking certification. It will need to be personally and professionally rewarding for those taking part. Ultimately, it will be designed with the profession, for the profession.

References

AITSL. (2011). *Australian professional standard for principals*. Melbourne, Victoria: Education Services Australia. Retrieved from www.aitsl.edu.au (last accessed on 9 July 2015).

Anderson, M., Gronn, P., Ingvarson, L., Jackson, A., Kleinhenz, E., McKenzie, P., Mulford, B. and Thornton, N. (2007) *Australia: Country background report. DECD improving school leadership activity*. A report prepared for the Australian Government Department of Education, Science and Training. Melbourne: ACER.

Branch, G. F., Hanushek, E. A., Rivkin, S. G. (2013). *School leaders matter: Measuring the impact of effective principals*. Education Next Online Journal. Retrieved from http://educationnext.org/school-leaders-matter/ (last accessed on 18 March 2015).

Caldwell, B. (2013) *National and international practice in voluntary certification for principals* Principals Australia Institute (PAI), Australia.

Dinham, Stephen (2008). *How to get your school moving and improving*. Camberwell, VIC: ACER Press.

Dinham, S., Ingvarson, L. and Kleinhenz, E. (2008). *Investing in teacher quality: Doing what matters most*. Melbourne: Business Council of Australia.

Dinham, S., Anderson, M., Caldwell, B. and Weldon, P. (2011). Breakthroughs in school leadership development in Australia. *School Leadership and Management*, 31(2), 139–154.

Goldring, E., Porter, A. C., Murphy, J., Elliott, S. N. and Cravens, X. (2007). *Assessing learning-centered leadership: Connections to research, professional standards, and current practices*. Retrieved from www.wallacefoundation.org/knowledge-center/school-leadership/principal-evaluation/Documents/Assessing-Learning-Centered-Leadership.pdf (last accessed on 18 March 2015).

Hargreaves, A., Boyle, B. and Harris, A. (2014). *Uplifting leadership*. New Jersey: Wiley Business Press.

Hopkins, D. (2011). *Instructional leadership and school improvement*. Nottingham: Faculty of Education, University of Nottingham.

Ingvarson, L. (2014). *Professional certification for accomplished school principals: Directions for Australia*. Australia: Principals Australia Institute (PAI).

Leithwood, K., Seashore-Louis, K., Anderson, S. and Wahlstrom, K. (2004). *Review of research: How leadership influences student learning*. New York: The Wallace Foundation.

Ministerial Council on Education, Employment, Training and Youth Affairs (MCEETYA). (2008). *The Melbourne declaration on educational goals for young Australians curriculum corporation as the legal entity for the MCEETYA, Melbourne*

NAESP and NASSP. (2013). *Rethinking principal evaluation: A new paradigm informed by research and practice*. VA: National Association of Secondary School Principals and National Association of Elementary School Principals

Northouse, P. (2007). *Leadership: Theory and practice* (4th ed.). Thousand Oaks, CA: SAGE Publications.

Robinson, Viviane, Lloyd, Claire and Rowe, Kenneth (2008). The impact of leadership on student outcomes: An analysis of the differential effects of leadership types. *Educational Administration Quarterly*

Shaar, J. (2000). *Manifesto as a contribution to a sustainable future.*, Santa Cruz, CA: University of California.

The Wallace Foundation. (2012). *The School principal as leader: Guiding schools to better teaching and learning.* New York: The Wallace Foundation.

10

Networking for Educational Equity: Rethinking Improvement Within, Between and Beyond Schools

Christopher Chapman

Introduction

Research tells us that higher levels of educational outcomes are associated with a range of positive outcomes including increased material wealth, healthier lifestyles and a lower likelihood of imprisonment (Teddlie and Reynolds, 2000). It would seem that giving every child the best chance of educational success is a prerequisite of a fair society, yet we know that despite decades of attempting to create socially just education systems, there remains a strong link between poverty, deprivation and academic achievement (Mortimore and Whitty, 1997).

This depressing situation means that a child from a socially disadvantaged background is more likely to leave formal education with poorer outcomes than his or her more advantaged counterparts and is likely to face a lifelong struggle involving a myriad of health, financial and social issues. It is time to rethink how we can tackle the steadfast relationship between socio-economic disadvantage and poor educational outcomes.

Towards More Equitable Education Systems

There is much to be proud of about most education systems, however, despite all our efforts, educational inequity remains one of the major concerns of our time (Payne, 2008). It seems that there are four key challenges facing most education systems around the world.

The first challenge is to change what we do 'within' schools. Traditionally, we have tended to focus on improvement within schools. Schools have been the primary unit of analysis. This has delivered some returns; at worst in some systems, tactically ratcheting up test scores at the expense of capacity building and at best in some systems, increasing schools' capacity to manage change for a longer term.

Improving the learning level is crucial and within-school approaches rightfully have a place within an improvement agenda, but we need to move from thinking about educational change purely in terms of school improvement—doing the same things more effectively—to thinking about it in terms of educational innovation and daring to think about doing new things which replace the current orthodoxies of practice. Furthermore, if we are to release the potential that exists within schools, we need to find new ways of moving knowledge, experience and expertise around them. Put simply, it is about finding new ways for teachers and leaders to share practice and learn together. However, for developing and refining approaches within school, collaboration is in itself not enough.

The second challenge is to develop education systems where schools work collectively to support each other's endeavour. Richer rewards will be gained from building collective capacity between schools through school-to-school collaboration. Furthermore, there is emerging evidence from a range of school-based networks to suggest that collaborative enquiry-driven approaches, underpinned by the intelligent use of performance and contextual data, can positively impact learning outcomes for marginalized and disadvantaged groups of students (Chapman et al., 2016). Stretching the focus from within to between schools is necessary but again insufficient for shift of focus.

The third challenge is to develop approaches that place schools at the centre of their communities and broaden public service provision. Only when we create a coherent set of services that create the context whereby children from the most disadvantaged backgrounds can effectively engage in the educational process, will the link between disadvantaged and low educational achievement be broken. It is clear that health, social and other public services have a major role to play in improving the access, aspiration and achievement of children from our most disadvantaged communities, and this is the area with the most untapped potential.

The fourth challenge is to create the conditions to make this possible. In order to achieve this, we need to create new ways of working within, between and beyond schools. This is not a simple task. The complexity of stretching from within- to between- and beyond-school approaches is a difficult and complex terrain, requiring a fundamental rethinking of roles and relationships within the system. Continuing as we have done in the past will only lead to a failure of implementation and continue to replicate educational inequity.

What Might within-, between- and beyond-school Improvement Look Like in Practice?

I now want to turn our attention to what within-, between- and beyond-school improvement might look like in practice. In doing so, I offer an overview of one of the city challenge initiatives in England, the Greater Manchester Challenge (GMC). A full account of this initiative can be found in the Chief Advisor's analysis of the programme (Ainscow, 2015). Although this example is bound in a particular context, the GMC managed to combine *within-*, *between-* and *beyond-school* perspectives to provide an instructive example of what might be done to move beyond the orthodoxy of thinking about school improvement as primarily a *within school* activity. This programme involved 10 school districts serving 600,000 students in about 1,150 schools and colleges between 2008 and 2011. The aim of the GMC was to develop a system that aspires to world-class standards of education and has the capacity to lead its own journey of improvement.

The initiative involved a partnership approach between national government, school districts and schools, with strong links to other stakeholders. The priorities of the programme were to improve:

1. *Access*: To address underperformance, so that all children and young people attend the schools they deserve.
2. *Aspirations*: To give all children and young people a sense of the positive opportunities open to them, by raising expectations about how good education across Greater Manchester could and should be.
3. *Achievement*: To make sure that all children and young people are able to achieve their potential, by breaking the link between the home backgrounds of learners and educational outcomes and life chances.

The strategy for the GMC was underpinned by the assumption that the system has untapped capacity to improve itself and that in order to unleash its potential, new ways of working would be required. And furthermore, to achieve this, the system required rethinking of relationships, roles and responsibilities. There were four key components of the strategy.

1. *Building leadership capacity*: To place school principals central to school improvement, by encouraging them to lead *within*, *between* and *beyond* schools, taking responsibility for the education of all children rather than only those attending their own schools. The National College of School Leadership set up a 'regional hub' working in partnership to develop National and Local Leaders of Education (there are now over 150 across the region) and a broader strategy involving peer-mentoring and coaching across the region. 'Hub' schools of various types have also emerged as important catalysts for change, encouraging leaders at all levels within schools to work across traditional subject and organizational boundaries. For example, 16 'Teaching Schools' have provided professional development programmes focused on improving classroom practice. Over 1,000 teachers across the region have taken part in these

programmes. School principals are encouraged to think holistically about educational and social service provision. For example, school leaders began to work more closely with social services to target children perceived 'at risk' from dropping out from school or suffering from domestic issues within their family setting.

2. *Families of schools*: Created in an attempt to stimulate discussion about progress and attainment within and between schools with similar socio-economic contexts, there are 58 primary families and 11 secondary, each of which has between 12 and 20 schools serving broadly similar communities. These cross-local authority groups quickly became a catalyst for sharing good practice *between schools* and tied in with the work of head teachers on leadership strategy. The performance map is indicated in Figure 10.1.

Figure 10.1
Performance Map

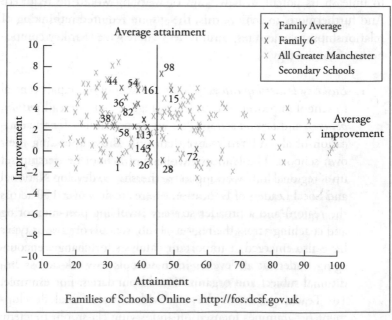

Families of Schools Online - http://fos.dcsf.gov.uk

Each school within the family is plotted on an improvement axis and an attainment axis. Clearly, there is usually
a spread of schools with some being identified as higher on
an improvement score and having high levels of attainment.
Principals within the family then begin to explore each other's
context and discuss possible explanations for these variations.
These conversations are sensitive and require appropriate
facilitation; however, they usually begin to provide interesting
insights and areas from which schools can cooperate to share
practice. For example, one principal explained that an outlier
mathematics department could explain their own strong performance. Conversely, another head explained their apparent
lack of improvement by a struggling mathematics department.
These two departments began working with each other
to share practice. This resulted in an improvement in both
department's performance and the identification of other
areas for collaboration.

3. *Key to success*: Focused on the improvement of around 160
   schools facing the most challenging circumstances with the
   lowest attainment, this strand of activity involved a team
   of experienced principals with a significant track record
   of improving the most challenging schools in the country,
   working with individual schools to undertake a detailed analysis of the context and the development of tactical and strategic improvement strategies to kick start and then sustain
   improvements. This highly contextualized approach developed a unique blend of internal improvement efforts combined with external support and facilitation. The pairing of
   schools drew on families of schools data and other sources
   to 'match' schools across various boundaries, thus unlocking
   their potential that had been previously restricted to a specific
   local authority or faith group. There is evidence which suggests that these arrangements have a positive impact on both
   schools in the partnership. This is not a transmission model
   of improvement.

4. *Workstrands* were set up to inject innovation and experimentation into the system. Each school district led on a workstrand

focused on an educational issue facing school districts, linking improvement efforts *beyond schools* to broader social and economic agendas. The workstrands facilitated further exchange of expertise, resources and learning from innovation and experimentation across local authorities. For example, the director of one school district, with a social services background, led on the teaching and learning workstrand. This programme involved developing experimental classrooms, lesson study and learning rounds *between schools* across the region. Those involved in it worked together on a range of interlinked projects and shared their work with colleagues through a series of events and seminars across the region.

Moving from the Margins to the Mainstream

For all this to move from the margins to the mainstream, a significant cultural shift is needed in how we construct professional identity of those tasked with delivering and supporting the education and the wider development of children within our societies. We have to rethink not only with whom we work, but also how and where we work. This involves the blurring of institutional boundaries and developing new ways of working.

Those of us working within schools need to develop a more outward-looking perspective, where working with colleagues from different institutions and sectors becomes second nature. We have to rethink not only with whom we work, but also how and where we work. It means that those of us who left schools and classrooms some time ago will be likely to find themselves back in them again, while those who never worked outside classrooms or schools will be required to do so for the first time. Frankly, it is no longer acceptable to hide in your classroom, school, town or city hall or university office replicating practices of the past. If the status quo prevails, we will continue to fail a significant number of our children.

References

Ainscow, M. (2015). *Towards Self Improving Schools Systems: Lessons from a City Challenge.* Routledge: London.

Chapman, C., Muijs, D., Reynolds, D., Sammons, P. and Teddlie, C. (eds.) (2016). *The International Handbook of Educational Effectiveness and Improvement: Research, Policy and Practice.* Routledge: London.

Mortimore, P. and Whitty, G. (1997). *Can School Improvement Overcome the Effects of Disadvantage?* Institute of Education: London.

Payne, C. M. (2008). *So Much Reform, So Little Change: The Persistence of Failure in Urban Schools.* Harvard Education Press: Cambridge.

Teddlie, C. and Reynolds, D. (2000). *The International Handbook of School Effectiveness Research.* Falmer Press: London.

11

Leading Professional Learning to Improve Schools in Challenging Circumstances in Russia

Serge Kosaretsky, Irina Grunicheva, Marina Pinskaya, Alma Harris and Michelle S. Jones

Introduction

The challenge of improving schools located in deprived contexts is one faced by many education systems around the world. The negative correlation between most measures of social disadvantage and school achievement means that improving schools in challenging circumstances is far from easy or straightforward (Maden and Hillman, 1996). However, this does not mean it is impossible. Evidence shows that schools in challenging circumstances can improve the levels of student performance and achievement but in order to secure and sustain this improvement, they must exceed what might be termed as 'normal efforts' (Maden, 2001).

It is well established in the research literature that leadership plays a key role in school improvement and this is acutely so for schools in difficult contexts (Hopkins, 2001). For schools that are struggling because of socio-economic factors, high-quality leadership and high-quality teaching matters more than ever (Muijs et al., 2004). The evidence from the international research base highlights that effective leaders exercise an indirect but powerful influence on the effectiveness of the school and on the achievement of students (Leithwood et al., 2004). It also shows that for schools in challenging circumstances, the quality of leadership is the key determinant of success or failure and for that to be most effective, leadership practice has to be widely and wisely distributed (Harris and Lambert, 2003).

A recent study of high-performing organizations reinforced that leadership is central to peak performance and that exceptional outcomes are mainly secured through a combination of collaboration and competition (Hargreaves et al., 2014). It also showed that schools that perform beyond expectations do so in the most difficult contexts by having leaders with high expectations, who provide an optimum level of support and challenge. Leadership is a pivotal component in the amalgam of high performance and, at best, is a formidable force for continuous improvement.

This chapter explores the role that leadership is playing in improving schools in challenging circumstances in Russia. It draws directly upon evidence from a study that identified schools in difficult circumstances in Russia and showed that they mainly performed at a lower level than schools in more affluent contexts. The study also highlighted the main contributory factors to low performance in schools in disadvantaged areas (Pinskaya et al., 2013). Subsequently, a research and development project is now focusing on schools in challenging circumstances in three regions in Russia, with the prime purpose of supporting improvement and change (Harris et al., forthcoming). This chapter focuses primarily, but not exclusively, on how leadership capacity is being built to support schools in difficulty at the school and local level.

To begin with, this chapter argues that the introduction of greater accountability into the Russian education system has resulted most recently in the clear identification of underachieving schools located predominantly in high-poverty areas. It also argues that one byproduct of a more transparent education system is that the powerful relationship between underperformance and disadvantage can no longer be denied. It is argued from empirical data that schools in disadvantaged areas tend not to reach the same level of performance in external examinations as the schools in the more wealthy areas of Russia do (Pinskaya et al., 2013).

This chapter concludes by discussing emerging empirical evidence from a contemporary school improvement project in three regions in Russia (Harris et al., forthcoming). It focuses particularly on the contribution of leadership to improvement and highlights how leadership at the municipal or district level is proving to be a critical component of success.

New Accountability

The Russian education system is highly centralized and remains a rigid hierarchy. This means that decisions are top-down and are made without involving participants at the regional and local levels. In the past few years, the principals' duties have shifted towards management or financial matters and away from pedagogical issues. According to the data of National Survey of the Economy of Education (2013), conducted in all federal districts of Russia and involving a representative sample of more than 1,000 teachers and 1,000 directors, there is a brand 'new' accountability for those working within the education system.

Unlike many other countries, the introduction of national systems of accountability in Russia is a relatively recent development. In 2005, the development of a national system of quality assurance was introduced which signalled a step change from years of state-controlled accountability. By introducing new measures of accountability and greater transparency, Russia entered a new educational era that created as many challenges as opportunities. The 'Russian System of Quality Assurance' (RuSyQA) was introduced to make the system much more accountable to its clients, that is, individuals, families, civil society and employers. For almost a hundred years, the system was accountable only to the state. Therefore, the importance and significance of this shift towards greater accountability, however imprudent or imperfect, cannot be underestimated.

Attempts to create a new Russian system of quality assurance were, to a great extent, viewed as an answer to most of the social and economic problems in the post-Soviet period. In 2009, the national Unified State Exam (USE) was introduced. This is centrally administered by the Russian Federation. The USE serves as the final school exam and also as an entrance exam for higher and secondary educational institutions. In the Soviet Union, each school had the right to administer its own final exams, which were not tied to universities that also had the right to develop and implement their own forms of entrance examinations. So, 2009 was the first year in the history of Soviet and post-Soviet education, when Russia had a benchmark against which schools and provisions at the municipal, regional and national levels were to be compared.

Introduction of the Unified State Examination (USE) has been viewed as one of the most important components in the democratization of education in the past decade. Every Russian student, regardless of social background and place of residence can apply to universities and participate in higher education. Now, students are enrolled in the universities on the basis of USE scores only, and the previous practice of giving bribes or paying for private tutors from chosen universities, to guarantee enrolment, is no longer practised. The USE results have become one of the main performance indicators for the Russian Federation government to assess the efficiency and effectiveness of regional education authorities as well as general performance of executive authorities of the subjects of Russian Federation.

Apart from the introduction of this unified exam, several other initiatives have been introduced to secure better quality assurance in education system in Russia. These include the introduction of public accountability at all levels of the system exemplified at the school level by the public reports of school principals. School governance bodies now take the lead and have compiled checklists that allow them to audit not just the academic outcomes but also the ethos and environment existing within a school (Vakhstain et al., 2009). However, at the school level there is no culture of working with data. For example, teachers do not use formative assessment as they are not familiar with it and according to the data of National

Survey of the Economy of Education (2013), 'classroom observation data' is the least rarely used source of information that schools use to judge the quality of teaching. While the process of regional or national inspection is not in place, the growing trends in assessment of school performance based on evidence and pre-specified criteria is an important departure from previous practice.

Not surprisingly, one of the consequences of increased accountability in the Russian education system has been the fact that inequality among schools has become acutely apparent. In Soviet times, such differences were not so visible, as there were no means of comparing schools and there was no available or reliable comparative measure. But now with the introduction of accountability mechanisms that are more akin to the West, the fissures and fractures in Russian education are much more visible. In terms of educational achievement, the differential performance of schools is a major source of contemporary concern as there are important implications for the country's future economic wealth and prosperity.

Inequality

While the powerful relationship between disadvantage and underachievement is well known and understood in the Western countries, until relatively recently in Russia it has not been explored (Pinskaya et al., 2013). In Soviet times, pedagogy was geared to equality. There were very effective mechanisms for supporting children from families with low cultural capital and 'making them equal' (Froumin, 1995). The national drive to maintain a system based on communist and collective principals along with centralized control meant that any differences were simply airbrushed out. A system of positive discrimination and strict meritocracy was created to support capable and hard-working students to succeed. However, in the post-Soviet era, this system of positive discrimination was dismantled and as a direct consequence the culture of supporting children with socioeconomic capital was replaced by a culture of fulfilling families' needs (Froumin, 1993).

According to the Global Wealth Report, Russia is far ahead of other major countries in terms of wealth inequality. It remains the case that one per cent of the richest Russians account for 71 per cent of all personal assets in the Russian Federation. In Russia, five per cent of the population owns 82.5 per cent of all personal wealth of the country (Global Wealth, 2012). As highlighted earlier, variation in educational opportunities in Russia prompted concerns about the country's future economic prosperity. Since 2000, international comparisons of educational achievement (e.g., Progress in International Reading Literacy [PIRLS] and Programme for International Student Assessment [PISA]) have demonstrated significant discrepancies in the comparative performance of Russian students linked to the economic and educational resources of their parents. The task of providing quality education and equal access for all children—regardless of the social, economic and cultural standing of their families—therefore is currently viewed as crucial for economic growth.

Research has shown that acquiring social capital along with the acquisition of social competencies leads to better life chances and greater individual productivity (Hanushek, 1971). Data also shows that the socio-economic status of students and the educational level of their parents combine to be a perfect predictor and indicator of a student's subsequent achievement. This is supported by data from the Universal State Exam (USE) which shows that graduates of more affluent city schools achieve higher scores in Russian, Computer Science and English. As a consequence, in Russia, it is currently the case that more affluent students have better chances to continue their education and are more competitive in the job market, as these skills are in high demand.

Evidence shows that if students from low-income families were equally distributed across all schools, and if all schools were all equally effective, it would still mean that social and cultural status remain powerful determinants of underachievement. However, while cultural and social factors are influential, the fact remains that the quality of schooling can significantly reduce the impact of poverty on subsequent attainment. In 2002, a World Bank project called 'Reform of the Education System' was based on the simple but powerful idea that schools are different and their social context explains the significant variation in the quality of education. This study concluded that

> A child's educational chances depends upon the social status of his or her parents and their education, on the family's economic standing, on the fact that the child happened to grow up in a village or in a city, in proximity or far from a good school ... children from a humble upbringing are pushed into 'cheap' schools. There is an actual worsening level of education for these young people .... This is a sore spot. This is where inequality arises and is then cemented; it starts here and continues through generations.

It is also clear from the international research evidence that the negative effects of social disadvantage upon subsequent achievement can be overturned. Evidence reinforces that the quality of education is a powerful force that can secure better outcomes, irrespective of a child's starting point. The large corpus of research within the school effectiveness and improvement field has repeatedly shown that highly effective schools can disrupt the connection between disadvantage and underachievement and improve the life chances of each student, regardless of individual capabilities and family context. This positive stance is particularly important for schools in poorer areas where majority of students come from disadvantaged families, as it implies that poverty need not result in poor attainment and achievement.

In Russia, however until recently, the external and internal causes of persistently deteriorating academic results in schools that operate in difficult social contexts had not been empirically explored. Consequently, a scoping study was undertaken and this proved to be the starting point for a research and development study that is currently focusing on improving schools in challenging circumstances in Russia.

Identification

The initial scoping study took place in three regions of Russia that differ significantly in terms of performance, geography, demographics and socio-economic characteristics (Tyumeneva, 2009).

A statistical analysis was undertaken based upon data from a stratified sample of 1,500 educational institutions in these three regions. The sub-sample for the field research comprised of 22 schools that all operated in difficult social contexts but were divided by academic achievement, into two groups: 'strong and weak'. *Consistently weak schools* were those that demonstrated consistently lower levels of academic performance than other schools over a sustained period. *Consistently strong schools* were those that demonstrated consistently high academic results in all categories for three consecutive years.

Education performance was measured using a range of indicators and schools were assigned into types using the SPSS two-step cluster analysis which allowed us to include in our analysis both continuous and discrete variables, and to work with large amounts of data. An analysis of variance was undertaken to start answering the question of causality of low performance. In other words, the research sought to seek explanations for a steady decline in the results of one school in challenging circumstances and the success of another school in equally challenging circumstances. These differences between groups of consistently weak and consistently strong schools were undertaken using dispersion analysis of the social aspects affecting these schools and an examination of the issues and factors relating to their performance.

In keeping with the broader literature on improving schools in challenging circumstances (Muijs et al., 2004), the analysis revealed that the most significant parameters on which successful schools differ from less successful schools can be attributed to the composition of their population. Analysing the data sets uncovered significant variation between school clusters. It showed that schools with lower performance scored much higher on the indicators of socioeconomic deprivation and household poverty. The research also found that students of high-performing schools were more likely to live in well-furnished apartments, as opposed to their counterparts. Essentially, differential performance was explained by degrees of material deprivation.

The research findings also reached the following conclusions:

1. Schools in Russia with consistently high results have the most favourable social contexts.

2. Schools in Russia with consistently low results have the highest percentage of non-native Russian-speaking students.
3. Schools in Russia with lower academic results have more students whose parents are out of work and do not have college degrees.

The data also showed that in underperforming schools, there was a lack of qualified teachers. Most teachers in the poorest performing schools were at the pre-retirement age, and generally, there was a lack of motivation among them to improve student-learning outcomes. There were also fewer library resources, less funds for equipment and a far lower share of the budget spent on teachers' salaries in such underperforming schools.

While such findings might seem unremarkable to those working in other countries and other educational settings, it is important to reflect upon the context where these findings have emerged. In post-Soviet Russia, this is the first time that empirical data has been available which categorically shows the relationship between disadvantage and the educational underachievement. It shows that not all schools in Russia are equal and that the life chances of certain young people are limited by their socio-economic context. The empirical evidence also shows that schools located in high- poverty contexts in Russia encounter more challenges than schools in more affluent areas, and most importantly, they often do not have the necessary physical, material and intellectual resources to deal with the range of problems they face. However, on the positive side, the data also demonstrates that there are schools that 'succeed against the odds' in challenging circumstances in Russia and that these schools embody the characteristics of effective schools widely known in the international literature (Chapman et al., 2011).

Leading for Improvement

Until relatively recently, the idea of schools being identified as operating in challenging circumstances or underperforming has not been widely acknowledged or systematically explored in Russia. The emergent findings now clearly show a clear and strong relationship between inequality and underperformance that can be summarized as follows: Schools operating under less favourable social conditions in Russia with minimal staff and material resources have less chances of being successful or improving their national examination results. The most common determinants of schools with consistently poor academic results are the degree of disadvantage, poor social context and the lack of social capital that they experience. School context has been identified as a major explanatory factor for poor performance.

The findings show that there are schools operating in difficult social contexts that provide their students with a high level of education (so that their academic achievements are in line with the more advantageously situated educational institutions). These schools employ consistent and systematic educational strategies that ensure effective teaching and learning. They also have leaders who understand that poverty is not an excuse for failure and who put in place the right combination of challenge and support.

The research findings showed that there are three basic elements of success for securing high performance in schools of challenging circumstances. The first is the absolute focus on high educational achievement and high expectations of teachers for all their students. Leaders in the most effective schools, irrespective of context, make every effort to develop students' academic motivation, put them on the path to reach their academic potential and support their interests as well as help them to succeed. The data showed that to facilitate better learning outcomes, effective schools in challenging circumstances are actively involved in projects and academic research, starting with first grade, and that this is related to themes that are accessible to students such as the history of their families or the school's neighbouring environment. In a number of schools, these research projects are conducted at a very high level with students participating in regional and national competitions, in the capital of their region and nearby cities. For example, the schools in Karelia work with institutes in St. Petersburg.

Second, effective leaders of schools in challenging circumstances also carefully build lines of support for students who need the most help. In such schools, students are given a chance after the school is over, to prepare for the national exam (which is especially important, as parents cannot always provide this help). Here, they get additional assistance from teachers on subjects that are particularly difficult for them. The most interested and abled children take additional classes to prepare themselves for academic examinations and competitions. These classes are available to students of all levels and grades. As schools often do not have their own materials and staff to provide these services, they often work in partnership with local art centres and libraries, and nearby sports and music schools. Close cooperation and collaboration with parents, as well as openness to work with other educational institutions, is another major reason for their success.

Finally and most importantly, effective schools in challenging circumstances have a positive culture, based on cooperation, collective decision-making and common goals for everyone in the school community. New teachers that come to the school receive help from the administration and their colleagues, and get a personal mentor to support them throughout their first year at the school. They engage in meaningful collaboration in the form of professional learning communities and focus their collective attention on improving the continually improving standards. Teachers in these schools are supported and encouraged to try out new pedagogies and to work with other colleagues to improve their teaching skills.

Without question, becoming a more effective school in challenging circumstances requires extraordinary efforts from the staff and the wider community. But effort alone, while necessary, is not sufficient. There also needs to be appropriate resourcing and support along with carefully selected strategies for improvement. It is here that the leadership role of the municipality is so important. Schools in challenging circumstances need external support and challenges in order to improve; they cannot do it in isolation. In many schools in the current study, it is clear that municipality is a critical contributor to raising standards. The presence, involvement and support of the municipality at the local level not only retains the spotlight on improvement, but also brings necessary resource expertise and guidance. This distributed leadership ensures that the job of improving schools is not down to the principal but is viewed as a shared endeavor among teachers, parents and the wider community.

More than a quarter of a century ago, the seminal study by Rozenholtz (1989) made it clear that what distinguishes high-performing districts or schools from those performing less well is the quality of their professional relationships and the degree of professional support. Thus far, the research findings similarly reinforce the importance of shared leadership as a route to better performance and outcomes. It highlights the pivotal importance of the municipal level in making improvements possible, but critically also makes it sustainable.

Coda

The literature on improving schools in difficult circumstances highlights over and over again that there are strategies that can support schools in challenging circumstances in their improvement efforts. These vary according to the school context and the various needs of the students. However, the literature also reveals that one common contributor to school success, irrespective of context, is the nature and extent of leadership. The emerging evidence shows that it is leadership at the municipal level that has the greatest impact on improving schools in the most challenging contexts in Russia. This requires further empirical investigation in the next data collection round.

For many young people in Russia, particularly those in deprived settings, school is not their best chance; it is their only chance. This is also the case in many other countries and contexts. Therefore, it is imperative that we look for solutions, however imperfect they may be, to improve schools in the most impoverished situations. Ultimately, if the goal is to improve the life chances of all young people in poverty, so they can succeed against the odds; it is undoubtedly worth the effort and unquestionably worth the journey.

References

Analytical Report. (2007). *Key findings of the international studies of educational achievement of students in PISA-2006*, p. 23, Analytical Report, Moscow.

Chapman, C., Harris, A., Muijs, D., Reynolds, D. and Sammons, P. (Eds.), (2011). *Challenging the orthodoxy? Perspectives on school effectiveness and improvement research policy and practice.* NL: Springer

Froumin, I. (1993). *The role of innovative schools in the educational reform in Russia. Context*, 5, 14–16.

———. (1995). The child's road to democracy. In J. Chapman, I. Froumin, D. Aspin (Eds.), *Creating and managing the democratic school.* London: Falmer Press.

Hanushek, E. (1971). Teacher characteristics and gains in student achievement: Estimation using micro data. *American Economic Review - American Economic Association*, 61(2), 280–288.

Hargreaves, A., Boyle, A. and Harris, A. (2014). *Uplifting leadership.* USA: Wiley Business Press.

Harris, A. and Lambert, L. (2003). *Building leadership capacity for school improvement.* Buckingham: Open University Press.

Hopkins, D. (2001). *Meeting the challenge: An improvement guide for schools facing challenging circumstances.* London: DfES.

Jamison, E. A., Jamison, D. T. and Hanushek, E. A.. (2006). *the effects of education quality on income growth and mortality decline* NBER (Working Paper No. 12652). Cambridge: National Bureau of Economic Research, Inc.

Leithwood, K., Louis, K.S., Anderson, S., and Wahlstrom, K. (2004). *Review of Research: How Leadership Influences Student Learning.* University of Minnesota: USA.

Maden, M. (Ed.). (2001). Further lessons in success. *Success against the odds—Five years on.* (pp. 307–339). London/New York: Routledge/Falmer.

Maden, M. and Hillman, J. (1996) *Success against the odds.* London: Routledge.

Muijs, D., Harris, A., Chapman. C., Stoll, L. and Russ, J. (2004), Improving schools in socio-economically disadvantaged areas: A review of the research evidence. *School Effectiveness and School Improvement*, 15(2), 149–175.

Pinskaya, M. A., Kosaretsky, S. G., Froumin, I. D., Harris, A. and Jones, M. (2013, May). Schools in difficulty: Identification, issues and strategies for improvement. *International Journal of Scientific and Research Publications*, 3(5), 1.

Rozenholtz, S. (1989). Teachers' Workplace: *The Social Organization of Schools.* Teachers College Press: New York.

Tyumeneva, Y. A. (2009), *Comparative evaluation of factors leading to success in PIRLS: A secondary analysis of data from PIRLS 2006 from the Russian sample* (Voprosy Obrazovanie No. 1).

Vakhstain, D., Konstantiovsky, D. and Kurakin, D. (2009). *Between two waves of monitoring (2007–2008). Trends in education development: 20 years of reform, and now what?* (pp. 164–165). Moscow: Universitetskaya Kniga.

World Bank. (2002). *Reform of the Education System.*

12

Developing Leaders for Schools in Singapore

Pak Tee Ng

Introduction

The National Institute of Education (NIE) is an autonomous institute within the Nanyang Technological University. It is the only university institution in Singapore dealing with teachers' education and school leaders' development. All teachers and school leaders in the country are trained here. In Singapore, effective school leadership is seen as a key to the successful implementation of system-wide reforms and school transformation (Ng, 2013; Tharman, 2006). Leaders in school, in their different roles, have to lead curriculum and pedagogical changes, and manage diverse stakeholders and staff members. School leadership development, therefore, is a priority for the education system.

This chapter highlights three key strategies, not commonly observed or implemented as a coherent package globally, in keeping NIE's leadership programmes relevant and responsive to its education system, against the backdrop of rapid changes in the Singapore education system. These three strategies are:

1. Emphasizing the development of leaders' ability to deal with complexity.
2. Strengthening theory–practice nexus through authentic school-based projects.
3. Enhancing university–schools–government partnership.

This chapter also explains how each strategy is put into practice, using specific leadership programmes at the NIE, as examples. Three programmes are mentioned in this chapter, namely the Leaders in Education Programme (LEP), Management and Leadership in Schools (MLS) programme and Teacher–Leaders' Programme (TLP). It should be emphasized that the strategies are implemented in all these programmes, but in different ways as appropriate.

Emphasize the Development of Leaders' Ability to Deal with Complexity

Due to rapid changes in the wider economy and society, school leadership today has become a much more demanding role (Fullan, 2007; Harris, 2013; Ng, 2013; Sergiovanni, 2009). It also has to focus on developing the professional capital and not just the human capital (Hargreaves and Fullan, 2012). Educational governance and leadership involves a high level of complexity, given the tensions and paradoxes within the education system (Hargreaves and Shirley, 2012; Ng, 2011). There are no simple, straightforward solutions to resolve these paradoxes and tensions, and they often cause confusion and indecisiveness in leaders (Handy, 1994). But leaders have to make tough choices between options that often 'pit one right value against another' (Kidder, 1995:16). Singapore requires school leaders who can thrive in a complex environment that offers both possibilities and challenges in policy interpretation and implementation.

Another factor that adds to the complexity of leadership is that in a dynamic landscape, leadership in a school has to be distributed (Harris 2008, 2009; Spillane, 2006). There are multiple sources of influence within a school, and distributed leadership theory calls attention to the idea of 'leader plus' (Spillane, 2006:3). Distributed leadership implies departure from the bureaucratic model to an interconnected approach to change (Leithwood et al., 2009). It involves building relational trust so that distributed leadership is genuine and not mere delegation (Day, 2009). Trust is the glue that makes for the effective distribution of leadership. The social interactions that become a critical part of distributed leadership practice are more important than a particular leadership function, because value is actually created through interrelationships and interactions between those in formal and informal leadership roles. Distributed leadership, in practice, involves brokering, facilitating and supporting the leadership of others (Harris, 2013; Spillane and Diamond, 2007). The 'catch' of course, is that the practice of distributed leadership based on social interactions and trusting relationships is complex and involves many elements of uncertainty. The complexity of trusting relationships and social interaction implies that various interests of different stakeholders are taken into consideration whilst keeping the central idea of shared agenda.

The LEP is a six-month milestone executive programme to prepare school leaders. It is a collaborative effort between NIE and the Ministry of Education (MoE) of Singapore. Each year since 2001, the MoE selects 30–40 vice principals (or MoE officers at the equivalent level) to participate in this prestigious programme. The participants have to successfully undergo a series of situational tests and selection interviews before being selected to become full-time candidates in the programme (Ng, 2013).

The LEP aims at developing principalship capability that is 'values-based, purposeful, innovative and forward-looking, and anchored on strong people leadership, strategic management skills and an appreciation of how principals could work effectively in a complex environment' (NIE, 2014a:5). The LEP prepares school leaders to deal with complex situations and engage in problem-solving or negotiations with staff and stakeholders with differing priorities. To do so, the programme emphasizes a continuous action–reflection loop that is based on the interactive nature of the 'minds' and 'roles' of school leadership.

How leaders think (their 'minds') affects how they act (the actions associated with their roles). That is how leaders apply their 'minds' to their 'roles'. But leaders also need to reflect on their actions in the various 'roles' to refine their 'minds'. This is a continuous and virtuous application-reflection spiral in the journey of school leaders, which helps them to appreciate the different pathways, generate multiple solutions and manage dynamic relationships in leading a school in an increasingly complex environment. (NIE, 2014a:5)

One key component of the LEP, the Creative Action Project (CAP), illustrates how the programme develops the ability of school leaders to deal with complexity. The LEP participants are attached on an individual basis to a local school in Singapore throughout the duration of the programme. This is of course a different school to the one which they come from. This arrangement exposes them to different facets of the education system. The principal of the attachment school serves as a mentor to the LEP participant. The CAP is a major undertaking by each LEP participant in the attachment school. The requirements of the CAP are (NIE, 2014a):

1. The LEP participants have to envisage what the attachment school will be like in 10–15 years' time. This requirement of the project challenges participants to examine current assumptions about education and to explore new and exciting concepts that can transform the school system in the future. Also, in terms of future challenges, participants need to consider global economic and geopolitical factors that can impact the development of the country.
2. They have to describe the major facets of the future school (e.g., location, curriculum, pedagogy and school structure), especially the ones that are very different from the current one.
3. They have to work with the principal and staff of the school to implement a component of this future school that is currently feasible and desirable, preferably in the area of curriculum, pedagogy and assessment. This can be done as a prototype (e.g., experimenting with one or two teachers and one or two classes). But they have to justify how the concept is scalable and sustainable.

4. They have to reflect on the implementation challenges of the prototype and possible implementation challenges in the scaling-up plan so as to develop operational savviness.

Although the theoretical foundation of the concept of 'complexity' is addressed in a course within the programme (Ng, 2011), the participants are exposed to the practical application of the knowledge in the CAP. The complexity of the project is due to multiple variables and uncertainties inherent in the process of conceptualization and implementation. The participants have to exercise their leadership strategically and systematically, addressing change management issues in an unfamiliar school with no comforting sense of certainty. With no position or authority within their assigned school, they have to be able to work with the incumbent principal, vice principal and teachers of their attachment school, selling a vision of the school (10–15 years down the road) and implementing a change as part of that vision (Ng, 2013).

Because they cannot approach the project in a linear and mechanical way, the LEP participants learn a few critical skills in dealing with non-linear and dynamic situations. In particular, they learn to conduct 'futuring'. The CAP requires the participants to critically examine future trends in education. They, therefore, develop the foresight necessary to move education into the future. To lead schools in the 21st century, school leaders need to continuously interpret the future to craft organizational responses strategically. They also learn to adapt and be flexible. The LEP only prescribes broad project parameters. The adaptive skills and flexibility learned by the participants are put into practise in carrying out the project in an unfamiliar context. Moreover, they learn to collaborate with other people. The LEP participants experience first-hand challenges of leading people without using authority and facilitating change without using position. This encourages participants to work in a collaborative way with stakeholders in their attachment school. The unstructured nature of the project is also a compelling antecedent to generating self-organizing dynamics among fellow participants for ideas and mutual support (Ng, 2013).

Strengthen Theory-practice Nexus through Authentic School-based Projects

Leaders, at various hierarchical levels in school, are expected to spearhead reforms and facilitate change. Theories, while important, require appropriate contextualization to be applicable in local situations. Therefore, NIE's leadership programmes strive to strengthen the theory–practice nexus, going beyond the academic rigour of knowing 'why' and 'what' to the 'how' of implementing changes in school. These programmes create the theory–practice nexus by involving participants in authentic school-based projects. It is clear from the discussion in the previous section that the CAP is a learning platform for achieving the theory–practice nexus. The CAP represents an authentic learning opportunity for LEP participants to implement a value-adding change in a school. In order to do so, they have to contextualize their acquired knowledge into real practices that suit the school. This experience gives them a deeper appreciation of how new knowledge ties in with school realities.

The MLS, which is a programme for middle leaders, offers another example to illustrate this strategy in practice. Middle leaders in school play a critical role in supporting their principal in a school-based reform and leading various aspects of it. Middle leaders help the school principals manage the work of colleagues or teams of colleagues (Gunter and Rutherford, 2000). They serve as co-leaders in their schools. They are expected to be champions of change and innovators in their own areas of work. The MLS is a programme for developing such school middle leadership. Launched in 2007, the MLS is a full-time, 17-week in-service programme for selected middle leaders of schools (primary, secondary and pre-university level), with each run currently taking in approximately 200 participants per cohort. Middle leaders are nominated by their principals to attend the programme. They receive full salary during their time at the NIE and their fees are fully borne by the MoE. This programme is offered twice a year, in January and July (Ng, 2009).

The Curriculum Project (CP) is a major group-learning task that the participants have to undertake in the MLS. Working in small teams of five–six members, the participants develop a school-based curriculum unit in response to an authentic curriculum issue in the school that their team is attached to. Guided by a curriculum tutor, the participants work collaboratively to design a curriculum package that can be implemented in the school. This project equips participants with the knowledge and skills that support the current policy initiative 'Teach Less Learn More', which seeks to move the education system from quantity to quality through school-based curricula and pedagogical innovations (Ng, 2008).

The CP requires the participants to design an innovative curriculum unit for the attachment school based on the following principles (NIE, 2014b):

1. The project must be an innovation that adds value to the teaching and learning in the school.
2. It must meet the needs of the school.
3. It must emphasize effective learning, formative assessment, flexibility in breadth and depth of knowledge to suit the students and must focus on the students' understanding and application of knowledge.
4. It must utilize instructional approaches that are specific and relevant to the objectives.
5. It requires the participants to reflect on their CP journey as part of their learning regarding change management.

The CP is a form of action learning (Marquardt, 1999). It provides a platform where theory and practice come together in an authentic way. It involves participants learning together from multiple sources. It also involves them designing the curriculum around various considerations and limitations such as school resources, student capability, staff capacity, vision and strategic plans of the school.

Through the CP, the participants begin to view curriculum building as a developmental process that entails ongoing research, theory generation and teaching practice. The project encourages team members to engage in a series of dialogues regarding curriculum development. These dialogues serve as discourse platforms to help them arrive at a better understanding of theories and how these theories can be applied in different contexts. The CP provides an opportunity for participants to hear from one another candid and informed opinions about issues of teaching and learning.

Enhance University-Schools-Government Partnership

The practice of the above-mentioned strategies is possible because of close tripartite partnership between the NIE, schools and MoE. Through such partnership, participants are provided with a programme that enables them to interpret policies in the light of theories and translate the knowledge and skills learned into practice in their schools.

To deal with many complex issues in modern societies, multi-organizational partnerships are often touted as a solution; as such partnerships combine multiple perspectives, tap into diverse abilities and enhance collaboration to achieve a common purpose (Kearney et al., 2007; Silka, 2004). This is also the case in education. More and more institutions and universities embark on partnerships with relevant government ministries to enhance the delivery of education services and the professional development of teachers (Laferrière et al., 2010; Taylor, 2008). Partnerships between university and government can bring about new ideas and invigorate development agenda to support state reforms (Julnes, 2006). But, such partnerships have also at times been devalued and dismissed as 'conceptually empty and merely political expedient' (Brinkerhoff and Brinkerhoff, 2011:12).

In Singapore, the partnership between NIE, MoE and schools is not an empty concept or a recent endeavour. Since independence in 1965, Singapore has implemented a nationalized system of schools, managed through the MoE, and NIE has been the only teachers' education institution in the country. It is, therefore, a partnership that started at the birth of modern Singapore, and is sensible for all parties to continue in order to cultivate mutual understanding and a good working relationship. Taking a leaf from the concept of coaching, such partnership implies that entities are 'entering the relationship as an equal learner' who 'require a willingness to listen, to change and adapt, and to connect and engage others in the learning journey' (Robertson, 2009:40).

Two examples illuminate the nature of this partnership. The first is that of the LEP. This programme is a collaborative effort between the NIE, MoE and schools. When the LEP underwent a programme revamp in 2011, the revised programme was jointly designed by NIE and MoE, taking into account school leaders' inputs (Ng, 2013). The way NIE professors work with MoE officials to design and implement the curriculum for the LEP reflects a synergy of governance and academia. The roles are different but complementary. As Ng (2013:68) elucidates:

> As the MoE has been tracking the performance and development of vice-principals, it is in a suitable position to convey to the NIE some recommended developmental needs of the LEP participants. The NIE augments these needs with additional inputs based on what will give Singapore school leaders an edge in leadership. In this way, the university–government partnership ensures that the programme can address critical practice areas that are currently important, and also more enduring theoretical areas based on scholarly inputs.

Schools are heavily involved in the process because they provide an 'incubating platform' for the CAP and principals serve as mentors to the LEP participants. A university–schools–government partnership as closely linked as that of NIE, schools and MoE, is in itself an innovative approach to school leadership preparation programmes rarely seen in other education systems. Indeed, NIE and MoE hold regular meetings in order to discuss the training and development of school leaders.

The second example is that of the TLP. A philosophy of school leadership development in Singapore is to develop teachers as leaders in their own right, especially in the teaching and learning domains. Teachers are powerful change agents and there are actually many ways by which teachers lead other teachers to improve teaching and learning, in direct and indirect ways, and through formal and informal leadership (Fairman and Mackenzie, 2014).

Singapore teachers, who are more interested in advancing their careers as a teacher, rather than as a school leader, can be promoted along the Teaching Track. The Teaching Track provides advancement for teachers who are keen to develop the pedagogical capability of the teaching profession. Teachers can be promoted to senior teachers (STs), lead teachers (LTs), master teachers (MTTs) and finally the pinnacle position of principal master teachers (PMTTs).

The professional development opportunities of teachers on the Teaching Track are articulated in the Teachers' Growth Model (TGM), launched in 2012 (MoE, 2012). The TGM recommends learning areas that facilitate teachers' professional growth according to the stages in their career. The TGM also articulates five outcomes of professional development, namely the ethical educator, competent professional, collaborative learner, transformational leader and community builder.

In line with the TGM, a suite of programmes called TLP was launched in 2014 to develop teachers as leaders. The TLPs replaced the older versions of the Senior Teachers Programme and Advanced Senior Teachers Programme. The main conceptual differences between the old and new programmes are alignment with the TGM and the degree of continuity between the programmes.

The TLP is actually a suite of three milestone programmes. TLP1, TLP2 and TLP3 cater to the development of STs, LTs and MTTs/ PMTTs, respectively. TLP1 and TLP2 are full-time milestone programmes. For 10 weeks, participants are immersed in a learning environment that encourages them to examine established pedagogy in the light of more recent pedagogical reforms such as assessment literacy and Information and Communication Technology (ICT). They are also encouraged to reflect upon the issues of professional ethos, their scope of influence and the meaning and substance of teacher leadership. TLP3 is still in the initial stages of development at the time of writing. The content of the programmes reflects the current educational reforms, initiatives and practice concerns. For example, the TLP1 comprises various components, which are currently emphasized in the education profession, including curriculum leadership, assessment literacy, mentoring and coaching, teacher researcher, integration of ICT into curriculum and team leadership.

Of course, no partnership is smooth-sailing in all ways. There are various challenges to be resolved and overcome. There is a great degree of negotiation involved to maintain the balance between addressing 'differing organization cultures while maintaining the strengths of stakeholders' (Kearney et al., 2007:76). Established bureaucratic structure and culture in both universities and the government makes working together challenging (Kearney et al., 2007). The challenge in this partnership between NIE, MoE and schools is therefore, finding a common ground on which academics, government officials and school practitioners share their unique perspectives in a constructive and mutually edifying manner. Academics must develop the skills and aptitude to understand issues from practitioners' and government's perspectives. Officials must learn to approach issues unshackled by bureaucratic concerns, but also analyse issues based on education theories and ground practicality. Practitioners have to understand the government's policy intentions and allow theories to guide practice. This is an ongoing journey in Singapore.

Conclusion

This chapter described how NIE continues to enhance its leadership programmes with the following three strategies:

1. Emphasizing the development of leaders' ability to deal with complexity;
2. Strengthening the theory–practice nexus through authentic school-based projects and
3. Enhancing university–schools–government partnership.

Various prominent scholars in teacher education have recently advocated that programmes for teacher education need to develop a clear vision of teaching and learning (e.g., Darling-Hammond, 2007). Many programmes have indeed responded correspondingly in their visions and course offerings, but left the andragogy relatively untouched (McDonald and Zeichner, 2009). Teacher educators are left to their own devices within their own isolated courses. However, in pursuing the three above-mentioned strategies, teacher educators in NIE are brought into close proximity with schools and MoE. There is intensity in the interaction amongst the three parties. There is little chance of isolation. If education is indeed a complex business, then there is a need to prepare ordinary people in the field, to do extraordinary work. Singapore's approach to preparing school and teacher leaders is aligned with that need. Teacher educators at the NIE are required to continue enhancing their roles as clinical educators, not only to explain theories in abstract but also to provide an authentic platform for the integration of theory and practice on the ground.

The preceding discussion merely sets out the key strategies of leadership programmes in Singapore. Actual operations are understandably more complex than what is described in this chapter. However, it is hoped that the case of Singapore may both enrich the work of other jurisdictions and encourage ongoing efforts, not only to further understand school and teacher leaders but also to devise strategies to support their learning that is closely linked with practice.

References

Brinkerhoff, D. W. and Brinkerhoff, J. M. (2011). Public–private partnerships: Perspectives on purposes, publicness, and good governance. *Public Administration and Government*, *31*(1), 2–14.

Darling-Hammond, L. (2007). *Powerful teacher education*. San Francisco, CA: Jossey-Bass.

Day, C. (2009). Building and sustaining successful principalship in England: The importance of trust. *Journal of Educational Administration*, *47*(6), 719–730.

Fairman, J. C. and Mackenzie, S. V. (2014). How teacher leaders influence others and understand their leadership. *International Journal of Leadership in Education: Theory and Practice*, *18*(1), 61–87.

Fullan, M. (2007). *The new meaning of educational change* (4th Edition). New York, NY: Teachers College Press.

Gunter, H. and Rutherford, D. (2000). Professional development for subject leaders: Needs, training and impact. *Management in Education*, *14*(1), 28–30.

Handy, C. (1994). *The empty raincoat: Making sense of the future*. London: Random House.

Hargreaves, A. and Fullan, M. (2012). *Professional capital: Transforming teaching in every school*. New York, NY: Teachers College Press.

Hargreaves, A. and Shirley, D. (2012). *The global fourth way: The quest for educational excellence*. Thousand Oaks, CA: Corwin Press.

Harris, A. (2008). *Distributed leadership: Developing tomorrow's leaders*. London: Routledge.

———. (2009). *Distributed leadership: Different perspectives*. The Netherlands: Springer.

———. (2013). *Distributed leadership matters; potential, practicalities and possibilities*. Thousand Oaks, CA: Corwin Press.

Julnes, P. (2006). University-government partnerships in support of state reforms: Lessons from the Caribbean. *Journal of Public Affairs Education, 12*(4), 439–460.

Kidder, C. (1995). *How good people make tough choices: Resolving the dilemmas in ethical living*. New York: William Morrow.

Kearney, K., Self, M. J., Bailey, L., Harris, E., Halcomb, S., Hill, B. and Shimp, U. (2007). Building an academe and government partnership for workforce education: Challenges and possibilities. *Journal of Industrial Teacher Education, 44*(3), 71–91.

Laferrière, T., Montané, M., Gros, B., Alvarez, I., Bernaus, M., Breuleux, A., Allaire, S., Hamel, C. and Lamon, M. (2010). Partnership for knowledge building: An emerging model. *Canadian Journal of Learning and Technology, 36*(1), 1–20.

Leithwood, K., Mascall, B. and Strauss, T. (2009). *Distributed leadership according to the evidence*. London: Routledge.

McDonald, M. and Zeichner, K. (2009). Social justice teacher education. In W. Ayers, T. Quinn and K. Stovall (Eds.), *Handbook of social justice in education*. Mahwah, NJ: Lawrence Erlbaum.

Marquardt, M. J. (1999). *Action learning in action: Transforming problems and people for world-class organisational learning*. California: David-Black Publishing.

Ministry of Education (MoE). (2012, May 31). *New model for teachers' professional development launched*. Press Release. Retrieved from http://www.moe.gov.sg/media/press/2012/05/new-model-for-teachers-profess.php. Last accessed on 20 June 2015.

National Institute of Education (NIE). (2014a). *LEP 2014 handbook for participants*. Singapore: National Institute of Education.

———. (2014b). *MLS Jan 2014 handbook for participants*. Singapore: National Institute of Education.

Ng, P. T. (2008). Educational reform in Singapore: From quantity to quality. *Educational Research for Policy and Practice, 7*(1), 5–15.

———. (2009). The development of school middle leaders in Singapore: The management and leadership in schools programme. *Asian Journal of Educational Research and Synergy, 1*(1), 31–44.

———. (2011). How participants understand complexity theory through a school leadership programme in Singapore. *International Journal of Complexity in Leadership and Management, 1*(3), 301–313.

———. (2013). Developing Singapore school leaders to handle complexity in times of uncertainty. *Asia Pacific Education Review, 14*(1), 67–73.

Robertson, J. (2009). Coaching leadership learning through partnership. *School Leadership & Management, 29*(1), 39–49.

Sergiovanni, T. J. (2009). *The principalship: A reflective practice perspective*. Boston: Pearson.

Silka, L. (2004). Partnerships within and beyond universities: Opportunities and challenges. *Public Health Reports, 119*(1), 73–78.

Spillane, J. P. (2006). *Distributed leadership*. San Francisco, CA: Jossey-Bass.

Spillane, J. P. and Diamond, J. B. (2007). *Distributed leadership in practice*. New York, NY: Teachers College Press.

Taylor, A. (2008). Developing understanding about learning to teach in a university–schools partnership in England. *British Educational Research Journal, 34*(1), 63–90.

Tharman, S. (2006, December 28). *Building on Individual and Collective Leadership in Our Schools.* Speech by Mr. Tharman Shanmugaratnam, Minister for Education and Second Minister for Finance at the Appointment Ceremony for Principals. Retrieved from http://www.moe.gov.sg/media/speeches/2006/sp20061228.htm. Last accessed on 20 June 2015.

SECTION 3

Leader and Learner Level

Leading Futures: Leading Learning

This final section gets right to the heart of the matter and looks at the actual work and practice of a school leader. Chapter 13 by Karen Edge breaks new ground by exploring the recruitment, retention and progression of Generation X leaders. This is a fresh perspective because a majority of research studies have focused considerable attention on baby boomers, those leaders now in their 50s rather than those under 40 years of age. This chapter throws some important challenges and issues that point to a redefinition of leaders and leadership in the future. One point to note is the way these young leaders deal with accountability and technology, not as an imposition but as a natural process which they take in their stride. Also, many do not see the role of principals as a job for life. This brings its own set of challenges and the empirical findings from this study are the clearest indication yet that a future principal will be markedly different from those in the past.

Chapter 14 by Jim Spillane also sets out some challenges and similarly points to a redefinition of what we mean by leadership. In this chapter, he argues that rather than focusing on the traits and behaviour of individual leaders, we need to focus on leadership as practice. He argues that this practice includes the leader, follower and the situation. He also advocates a move away from the charismatic leader, hero or heroine to a more nuanced, accurate and empirically based analysis of leaders and what they do. While it is acknowledged that this is a more difficult research proposition because of the complexity of social interactions, he argues that unless the challenge is met, we will be simply recycling the same old accounts of individual leaders and their actions that inadequately represent leadership as practice.

In this final section of the book, we also return to the argument made in the Introduction that with increased emphasis on comparative performance, it is easy to forget the context and to lose sight of the learner. As we explore leadership through different lenses and different perspectives, it is important to remember that ultimately the purpose of educational leadership is to make a difference to learning and learners. Whether we subscribe to the label 'instructional leadership' or not, the fact remains that the best school leaders focus on learning and teaching first and then on administration and management tasks second. Wherever they are in the world, our best leaders put learners at the heart of their leadership practice.

Hence, the two final chapters, 15 and 16, focus on two important aspects of contemporary learning—pedagogy and technology. Chapter 15 by David Reynolds and Daniel Muijs looks at what we mean by effective pedagogy. To be an instructional leader requires detailed knowledge of pedagogical processes that surpass simply knowing how to undertake routine supervision or supportive coaching. The authors argue that *instructional leadership* is required if leadership is to affect the learning level and that this instructional leadership requires principals and other school leaders to actively engage with pedagogy, curriculum and data through visioning, strategizing, structuring, developing and monitoring. They also propose that, in the future to be most effective, teachers will need a far broader pedagogical repertoire to meet the needs of the 21st century learners and the increasingly complex technological world. The final chapter by Jill Jameson focuses on the way technology is shaping pedagogy and argues that digital innovation poses challenges and opportunities for 21st century learning.

13

Generation X Leaders in Global Cities: Emerging Perspectives on Recruitment, Retention and Succession Planning

Karen Edge

Global Cities (Sassen, 1991) are ranked annually by *Foreign Policy* in relation to their relative standing as international centres of influence. As focal points of innovation and international trends (Sassen, 1991), Global Cities are often found to be the epicentres of new practices and policy advances across sectors. While there is not yet an international ranking of educational Global Cities, there are cities whose policy and practice interventions and experiences stimulate ripple effects of discussion and debate. We believe that London, Toronto and New York City often serve this role. Each city has been placed in the top 10 of the *Foreign Policy* Global Cities Index and has featured at the centre or forefront of major international trends in educational research, policy and practice.

In the education sector, large cities often experience a high volume of staff turnover (McKinney et al., 2007) related to the challenging economic circumstances which makes recruiting and retaining staff members problematic (BBC, 2009). As our research specifically focused on the work of school principals or head teachers, we were intrigued and concerned about the growing policy and practice discussions associated with school leader shortages. In education over the past decade, many large urban centres have faced significant leadership shortages attributed to teachers' disinterest in the school leader role (Gronn and Lacey, 2004) and escalating principal retirement rates (Howson, 2008). Consequently, in London for example, leaders are stepping into principal posts at a much younger age than their predecessors (DCSF, 2009). Anecdotally, other Global Cities are also experiencing ever-growing cohorts of young school leaders. However, little research exists that examines the experience or influence of this new generation of leaders. These Generation X (GenX) leaders, born between 1966 and 1980, may in fact have a distinctly different approach to their careers, lives and leadership than their predecessors—baby-boomer leaders—who were born between 1946 and 1965.

As the current school leadership knowledge base has largely been generated with evidence from baby-boom-era leaders, system-level policy and practice work drawing on existing research may often exclude consideration of the younger leaders' experience and aspirations. As these new leaders guide school systems into the next era of reform and improvement, a rather urgent need for evidence is clear.

Our Study

In response, our current research explores the nexus of Global Cities, school leadership and GenX. Our three-year Economic and Social Research Council-funded study examines the careers, experiences and aspirations of cohorts between 20 and 25 young principals and vice principals in each of the three top 10 Global Cities—London, New York and Toronto (*Foreign Policy*, 2009). Our overall research project focuses specifically on GenX leaders under 40 years of age. These GenXers are known for their global mindedness, collaboration (Smola and Sutten, 2002), mobility (Duscher and Cowin, 2004) and pragmatism (Zemke et al., 2000). We believe that the emergence of this new generation of leaders marks a plausible and important shift in many aspects of leadership.

Also, as much of the educational leadership research literature has been derived from experienced and, more than likely, older school leaders, it is possible that GenX leaders have rarely been included in research studies, beyond those looking at novice principals. Barring some recent studies of new or novice educational leaders which may, by nature of the timing of the study, explore young leaders' experience (Spillane and Lee, 2014), there has been little research exploring the experience and aspirations of those from GenX (Stone-Johnson, 2014). Given their potential current and future influence, our study makes a unique, timely and important contribution.

This chapter presents our preliminary reflections on the emerging patterns from the analysis of individual semi-structured interviews and career-mapping exercises from over 60 principals and vice principals in the New York City, London and Toronto. We begin this chapter with an overview of our research programme examining the work, life and career trajectories of GenX school leaders in the three cities. Second, we provide a brief review of the literature that has informed the design of the study on Global Cities, urban education, the role of school leaders, and GenX characteristics and work patterns. Third, we introduce our methodology including the design and implementation of our city-based network events, focus groups and individual interviews with our cohorts of GenX-school-leader participants in each city.

Fourth, we present key observations from our first year of the project including the resilience of these young leaders with regard to the pace of policy change and intensified accountability structures, the importance they place on achieving a healthy work-life balance, the implications of their decision to start families later in life and begin their leadership careers earlier and their reluctance to commit to a lifetime career as a school leader. Finally, we draw these initial and emerging themes together to suggest future implications for leadership policy and practice in all three of our Global Cities. In order to foreshadow the breadth and potential policy implications of the findings, we highlight four specific areas: young leaders' views on accountability, on age and leadership, on leading and on managing work, life and family.

A Brief Review of the Literature

Global Cities

Global Cities are sites of innovation, migration and influence. In educational terms, based on our current research in London, New York and Toronto, these Global Cities are experiencing an increase in the number of young school leaders taking the helm of state-funded primary and secondary schools.

Urban Education

Within current discussions of school-level leadership in Global Cities, and in urban jurisdictions more generally, there is an almost an inextricable link between discussions of urban education and poverty (Raffo et al., 2010). While there is no denying that there are pockets of wealth and poverty in every large urban city, the discussions related to state-funded education almost always centre on challenge (Chapman, 2008) and disadvantage (Smyth and McCoy, 2009). Educational leadership research has followed suit, with an increasing focus on leadership in challenging circumstances (Harris, 2002) and leadership in areas of disadvantage (Day et al., 2009).

Role of School Leaders

At the same time, there has been a growing chorus of evidence empirically linking the work of school-level leaders and student outcomes. An increasingly explicit agreement exists that school leaders are second only to teachers in the influence they exert on their students' learning and results (Day et al., 2009; Leithwood and Jantzi, 2008; Robinson et al., 2008).

Generation X

GenX leaders have experienced the most rapidly expanding technological era and are recognized as globally minded, techno-literate, informal and pragmatic (Zemke et al., 2000). These oft-shared traits shape GenXers' desire for collaboration (Smola and Sutton, 2002), mobility (Duscher and Cowin, 2004), diversity and more experimental structures in organizations (Kunreuther, 2003).

Research Strategies

Our study aims to develop a preliminary understanding of GenX school leaders by examining their career trajectories (Gronn, 1999), professional identity formation (Busher, 2005; Luhrmann and Eberl, 2007) and their own perceptions of the intersections of race, ethnicity and gender, on the basis of their experience and work.

In the first year of our research, we established a 10–15 member advisory group (AG) that comprised of leaders from government, academia and leadership-related organizations in each city. These AGs meet twice a year to discuss the study and to examine the ongoing developments and preliminary findings. We also established cohorts of 20–25 young principals and vice principals in each city. Participants were initially recruited through an email invitation either directly from our team or through one of the many support organizations working with young leaders in each city. The invitation outlined the broad aims of the research and invited them to participate in network event or focus group discussions and future interviews.

The network events provide our GenX leader colleagues a chance to mingle and learn about the project, engage in data-gathering tasks in support of the research and, in the later stages of the project, examine data from all three cities to reflect on its accuracy and implications.

Interviews and Career Mapping

We conducted an annual 60-minute individual interviews with 20–25 young leaders in each city. The first-year interviews examined, in more detail, the factors that influenced their career choices, experiences and ambitions for the future whilst simultaneously exploring the possibility of an emerging model of GenX Global City leadership. To understand more about young leaders' career experiences and trajectories, participants were guided to develop individual personal career paths denoting the number of leadership positions they had held, their defining moments and any training and career breaks. Participants also noted the nuances of the transitions between jobs and the influence of mentors and advocates along the way. Upon completion of their trajectory, participants discussed their career paths in their first annual interview to explore any interesting patterns and provide more details on their professional journeys. Second-year interviews explored professional identity, work-life balance, talent-spotting strategies and approaches used to build staff capacity.

Interview Analysis

At this stage, members of our team worked to analyse the first annual young leader interviews and career trajectories individually, within and across cities. All data was entered into Dedoose (an online social science data analysis programme) using a multi-staged coding process and structure (Miles and Huberman, 1994). The overall coding strategy involves working from the transcripts as well as the original interview questions to creating a wide-ranging coding infrastructure, capturing both intended and unintended data. To address the challenges of an international data set and research team, each interview was fully coded by two members of the team to ensure a higher level of reliability across the evidence set. In the final stage of analysis, we examined, wherever applicable, individual participants' evidence across both years of the project. This chapter is drawn from our preliminary analysis of the first-year young leader interviews in the three cities.

Charting the Contextual Policy Landscape

We strongly believe that the experience of our young leader participants is firmly tied to the structures and support presented by the accountability and greater policy contexts within which they work. To understand if and how leadership experience and future career aspirations are influenced by policy, we developed a multi-strand, in-depth analysis of the leadership policy and practice context in each city. First, we developed a structural profile of each education system that included the role of national or state (e.g., department of education), middle tier (e.g., district) and local structures (e.g., networks and families of schools). Structural profiles also include information on the general student population, number and type of schools and leadership demographics. Second, based on the review of policy documents and academic literature, we generated a 10-year city-based policy timeline for key policy enactments that influenced the role and work of school leaders. The overall policy analysis and presentation of the city-based policy trajectories reflect key dates, actors, goals, supports, implementation and accountability strategies of each policy. Finally, policy trajectories note the introduction or refinement of leadership development priorities, strategies and programmes.

Mapping the Policy and Practice Actors

Along with our city-based policy analysis, we tracked the overall nature and function of policy and practice leaders in each city. Our goal was to establish a clear understanding of both governmental and non-governmental or philanthropic actors involved in leadership policy and practice. Based on this evidence, we have also created an overall map and comparative analysis of the leadership organizations and programmes in each city.

Key Preliminary Findings

The preliminary observations in this chapter are drawn directly from the analysis of the individual interviews conducted with each of our participants. As we move into the final year of data collection, recurring patterns noted here emerge from the evidence within and between the cohorts of leaders in each city. Here, we highlight some of the most interesting and pressing trends among our small sample of GenX leaders. As this chapter marks the first formal sharing of our preliminary findings, we focus on some of the most eye-catching findings from our early data including young leaders' perspectives on accountability and their views on age and leadership, on leading and on managing work, life and family.

Young Leaders' Views on Accountability

Leaders in our study are not intimidated by accountability, data or the seemingly relentless drive for school improvement. This is not surprising given that this new crop of school leaders has 'grown up' in the current high-stake accountability environment. While our leaders can see the benefit of accountability via testing and inspection, they express concern about the influence on the lives of students, teachers and leaders. Some of our young women leaders in

London are worried about the timing of inspections and their careers as school leaders. One or two leaders discussed the need to plan their future families around inspection cycles to ensure they are in post when the inspection team arrives. The stress that highly pressurized accountability structures place on the personal lives and choices of principals and the aspirations of future leaders is the cause for some concern. This is definitely the case in London and to a lesser degree in the New York City. There is also an emerging discussion amongst some of our female leaders who are concerned that leadership and parenthood are not compatible and are consequently planning to remove themselves from leadership career paths or to not vie for the top jobs.

Young Leaders' Views on Age and Leadership

Our participating leaders share their views on the challenges and opportunities of being young leaders in a Global City. Advantages include being open to new ideas, having stamina, being innovative and relating to younger staff and students. Young leaders also believe that their high energy levels are beneficial, if not necessary, to sustain a school leadership career in a Global City. In all Cities, the negative aspects of being a young leader relate specifically to adverse and inaccurate perceptions about their experience and/or ability and needing to work harder than their colleagues to build credibility.

Young Leaders' View on Leading

Consistently, our participating leaders describe developing staff and building relationships as the most important skill for leading contemporary urban schools. In turn, with only a few exceptions, they describe themselves as collaborative in their approach to leadership with an awareness of how they need to bring people together, identify individual and collective skills gaps, and work together to deliver their goals. In interviews, leaders quickly follow up with the rationale for their collaboration and strategies for building relationships across their schools. Our future analysis will explore how and why the leaders developed this commitment to collaboration and its implications for their teachers and schools.

Young Leaders' View on Managing Work, Life and Family

The leaders in our study are at an interesting place in their careers and lives. They are generationally predisposed to wanting to find a balance that keeps their home and work lives sustainable. In London, more so than in Toronto but similar to the situation in New York, leaders feel pressured to work late and at weekends simply to keep up with daily tasks and responsibilities. There are more single leaders in London and New York and often, leaders suggest, it is work-life balance that keeps them from being able to prioritize their personal lives. The cohort of participating leaders has, for the most part, delayed having children while taking on leadership posts earlier. This presents an interesting nexus of work and family which has traditionally existed only for men leaders. Now, women leaders may often have toddlers or young school-age children while serving as deputy head teachers or head teachers, which creates new pressures and tensions for work-life balance. Our evidence show that the desire of young leaders to find a balance that suits their own personal and professional aspirations is one of the most important challenges. Many of our young leaders in New York and London have stated that if they cannot find a suitable balance, the longevity of their school leadership careers may be affected.

Final Thoughts and Conclusions

As we are currently heading to the final stages of analysing the within- and between-city patterns in our evidence, this chapter presents snippets of our emerging findings. At the moment, there are a few red evidentiary flags that warrant deeper analysis and exploration with our research participants and AG members. These areas of caution and concern include future career aspirations and retention, women in leadership and retention, the quest for work-life balance and the middle tier and diversity of leadership cadre, described further.

Future Career Aspirations and Retention

Majority of young leaders suggest they may not be in their roles in five to ten years. While many members of our cohort indicated that they might remain in their school leadership positions, some suggested that they were already thinking about alternate options beyond their schools. The expectation of multiple careers and jobs attributed to GenXers appears to be influencing school leaders also. However, this appears to be less so in Toronto, where the landscape of potential post-principalship career options is more limited than in London and New York. This may even cause more significant leadership recruitment challenges in the near and distant future.

Women in Leadership and Retention

In London, more than the other cities, a number of young women leaders express their worry that school leadership is not compatible with family life. This may cause young women to withdraw themselves from their career paths in advance of families and promotions.

The Quest for Work-life Balance

The importance of work-life balance appears to be escalating for all leaders. Leaders also struggle to find role models who can demonstrate how to achieve it and remain successful in all spheres of life and work. This has significant implications for young leaders' desires to remain in post and is starting, in some jurisdictions, to gain traction from governments and principal organizations as an important research and discussion point.

The Middle Tier and Diversity of Leadership Cadre

Each city has a racially different experience of the role of the middle tier, including school districts, within the education system as a central point of recruitment, development and retention of young leaders varies greatly between cities. Similarly, we have also noted the potential role of the middle tier, including districts, in potentially promoting an escalation in the breadth of diversity amongst a leadership cohort.

Our early findings suggest that GenX school leaders may, in fact, be approaching their careers and lives in ways that may necessitate new strategies to support their recruitment, development and retention. Our own research will continue to examine the nuances of these differences with an eye on practical and innovative strategies to make the most of the educational opportunities presented by this new generation of leaders.

References

BBC. (2009, January 13). *Cash for working in tough schools.* Retrieved from http://news.bbc.co.uk/1/hi/education/7824959.stm (last accessed on 23 July 2012).

Busher, H. (2005). Being a middle leader: Exploring professional identities. *School Leadership and Management, 25(1)*, 137–154.

Chapman, C. (2008). Towards a framework for school-to-school networking in challenging circumstances. *Educational Research, 50(4)*, 403–420.

Day, C., Sammons, P., Hopkins, D., Harris, A., Leithwood, K., Gu, Q., Brown, E., Ahtaridou, E. and Kington, A. (2009). *The impact of school leadership on pupil outcomes.* Department of Children, Schools and Families (Research report No. RR108). London: DCSF.

DCSF (2009). *School workforce in England (including pupil: teacher ratios and pupil: adult ratios)—provisional.* London: DCSF.

Duscher, J. and Cowin, L. (2004). Multigenerational nurses in the workplace. *Journal of Nursing Administration, 34(11)*, 493–501.

Foreign Policy. (2009). *The 2008 Global Cities Index.* Retrieved from: http://foreignpolicy.com/2009/10/06/the-2008-global-cities-index/ (last accessed on 7 July 2015).

Gronn, P. and Lacey, K. (2004). Positioning oneself for leadership: Feelings of vulnerability among aspirant principals. *School Leadership and Management, 24(4)*, 405–424.

Gronn, P. (1999). *The making of educational leaders.* London: Cassell.

Harris, A. (2002). Effective leadership in schools facing challenging circumstances. *School Leadership and Management, 22(1)*, 15–27.

Howson, J. (2008). *The state of the labour market for senior staff in schools in England and Wales.* Oxford: Education Data Surveys.

Kunreuther, F. (2003). The changing of the guard: What generational differences tell us about social-change organizations. *Nonprofit and Voluntary Sector Quarterly, 32*(3), 450–457.

Leithwood, K. and Jantzi, D. (2008). Linking leadership to student learning: The contributions of leader efficacy. *Educational Administration Quarterly, 44*(4), 496–528.

Luhrmann, T. and Eberl, P. (2007). Leadership and identify construction: Reframing the leader-follower interaction from an identity theory perspective. *Leadership, 3*(1), 115–127.

McKinney, S. E., Berry, R. Q, Dickerson, D. L. and Campbell-Whately, G. (2007). Addressing urban high-poverty school teacher attrition by addressing urban high-poverty school teacher retention: Why effective teachers persevere. *Educational Research and Review, 3*(1), 001–009.

Miles, M. B. and Huberman, A. M. (1994). *Qualitative data analysis: An expanded source book.* Thousand Oaks, CA: SAGE Publications.

Raffo, C., Dyson, A., Gunter, H., Hall, D., Jones, L. and Kalambouka, A. (2010). *Education and poverty in affluent countries.* London: Routledge.

Robinson, V., Lloyd, C. and Rowe, K. (2008). The impact of leadership on student outcomes: An analysis of the differential effects of leadership types. *Educational Administration Quarterly, 44*(5), 635–674.

Sassen, S. (1991). *The global city: New York, London, Tokyo.* Princeton: Princeton University Press.

Smola, K. and Sutton, C. (2002). Generational differences: Revisiting generational work values for the new millennium. *Journal of Organisational Behaviour, 23*, 363–382.

Spillane, J. P. and Lee, L. C. (2014). Novice school principals' sense of ultimate responsibility problems of practice in transitioning to the principal's office. *Educational Administration Quarterly, 50*(3), 431–465.

Smyth, E. and McCoy, S. (2009). *Investing in education: Combating educational disadvantage.* Dublin: Economic and Social Research Institute (ESRI).

Stone-Johnson, C. (2014). Not cut out to be an administrator: Generations, change, and the career transition from teacher to principal. *Education and Urban Society, 46*(5), 606–625.

Zemke, R., Raines, C. and Filipczak, B. (2000). *Generations at work: Managing the clash of veterans, boomers, xers, and nexters in your workplace.* New York: AMA Publications.

14

Getting Beyond Our Fixation with Leaders' Behaviours: Engaging with Leading Practice for Real

James P. Spillane

Introduction

In most societies we develop an early fixation with heroes (and sometimes heroines). Their charisma, gallant acts and supernatural traits are the subject of folklore, fiction and non-fiction; even writings that fall under what are refered to as social science. Indeed, much of the literature on leadership is leader-centric, focusing on the traits, characteristics and behaviours of leaders.

For more than a decade now, several scholars, myself included, have been arguing for and theorizing about a distributed perspective on organizational leadership. At its most rudimentary level, a distributed perspective involves two key aspects: the principal-plus and the practice aspects. In this short chapter, I am concerned chiefly with the practice aspect, an aspect that has received short shrift from those writing about leadership from a distributed perspective, though there are some exceptions. I do so because I see the practice aspect having the potential to counterbalance our pre-occupation with the behaviours and traits of leaders. A practice orientation to school leadership focuses on *how leadership actually gets done*: *What* people actually do *together*, *how* they do it and *why* they do it.

Framing the Practice of Leading

A distributed perspective casts the *practice* of leading as a central pursuit in research and development work on organizational leadership. But it does more because a distributed perspective also frames practice in a particular way, one that goes beyond equating leadership practice with the action or behaviour of individual leaders. Specifically, from a distributed perspective, the practice of leading is fundamentally about interactions—someone acts, someone else reacts and so on. So an exclusive focus on individual actions or behaviours, in documenting empirically or indeed developing the practice of leading, is entirely insufficient.

To underscore the importance of interactions in the study of leading practice, consider the performance of a dance, for simplicity let's say a 'two-step'. The individual actions of each partner are indeed essential to the practice of the two-step. Still, it is necessary to get beyond the actions of each of the partners in order to describe the practice of the two-step because the practice or performance of the dance is in the interactions of the two partners. It is *in-between* them! Consequently, it is imperative to examine the interactions in order to capture the practice. And, of course, an aspect of the situation—the music—contributes to defining the practice by providing the rhythm.

What does it mean then to study the practice of leading when taking a distributed perspective? Several things are involved like first, the interactions among leaders are critical to understanding the practice of leading, both formally designated organizational leaders (e.g., principal, assistant principal and teacher leaders) and organizational members who lack such designations but exercise influence over other organizational members related to the organization's core work. Second, interactions among leaders and followers are also critical in documenting the practice of leading because followers, by virtue of how they react, co-produce practice with leaders. Contrary to popular thinking, leadership practice is not something that is done to followers. Third, human interactions are mediated by aspects of the situation such as organizational routines, protocols for doing the work, language, norms and so on. By framing and focusing interactions among leaders and followers, aspects of the situation define the practice of leading. Thus, to understand the practice of leading, we have to attend to the web of interactions among leaders and followers as enabled and constrained by often taken-for- granted aspects of their situation.

Entailments for Research

Most writing about leadership from a distributed perspective fail to engage with the practice of leading (or even managing for that matter), and often those who attempt to only rarely engage the practice of leading (and managing) from anything more than an individual behaviour or action perspective. Fewer still, try to engage seriously, in either research or development work, with how aspects of the situation are both constituted of and constituted in practice.

There is good reason for this. Studying practice as social interactions mediated by aspects of the situation is difficult and time consuming. It involves empirically documenting leading practice in real time and historical time. It involves attending to the micro and the macro simultaneously and acknowledging the bi-directionality of relations among these levels. Thus, a multi-level approach is necessary. It involves grappling with how the situation (both proximal and distal aspects) affords and constrains the here-and-now interactions we observe as researchers and at the same, struggles to appreciate and document how the same situation is reproduced and sometimes transformed into these here-and-now interactions in practice. A tall order some would argue but essential if we are to do solid empirical research on the practice of leading. Further, a key component of this work involves developing and validating new research approaches and measures. It is not just about carrying out research on leading practice.

Entailments for Development

My argument for focusing on the practice of leading also has entailments for what we commonly refer to as development work on school leadership. The dominant approach to develop leadership is to develop leaders—their knowledge and skill or what economists refer to as human capital. And the typical approach is to develop individual leaders. Such an approach has its merits but also has limitations especially if we frame practice, as I have, from a distributed perspective.

What would it mean to take a distributed perspective to leadership development? Several things by way of sparking a discussion: First, rather than focusing chiefly on developing individuals in both the pre-service and in-service preparation of school leaders, we might seriously entertain what it would mean to develop groups or teams of leaders for a school. Second, if aspects of the situation fundamentally define practice (in much the same way that individuals do), then investing time and effort on the design and redesign of the key aspects of the situation of leadership in schools and school systems should be a central focus of our leadership development efforts. Many Comprehensive School Reform models, for example, do just this. Work on things such as lesson study and learning walks also do versions of this by designing organizational routines intended to support the practice of leading and managing instructional improvement. Third, our leadership preparation and professional development programmes might focus on cultivating a diagnostic and design mindset in school leaders so that they see improving the *practice* of leading as a central pursuit in their work. Such an approach would contrast sharply with the implementation of the mindset that dominates many leadership development programmes. This would involve preparing school leaders to do both diagnostic and design work.

Conclusion

In this chapter, I have argued for focusing our attention, as researchers and developers with an interest in school leadership and management, on the practice of leading and managing instructional improvement in schools. I have sketched very broadly the entailments of such a stance for our field, and in doing so I acknowledge the difficulties of such an approach. Chief among these difficulties is letting go of our fixation with heroes and heroines.

Some might read this chapter as suggesting that the school principal is less relevant to research and development work on leadership. Such a reading would be wrong. Research suggests, including research conducted from a distributed perspective, that the school principal is critical in efforts to improve schools. There is no evidence to suggest that this is likely to change any time soon. Engaging seriously with the practice of leading, as researchers and developers, does not mean abandoning the critical role of the principal. Rather, it means expanding how we understand school leadership pressing us to get beyond the behaviours of the school principal and examine how it is in the interactions among the principal and other leaders that we can begin to develop an appreciation for leading practice.

15

Leading Effective Pedagogy

David Reynolds and Daniel Muijs

Introduction

In terms of acquisition of basic skills and knowledge, we have a wealth of information about the usefulness of the direct instruction model (Muijs et al., 2014). Literally, hundreds of studies have shown that there is 'added value' in terms of student achievement if the teachers do or possess the following:

1. Have high, positive expectations of what students can achieve.
2. Create an ordered, structured classroom where there is discipline and rules are well understood.
3. Emphasize the importance of academic achievement over other goals.
4. Manage time well with efficient lesson transitions, where lessons' start and finish times are adhered to.
5. Are clear in their rules and in the obligations expected of students.
6. Provide quality feedback both with the lesson and to students in areas such as homework.

7. Vary instructional practices within the formal class setting, to promote interest and use the presentations of students in classroom activities to also provide variety.

8. Maintain a high (+90%) level of students' 'time on task' and attention within lessons.

9. Use frequent, rich and appropriate questioning to stimulate students' mental processes and use higher order questions, particularly.

10. Maintain a supportive and relaxed, yet task-orientated, classroom climate.

This 'basic' pedagogy appears particularly important for giving foundations to younger children, for the teaching of 'transmission' subjects like mathematics and for the cognitive development of children from lower social classes who may respond particularly to the structure, support and involvement of the teacher in 'pushing' them to achieve in ways that their families and communities may not be doing (Muijs and Reynolds, 2011).

But we do need to acknowledge a number of limitations of this model of pedagogy, such as:

1. Older children may need pedagogy that encourages them to self-learn, develop skills and move towards a more 'enquiry-orientated' set of skills, appropriate for generating knowledge rather than just retrieving it.

2. The social outcomes in areas such as students' self-concept, self-esteem, capacity to relate to others and generally the sets of skills associated with having a positive personal 'affect' may not necessarily be developed by methods such as 'direct' pedagogy that focuses upon the academic.

3. Students need to have the opportunity to develop through individual and group practices, the opportunity to reinforce and develop whatever they might be taught in formal settings.

It is sensible, therefore, to support a 'suite of methods' that fall within the term 'basic pedagogy'. It is also sensible to use structured, collaborative small group works which develops both social skills and the capacity to work with others. Academically, small groups can be valuable to students developing their thinking in interaction with their peers (Muijs et al., 2014).

Peer thinking, where students help each other learn 'one on one', is also shown by research to be powerful, since there is learning for the students doing the teaching as well as for the students being taught.

What Will Future Pedagogy Look Like and Necessitate?

It is clear that the skills necessary for the 21st century living and intellectual or personal growth may not necessarily come through our existing commitment to 'basic' direct instruction models for the following reasons:

1. The pace of change means that knowledge is more rapidly redundant, necessitating concentration upon how students may access the 'new' knowledge that emerges.
2. The easy availability of 'knowledge' through increasingly sophisticated search facilities within Information and Communication Technology (ICT) puts a premium on the possession of the 'skills' necessary to access and create new knowledge.
3. The increasing opportunities to acquire knowledge and skills in multiple settings suggest a need to develop 'learning–to-learn' skills that are appropriate to these multiple settings.
4. Increasingly sophisticated Information Technology (IT) is offering both rich learning opportunities and the creation of communities of learning or learners independent of geographical boundaries.
5. IT itself is permitting a redesign of learning to encompass images as well as sounds and words and a blending of distinctions between 'knowledge' and 'skills', learning and enjoyment, the cognitive and the social and the individual and the group.

6. The redundancy of knowledge and the opportunities for education throughout life means that self-regulated learning is necessary to take advantage of these opportunities.

Metacognitive approaches to pedagogy reflect all these necessities and are related to what we call 'thinking about thinking' or what has also been called 'higher order thinking'. In these formulations, individuals acquire knowledge of their own capacities or needs as learners, learn what cognitive strategies maximize this and know when to apply different learning methodologies. Activities involve planning, learning, setting goals, activating prior knowledge, selecting new strategies and allocating appropriate resources. Monitoring a self-regulated process is also necessary (Veenman et al., 2006).

Evidence suggests that embedding metacognitive approaches within the existing curricula is preferable to using context-free approaches as 'stand-alone' (Muijs et al., 2014).

The new approaches need large-scale training programmes to ensure that they are 'blood stream' rather than 'bolt-on' in terms of teacher practices, and also need to be part of the setting wherever learning takes place—whether school, community, factory or home. Additionally, any evaluation of learning gained over time—as with the present accreditation systems in Britain, for example, General Certificate of Secondary Education (GCSE), 'A' levels, degrees, etc.—needs to assess the extent to which metacognitive outcomes have been achieved.

The revolution in our understanding of the brain that takes place in the field of cognitive neuroscience also has implications for future pedagogy. Specifically, it seems that

1. The brain may be influenced by nutrition, sleep patterns, hydration and stimulation, suggesting that 'learning' needs to involve learning brain potentiating in addition to skills and knowledge.
2. The cerebellum is increasingly seen as a part of the brain that makes the skills learned to be automatically employed (automaticity) with this region of the brain necessitating

potentiation through stimulation of motor functions and the visual system.

3. The brain's own working memory, in which inputs are stored for short term before being transferred to the long-term memory, imposes restrictions upon the nature of learning. Neither 'over-learning' nor 'over-teaching' seem to be functional; therefore, 'discovery'-orientated approaches that require a lot of brain need to be balanced with mechanisms, collaborative ones probably, that do not overburden because work is shared out.

Pedagogy: The Leadership Tasks

The importance of pedagogy as rapid developments outlined above mean that both pedagogy and pedagogical changes highlight the importance of instructional leadership and, in particular, the need for leaders to focus on pedagogy (Hallinger and Heck, 1998; Leithwood and Riehl, 2003).

The first key task of a leader in this respect is *developing the pedagogical vision* for the school. Educational effectiveness research has shown that students, and in particular those from more socially disadvantaged backgrounds, benefit from a consistent pedagogical approach across the school (Muijs et al., 2004). An instructional leader therefore, needs to have a clear view on effective pedagogy and some solid knowledge of general effective teaching strategies. The pedagogical vision needs to include principles of effective teaching, behaviour management and classroom environment, including elements, such as the use of learning assistants, ICT, assessment and reward systems, as well as teaching methods, such as direct instruction or learning to learn.

The instructional leader also plays an essential role in setting the *strategies* around pedagogy. This entails the development of improvement plans and specifics of how pedagogical change and/or maintenance are going to be managed. This includes plans for training and development, monitoring and assessment, and communication.

A clear implementation plan, therefore, needs to be in place, which includes processes for monitoring and introduction. Clear timelines and milestones need to be set to allow proper evaluation and to create the necessary momentum for any change of plans. It may be desirable to roll out any changes in waves (e.g., by year group or subject), or to test developments by using small-scale experiments (Muijs, 2010b). The leader has to establish a change in the coalition of influential supporters in the school and needs to have in place contingency plans in case the strategy does not work, as well as plans for dealing with recalcitrant or incompetent members of staff.

In order for pedagogical strategies to be successful, necessary *structures* need to be in place. Such structures can be physical, as in IT or building requirements (such as in the case where a move from open to closed classrooms or a move to blended forms of learning is required). In many cases, however, they are related to human resources, such as building planning and professional development time into the timetable, enabling key appointments and structures for professional development such as observation training or related to motivation, for instance in terms of rewards for achieving specified goals or pay related to pedagogical performance.

In many cases, a pedagogical strategy requires the professional *development* of staff, which includes retraining of the existing staff in new or improved approaches or the induction and training of new staff in the pedagogical practices of the school, a key task in maintaining the consistency necessary for effective schools. Apart from building in the necessary time to do this, it is essential that principles of effective professional development are followed. Too often a one-size-fits-all model is used which schools would not employ with their students, but find it suitable for adults. However, as Antoniiou and Kyriakides (2011) have shown, effective professional development of teachers also needs to take into account their current level, with training tailored to this. Deciding on what type of professional development to opt for is also a leadership decision—be it externally brought-in, internally developed or co-constructed with other schools or organizations, such as a university.

Finally, *monitoring* of pedagogy is an important aspect of effective instructional leadership. A culture of peer monitoring and observation, as well as monitoring and observation by management, needs to be in place, so that less effective practice can be dealt with and mutual learning can take place. Observation systems need to be valid and reliable, and tailored to the desired pedagogical strategies. In addition, attainment requires careful monitoring to ascertain that any developments made have the desired impact on learning. Where possible, a rigorous approach in evaluating the relationship between pedagogies and attainment is desirable. A useful part of monitoring is also to gain views of key stakeholders, in particular the students and, where appropriate, parents.

The Role of the Curriculum

Along with *how* we teach, *what* we teach is also important for the development of our students. Curriculum content has always been a contentious aspect of education, but one that inevitably falls in the orbit of educational leaders as they work on developing appropriate classroom contexts. Therefore, instructional leaders are required to have views and policies on key areas of curriculum in their schools (although usually within given systemic parameters, such as national curricula). These include: choice of subjects to be offered, choices on subject content and types of curricula to be devised.

Curriculum Subjects

A key element of creating the learning environment in schools (especially in the secondary phase) is the choice of subjects to offer. Here, national contexts and policies may offer schools more or less freedom, with typically a 'core' of subjects required, usually including mathematics and national language(s) and sometimes science, with more or less discretion over the selection of other subjects.

Decisions on what subjects to prioritize are key to the identity and focus of the school, with some policies, such as the creation of 'specialist schools' in England under the Labour government, specifically aimed at strengthening such identities and foci. Subject mix is also important with regard to meeting the needs of the community that the school serves. Thus, for example, a group of schools in a rural location in England formed a federation to allow them to collectively hire an itinerant chef to deliver hospitality courses aimed at developing students' skills to work in the locally dominant tourism industry (Muijs, 2008). There is also a need to consider the views of stakeholders such as local employers and parents, as well as the requirements of further and higher education entry. In systems where school choice operates, subject portfolios are also potentially important marketing tools, with different choices attracting potentially different parents and students.

Of course, these choices are significantly constrained by a number of environmental and organizational factors. Staffing is a key issue, in particular where more specialist subjects are chosen, as the requisite human capital needs to be available to effectively teach the subject (and it is here that subject knowledge of course becomes important). School size may also be a constraint in terms of adequate numbers choosing options, a factor that may also be susceptible to 'subject fashions'. The students whom the school attracts in the first place again may constrain what a suitable subject mix would look like, with some likely more suited to a heavily academic mix than others.

Along with the subjects to be offered, decisions also have to be made regarding the amount of time spent on each subject, when they will be delivered and to which year groups. State and exam requirements may again constrain the level of freedom in this regard, although in almost all systems there is at least some discretion to the school to vary the mix.

Curriculum Content

Along with the mix of subjects, key decisions need to be made around the content of subjects delivered in the school. Again, the extent to which schools are free to vary differs significantly between education systems, although it tends to be smallest in 'core' subjects and largest in option choices.

As the full breadth of possible content in a given subject cannot, in most cases, be covered during the school years, an important element of the curriculum is what exactly is covered in each subject. This is frequently a contentious issue, as shown by recent arguments in England around history (Paton, 2014) and English literature (Adams, 2014), in the USA around the 'Common Core' curriculum (Dreilinger, 2014) and internationally around HE economics curricula.

As these arguments demonstrate, subject content is frequently subject to the influence of stakeholder groups, including business, subject teachers' organizations, academia, and religious and political groupings. Parents and teachers in the school may also have strong views on the content of certain subjects (such as religious education or sex education) as what is covered will of course have potentially major influences on students' knowledge and behaviours. Content choices also have far-reaching consequences for the school as an organization, not least in terms of sourcing teaching materials, such as textbooks, and aligning with suitable standards and examinations where this is possible. It is, therefore, not surprising that many national governments prescribe subject content to at least some extent in the few subjects deemed key to national development, culture or identity, so schools are operating in a constrained environment in this regard. A key consideration here is of course what is required in terms of national assessment systems, and in most cases what is taught will closely mirror what is assessed.

An important choice that schools have to make is whether to opt for a more or a less academically demanding curriculum. This is a particular issue for schools serving disadvantaged areas. In many cases, there is a stronger need to remedy weaknesses in language and numeracy, which tend to lead schools to a curriculum focused on basic skills. This is a rational decision, and one which has received some support from studies showing that high-performing schools in disadvantaged areas focus on basic skills within a strongly focused curriculum (Muijs et al., 2004). However, the risk here is that students will be disadvantaged over the mid-to-long term compared with peers in more advantaged areas, who have had access to a richer and more academic curriculum that is more conducive to successfully completing post-compulsory education at a high level; there is some evidence that approaches emphasizing an advanced skill curriculum can be successful, provided they are accompanied by suitable scaffolding and support (Muijs et al., 2004).

Importantly, many of the developments mentioned in the section on pedagogy also affect curricular choices. Thus, the increased need for information processing skills should affect both the subjects offered and the specific content of the existing subjects, while the ubiquity of IT is leading to programming becoming a core subject in a number of countries. It is, therefore likely, that both policy-makers and school leaders will need to focus on redesigning their curricula to adapt to this changing world.

Curriculum: The Leadership Tasks

The five leadership tasks identified in terms of pedagogy are also present when it comes to curriculum.

Vision is again important and a key leadership task will be to consider the nature of the school, its community and broader society, and to consider what curriculum should reflect this. In terms of subject choices, decisions need to be made around specialization, breadth and depth which reflect a particular curricular vision, again pointing to the need for the principal to be an instructional leader. However, especially with regard to curricular decisions, the input of stakeholders is the key, as is the input of all staff in the school, which becomes particularly clear when one considers subject content, as no individual leader can possess sufficient expertise in all subjects taught in the school.

Again, vision needs to be turned into *strategies*. If the school is to specialize in a particular area, how are we going to ensure that we have the right mixture of human capital in place to deliver this curriculum? How are we going to ensure that stakeholders are aware of the change? How we will develop buy-in and support? Are there financial or other resources that we can tap into? As with pedagogical change, any major curricular change will, therefore, require a clear plan.

Curriculum decisions need to be carefully considered in terms of the *structural* changes they might require. Opting for a strongly science-based specialism or offering a range of vocational subjects will often require significant investment in terms of specialist equipment such as science labs, workshops or simulated work spaces (e.g., hairdressing salons). All curricular decisions also impact on timetabling, a major issue in many schools and one that too often acts as a restraint on change.

Ensuring that staff are able to deliver the chosen curriculum may again require their professional *development*, which can include retraining of the existing staff in new or improved approaches, or the hiring of specialists in new curricular areas. As with pedagogy, it is, of course, necessary to *monitor* the impact of any curricular changes, in terms of student outcomes, learning and satisfaction, stakeholder views and practical delivery. However, it is, of course, equally important to monitor existing curricula, which may be subject to inertia effects that are problematic in a rapidly changing world. It is important to monitor environmental and policy changes, not least those made by examining organizations, to ensure the curriculum is suited to the current and future needs (Hopkins et al., 2014).

The Importance of Data-based Decision-making

A recent development in education has been the increased realization of the importance of data-based decision-making. As Schildkamp et al. (2012a:123) point out, 'School leaders and teachers can use data (e.g., information on the functioning of their school) to change teaching, address existing (*ineffective*) programmes in their schools, and improve the functioning of the school in terms of increased student achievement'. Data use has, thus, become a key component of school improvement efforts, and has, long been the case in other sectors such as business, become a key driver of the management of educational organizations.

Schools increasingly collect a range of useful data. Obviously, attainment data, preferably collected regularly for all subjects and departments, allows school leaders to monitor effectiveness and progress, and to compare this between subjects and in some cases teachers. Of course, this needs to be done in a non-mechanistic way, taking into account contextual factors (such as differential growth rates observed in some subjects, student intake in different subjects or classes and test difficulty in different areas), but has been shown to lead to significant scope for improvement (Schildkamp et al., 2012b). However, increasingly, schools have access to additional data, such as surveys of parents which can provide useful data on perceptions of the school locally and surveys of staff that are of great value to pedagogical monitoring, staff development and classroom observations. Schools will then possess a range of data that can be used for a variety of school improvement and professional development purposes and can, as has been the case in other areas of society, potentially have a major impact on the effective and efficient functioning of the organization. The role of leadership and management are the key here, both in creating a culture in which data use is the norm and in creating structures and systems in which staff knows how to analyse, interpret and use data. In addition, leaders themselves need to understand data and use it to monitor the progress of their school and to develop improvement plans based on proper analysis of the existing strengths and weaknesses and capacity in the school.

Of course, this is not the only function of data in schools. Increasingly, data is used to plan and set individual targets for students, which helps both students and teachers to plan their learning and monitor progress using ambitious but achievable goal setting. This approach has been found to be effective in terms of improving student attainment, although a possible downside is the labelling of students leading to an underestimation of their potential. It is, therefore, crucial that the data used for target setting is valid and reliable, and that there is some flexibility in approaches. This requires some understanding of the limitations of data and, therefore, a basic statistical literacy. A data coordinator in the school may take on the role of developing this or of explaining data in a way that allows teachers to realize both the strengths and limitations thereof.

The role of the principal has been found to be the key in developing data-based decision-making in schools, and again their activities can be looked at through the lens of the five key leadership activities. In terms of *vision*, school leaders need to be advocates for and themselves model data-based decision-making in order for the school staff to buy in to this approach. Where this is not the case, attempts to develop data-based decision-making tend not to be successful. *Strategies* need to be in place to develop a data-based system, as a range of decisions are required, such as whether to appoint a member of staff as responsible for data as happens in many schools in the UK, which staff members to involve in data collection and analysis, what sources of data (tests, observation, etc.) to use and what instruments to use (e.g., what observation schedule and what tests). *Structures* such as appropriate IT and data management systems as well as staff capable of using them and interpreting results need to be put in place, whereby it is important to ensure that key structures such as data protection and privacy are assured. Data systems also usually require some quality assurance systems to ensure reliability and correct errors. Professional *development* is important, as in other aspects of instructional leadership, to enable staff to understand the data being used. This can take the form of the so-called data teams, where groups of staff engage in analysis of data around a problem and formulate improvement plans based thereon (Schildkamp et al., 2012). Finally, data use and systems require continuous *monitoring* to ensure they are appropriately used, reliable and developed in light of the ongoing and future needs of the school.

Final Words

It is posited in this chapter that *instructional leadership* is required if leadership is to affect the learning level, and that this instructional leadership requires principals and other school leaders to actively engage with pedagogy, curriculum and data through visioning, strategizing, structuring, developing and monitoring. However, what is clear is that the demanding and multifaceted nature of these tasks means that it will be hard for the principal to assume this role individually. This is why, increasingly, researchers and policy-makers have called for a move towards more distributed forms of leadership.

Distributed leadership implies that the practice of leadership is *stretched* within or across an organization and that there are high degrees of involvement in the practice of leadership (Spillane et al., 2001). This 'deep leadership' is co-constructed through joint practice, drawing in part on a yet untapped leadership potential and underdeveloped resources for collaboration and coordination. In this sense, distributed leadership is 'an emergent property of a group or network of individuals in which group members pool their expertise' (Gronn, 2000:23). Increasingly, the evidence for distributed leadership, like instructional leadership (indirectly) being related to student outcomes and to school improvement has grown (Harris and Spillane, 2008; Muijs, 2010a). We would, therefore, suggest that the model through which we can best develop the learning level is a form of *distributed instructional leadership* in which a range of teachers and other school staff are involved in the key components of instructional leadership mentioned above.

What remains important, however, is to ensure that leadership adapts to the changing role of teachers, schools and learning, and acts as a facilitative environment for these.

It is highly likely that the teacher will have a much more demanding role in the future than ever in the past. Basic 'direct instruction' models will still be needed—children will not discover Pythagoras' theorems for themselves! But students need to acquire 'learning-to-learn' skills in addition to knowledge and the 'metacognitive' or 'learning to think about thinking' strategies also. They will need IT to be a mainstreamed part of their learning experiences, not a session in a special room or subject. They will also need to learn through interaction with other students in collaborative groups and 'one-on-one' settings, and will need to know how to maximize their 'brain quality' and to not overburden themselves.

So, teachers will need enhanced repertoires of skills themselves to potentiate enhanced numbers of learning outcomes from their students. They themselves will need to be 'lifelong learners' to keep up with advances in knowledge from developments in IT, in cognitive neuroscience and in metacognitive discoveries and practices. This is probably best done by ensuring that teachers are themselves trained as researchers, with core courses in instructional methodology and research methods taking place within all pre-service teacher preparation programmes and within in-service continuing professional development too. Teachers need to find space and time within their busy professional lives to undertake the disciplined professional and collaborative development that will produce a 'thinking profession'.

One last set of changes complicates matters enormously—the increasing need for schools to cater to some of the consequences of broader patterns of social, cultural and economic changes. The possibility of maintaining and enhancing (indeed as we have outlined here), a conventional academic orientation within educational processes has been seriously compromised by the dissolution of community and family structures and the effects that this has on the role of schools. The pressing need to do something to prevent the looming global environmental crisis also means an enhanced role for teachers and schools. Historically, educational systems and teachers have been the 'waste paper basket' of social policy and have had their roles stretched considerably. This has itself generated difficulty in adapting, which may well continue.

However, the rise of educational effectiveness movement and the large quantity of material now available about 'what works' means that we now have multiple sources of help to give to teachers to help them cope with their stretching new roles. Knowledge bases about effective pedagogy, effective schooling, effective leadership and novel bodies of knowledge about metacognition and the brain, all exist in accessible formats. We need to ensure that all teachers can gain access to these bodies of knowledge before the scale of their task overtakes them, and therefore us.

All this makes the role of instructional leadership even more crucial, as the task of developing and retraining teachers to cope with this greatly complex role is non-trivial and requires a high level of leadership support across all four areas: for developing a vision and strategy to enable change, for creating structures that provide teachers the time required for professional development, for developing effective professional development and for monitoring progress (Reynolds, 2010).

References

Adams, R. (2014). Michael Gove hits back in row over GCSE syllabus. *Guardian.* Retrieved from http://www.theguardian.com/politics/2014/may/27/michael-gove-denies-ban-of-american-novels-from-gcse (last accessed on 27 May 2014).

Antoniiou, P. and Kyriakides, L. (2011). The impact of a dynamic approach to professional development on teacher instruction and student learning: Results from an experimental study. *School Effectiveness and School Improvement, 22*(3), 291–311.

Aughinbaugh, A. (2012). The effects of high school math curriculum on college attendance: Evidence from the NLSY97. *Economics of Education Review, 31*(6), 861–870.

Dreilinger, D. (2014). Common core on the brink in Oklahoma: Reports. Retrieved from http://www.nola.com/education/index.ssf/2014/05/common_core_on_the_brink_in_ok.html (last accessed on 28 May 2014).

Gronn, P. (2000). Distributed properties: A new architecture for leadership. *Educational Management and Administration, 28*(3), 317–338.

Hallinger, P. and Heck, R. H. (1998). Exploring the principal's contribution to school effectiveness: 1980–1995. *School Effectiveness and School Improvement, 9*(2), 157–191.

Harris, A., and Spillane, J. (2008). Distributed leadership through the looking glass. *Management in Education, 22*(1), 31–34.

Hopkins, D., Stringfield, S., Harris, A., Stoll, L. and MacKay, T. (2014). School and system improvement: A narrative state-of-the-art review. *School Effectiveness and School Improvement, 25*(2), 257–281.

Leithwood, K. A. and Riehl, C. (2003). *What do we already know about successful school leadership?* AERA Paper Task Force on Developing Research in Educational Leadership.

Muijs, D. (2008). Collaboration in a rural school district. *Improving Schools, 11*(1), 61–73.

———. (2010a). Leadership and organisational performance: From research to prescription? *International Journal of Educational Management, 25*(1), 45–60.

———. (2010b). Changing classroom learning. In A. Hargreaves, A. Liberman, M. Fullan and D. Hopkins (Eds.). *Second international handbook of educational change* (pp. 857–869). New York: Springer.

Muijs, D. and Reynolds, D. (2011). *Effective teaching.* London: SAGE Publications.

Muijs, D., Harris, A., Chapman, C., Stoll, L. and Russ, J. (2004). Improving schools in socio-economically disadvantaged areas: An overview of research. *School Effectiveness and School Improvement, 15*(2), 149–176.

Muijs, D., Kyriakides, L., van der Werf, G., Creemers, B., Timperley, H. and Earl, L. (2014). State of the art—Teacher effectiveness and professional learning. *School Effectiveness and School Improvement, 25*(2), 231–256.

Paton, G. (2014). Less time for 'Hitler and the Henrys' in history A-level. *Telegraph.* Retrieved from http://www.telegraph.co.uk/education/educationnews/10841616/Less-time-for-Hitler-andthe-Henrys-in-history-A-level.html (last accessed on 19 May 2014).

Reynolds, D. (2010). *Failure free education? The past, present and future of school effectiveness and school improvement.* London: Routledge.

Schildkamp, K., Ehren, M. and Lai, M. M. (2012a). Editorial article for the special issue on data-based decision making around the world: From policy to practice to results. *School effectiveness and School Improvement, 23*(2), 123–131.

Schildkamp, K., Rekers-Mombarg, L. and Harms, T. J. (2012b). Student group differences in examination results and utilization for policy and school development. *School effectiveness and School Improvement, 23*(2), 229–255.

Spillane, J., Halverson, R. and Diamond J. (2001). Investigating school leadership practice: A distributed perspective. *Educational Researcher, 2001*(30), 23.

Veenman, M. V. J., Van Hout-Wolters, H. A. M. and Afflerbach, P. (2006). Metacognition and learning: Conceptual and methodological considerations. *Metacognition and Learning, 1*, 3–14.

16

Leading Future Pedagogies

Jill Jameson

Introduction

Sharply rising global use of mobile information and communications technology (ICT) and a relative lack of informed pedagogic e-leadership of ICT in education coupled with fierce international competition for achievement and a trend towards increasing accountability (to meet targets via audit and high levels of youth unemployment) means that schools now face significant challenges in responding to the needs of future generations of the 21st century learners. This chapter briefly outlines four key trends relating to the above issues, particularly in the context of pedagogic applications of technology development, and then considers these challenges in a global context.

Significant Growth in Global Mobile Technologies, the Internet and Social Media

The initial observation on the challenges of leading future pedagogies is that nearly everyone everywhere seems to be on a mobile phone using the Internet nowadays. Official statistics on global mobile phone usage record that 91 per cent of all people on earth now have a mobile phone. The Internet company Super Monitoring observes that globally the average first usage of mobile phones is now at the age of 13 (Super Monitoring, 2013), a fact that is highly relevant to all schools, but particularly those not yet equipped or resistant to the use of mobile learning (m-learning) for school pupils. If the use of these devices is so prevalent in the general population, notably affecting young people's lives on a daily basis, then why are we not using them more for pedagogical purposes in education? The International Telecommunication Union (ITU) observed at the end of 2013 that there were 6.8 billion mobile-cellular subscriptions globally. Super Monitoring has now, however, exceeded even this figure in estimating that now there are already more mobile devices than people on the planet, that is, 7.2 billion.

Furthermore, in relation to the proliferation of the Internet, the ITU reported in 2013 that about 2.7 billion people, almost 40 per cent of the world's population, are online, with 31 per cent of the developing and 77 per cent of the developed world able to access the Internet (ITU, 2013a); earlier in 2013, Meeker reported an eight per cent year-on-year growth in the Internet (Meeker, 2013)—a massive continuing growth. The Real Time Statistics Project reported in 2014 that more than 48 per cent of the world's 2.8 billion people on the Internet are living in Asia, a fact that is highly relevant to this book and its 'eye on Asia' (Real Time Statistics, 2014). In relation to the statistics on global usage of social media applications, the figures are even more staggeringly impressive, but I am not going into the detail, as the reporting of general global statistics is not our main purpose here. This chapter is concerned with discussing the future of education in relation to educational technology. For education, there are not only many positive, indeed transformational potential aspects to this trend of incessant worldwide uptake of mobile technologies, Internet access and social media, but also worrying aspects that need to concern us in planning for the effective future of education in schools. Here are some of the concerns.

First, although mobile devices offer significant potential learning opportunities for current and future classroom use, UNESCO has found in its research on m-learning technologies globally (UNESCO, 2012) that many teachers, parents and indeed sometimes pupils themselves are resistant to the use of mobile technologies at school and in fact feel that there is a stigma attached to the usage. Second, UNESCO has found that there is insufficient attention paid to m-learning as yet in national, regional and local education policies, and that there is a significant lack of appreciation of the potential for m-learning, to facilitate improvements in pedagogical effectiveness for pupils in the classroom. And yet, as is clear from an abundant number of studies on the role of ICT, e-learning and m-learning in enriching both pedagogy and learning (De Freitas and Jameson, 2013), the opportunities provided by Web 2.0 interactive learning through mobile and related ICT devices for improved education are many and varied, for all schools and particularly for populations who have difficulties with traditional face-to-face access to education, such as those in poorer rural communities equipped only with mobile phones rather than broadband Internet access.

Third, there is lack of in-depth knowledge about the effects of this massive trend towards mobile communications on and within education. As UNESCO, the European Union and the World Bank acknowledge, we—the human race—are far better at collecting general global statistics on Internet users and mobile phone subscriptions managed by private telecommunications companies than we are at gathering specific, accurate, detailed statistics on pedagogic uses of ICT and e-learning in education. So, although there are global, countrywide, regional and local committees, initiatives, policies and strategies aplenty to collect this data, there is a lack of planned focused action to do so, on a daily basis, systematically and rigorously. Compared with the profit-driven, media-rich, rigorously collected, constantly monitored and daily available data on commercial mobile phone subscriptions and usage, on Internet traffic, on Google searches and on an incessant stream of continuously refreshed data about the hourly use of social media, we are relatively speaking still in the dark about how these trends are really affecting education in schools locally. Apart from a few international research studies which have become outdated relatively quickly, the data is significantly lacking, as the World Bank ruefully admits in reporting on global statistics on ICT in Education that:

> [I]t can often be difficult to present evidence-based policy advice related to ICT use in education to inform large scale investments in educational technologies across an education system based on hard, rigorously collected data for the simple reason that there is actually not a lot of rigorously collected, globally comparable data out there. (Trucano, 2012)

Lack of Awareness and Interest in Pedagogic E-leadership

To add to this picture, in education, there is apparently a distinct lack of awareness and interest in pedagogic e-leadership, which I term pragmatically, here, to be the distributed leadership meaning-making and influencing relational and decision-making processes (Jameson, 2005) involved in implementing e-learning effectively in the classroom for enhanced teaching and learning in education. Evidence of this comes from my work as the Lead Guest Editor for the 2013 Special Edition on e-Leadership of educational technology for the *British Journal of Educational Technology* (Jameson, 2013). Frankly, apart from a few outstanding examples of good practice led by some countries and some individuals, I was shocked at the paucity of information, awareness and responses relating to the global pedagogic leadership of ICT and e-learning for the enrichment of learning and teaching opportunities that benefit pupils in education.

Despite some excellent pockets of outstanding practices as well as some generally good and satisfactory or poorer practices, at a global level, regrettably we are still in our infancy as regards the understanding and development of leadership systems and practices relating to the effective pedagogic use of educational technologies. This is alarming, given the speed of rapid ICT developments—notably mobile technological development, and Internet and social media take-up—around the world. It seems that in education we are far behind business and particularly far behind leisure industries'—gaming, music and video—world trends, although, educators should be leading the field for the sake of our young people's education, to prepare them for the new world that they are entering into, in which ICT skills will be crucial for all aspects of daily communication and employment.

Where we are rapidly making progress globally at country-wide levels on developing our work on ICT in education, as yet we have shown more proficiency at writing technological strategies and policies for this and increasing investment in hardware and software than in investigating, understanding and implementing the ways in which new technologies can be really effectively used for learning and teaching for the benefit of children in the future. There is a risk that we are becoming too mechanistic, too techno-centric, in assuming that learning automatically occurs after we have written a policy and strategic plan to say it will, and that good teaching through educational technologies will automatically follow the allocation of up-to-date technical equipment and software. Unfortunately, as Cuban et al. (2001) have observed, too much enthusiastically purchased new computing hardware ends up unused in school cupboards, since merely increasing 'access to equipment and software seldom [leads] to widespread teacher and student use'. There is a need to develop detailed professional guidance on the effective pedagogic uses of advanced ICTs in education, to implement major ongoing staff development programmes, coaching and mentoring, to set up new online professional learning communities and for both senior managers and teaching practitioners to lead the way in using educational technology in a meaningful process that increases learning and builds on the existing good classroom practices.

This trend, I argue, is so crucial for the future of education that we are now entering the liminal area of a transformational zone relating to the global development and use of ICT and e-learning in which almost everything relating to both formal and informal education is now gradually but inexorably changing, while we seem to be burying our heads in the sand and continuing to teach as if to equip our pupils effectively for the last century. The impending changes that will result from the incessant uptake of new technologies lead me to suggest some important future recommendations for school leadership for effectiveness and improvement. I argue that a future potential crisis is gradually emerging for young people and that this has received too little attention as yet in relation to schools' leadership of the pedagogic aspects of technology development.

This convergence is occuring between the increasing global use of the ICTs discussed above, the international growth in youth unemployment and what I perceive to be a relative lack of informed and coherent e-leadership of pedagogic practice in schools. I am not talking at the level of individual leaders or particular schools, as we have examples of best practice in many different countries in which exceptional leadership teams and systems distributed across both formal and informal levels are making profoundly important contributions. An e-leadership framework to develop such examples of best practice is suggested in the appendix (Figure A1). In this, a

Figure A1
e-Leadership Framework

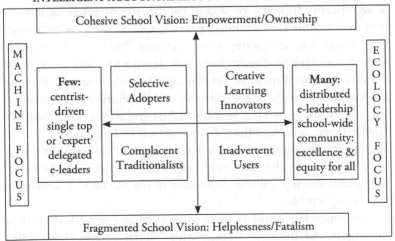

INTELLIGENT ACCOUNTABILITY TO DISTRICT/GOVERNMENT

Cohesive School Vision: Empowerment/Ownership

M A C H I N E   F O C U S

Few: centrist-driven single top or 'expert' delegated e-leaders

Selective Adopters

Creative Learning Innovators

Many: distributed e-leadership school-wide community: excellence & equity for all

Complacent Traditionalists

Inadvertent Users

E C O L O C Y   F O C U S

Fragmented School Vision: Helplessness/Fatalism

RIGID MICRO ACCOUNTABILITY TO DISTRICT/GOVERNMENT

cohesive school vision for e-leadership of advanced ICT adoption with a focus on living systems rather than machine-led solutions is suggested. Examples of this kind of work are already working well in some countries to improve school effectiveness and the achievement of pupils. However, I do not believe that such good practice is as yet very widespread.

A proposed e-leadership framework for schools is presented in Figure A1, to propose that intelligent accountability and a cohesive school vision for empowerment/ ownership of advanced ICT adoption in schools leads to creative learning innovations with a focus on living systems rather than a machine-led focus. Such a framework may be useful in facilitating the development of professional learning communities, staff training, mentoring and coaching for effective e-leadership of the implementation of advanced ICTs in schools.

Digital Divide: Significant Disparity of Access in ICT-enabled Education

A significant disparity of access to the Internet has differentiated ICT-enabled educational provision in schools, with broadband Internet access costing schools around 700 times more in the poorest countries in comparison with significantly low access costs in more developed nations. Yet this digital divide is rapidly altering, as broadband costs have dropped and mobile phone communication usage has vastly expanded, notably in Asia and Africa (ITU, 2013b). Furthermore, it is clear that 'digital natives' in ITU's terms (modified in recognition of critical literature), that is, young people aged 15–24 with more than five years' experience of using the Internet, are steadily driving a global expansion in the use of ICT across the developing world.

This emerging trend is interestingly reinforced by both school enrolment and domestic access, with 'digital natives' now informally and unexpectedly leading the way, taking on a digitally literate networked mindset in advance of the rest of the population. It seems that a global race by young people towards achieving ICT skills and networked connectivity is occurring, in the attempt to attain visible success and tangible rewards in an increasingly economically driven, competitive, instrumentalist and marketable global education landscape, in which high youth unemployment is an ever-growing threat. As Czerniewicz et al. (2009) observe of students in lower socio-economic groups who, despite numerous constraints, 'make a plan' to exercise their own sense of freedom in South Africa: "[C]omputers are the means to a 'better' life, to success in the market place and possibly to future financial security."

Innovative Disruptive Digital Technologies: Pupils Are Ahead of the Schools

Yet arguably there has been insufficient public acknowledgement of the importance of these massive global shifts occurring in technological development and access for young people and for schools, as the liminal zone stretching a gulf between more limited and more connected technology-enabled methods of learning and teaching has widened over the past few decades. Innovative forms of highly uncertain disruptive online technologies are gradually transforming educational and employment opportunities for young people equipped with smartphones, Internet access, social media applications and online support in this newly connected, spontaneous milieu. Mobile devices in particular have opened up previously inaccessible learning and job opportunities, even to those in remote rural communities and in the poorest regions (Czerniewicz et al., 2009).

For those with the confidence and connectivity to learn how to use new ICT resources, it is now theoretically possible to learn and earn 100 per cent online from any location, to teach oneself remotely through free opportunities for study in online courses run by elite institutions across the globe and to generate income from self-publishing or start-up innovations. These unprecedented opportunities are best achieved when reinforced by school ICT access, good pedagogic guidance and family support, but are even possible without this. As Mitra has demonstrated, there are circumstances in which, through 'minimally invasive education' (Mitra and Rana, 2001), digital resources can enable keen young people effectively to teach themselves valuable skills, regardless of socio-economic circumstances.

Yet as advanced ICTs, and our global fascination with them, gradually change all levels and facets of education in unpredictable ways for schools and families, in most cases they are, regrettably, sharply reinforcing social, gender, employment and income inequalities of the existing digital divides in a highly stratified global education system. From the use of web-based learning systems, virtual learning environments, social media applications, game-based learning, smartphones, iPads and digital notebooks in homes and classrooms to the application of online assessment tools and advanced Management Information System (MIS), more technologically connected schools in developed nations have experienced a massive expansion in ICT-enabled teaching, learning and administrative applications that are providing unprecedented benefits for their pupils. Accelerated growth in educational technology and social media usage is radically changing the environment experienced by such pupils, staff, schools and parents to the point that online 21st century technologies are now playing a more significant role in education than was ever envisaged. Emerging pedagogic and systemic digital innovations, variously interpreted as utopian and dystopian, offer significant opportunities for schools to design new pedagogic approaches, based on existing and new researches, to transform system-wide levels to accommodate and develop the strong interest shown by young people in technological innovations. While a critique of neoliberal technological determinism removes the normative expectation of techno-glamour relating to such ambitions, there is little doubt of their instrumental effectiveness in enabling learning and employment opportunities for young people desperate to achieve.

Conclusion

In the changing future landscape for schools, in which unpredictable spontaneous digital innovation will continue to accelerate, a genuinely collaborative distribution of pedagogic e-leadership tasks and responsibilities to all positional levels, both formal and informal, will be needed. This is a risk and a challenge for school leaders at all levels, particularly those in the classroom and at the top of institutions. But for young people to become all that they can be in achieving sound digital skills, learning and future employment, it is worth all the effort it will take.

References

Cuban, L., Kirkpatrick, H. and Peck, C. (2001). High access and low use of technologies in high school classrooms: Explaining an apparent paradox. *American Educational Research Journal, 38*(4), 813–834.

Czerniewicz, L., Williams, K. and Brown, C. (2009). Students make a plan: Understanding student agency in constraining conditions. *Research in Learning Technology, 17*(2), 1741–1629.

De Freitas, S. and Jameson, J. (2013). *The e-learning reader.* London: Bloomsbury.

ITU. (2013a). *Measuring the information society.* Report of the International Telecommunication Union, Geneva, Switzerland. Retrieved from http://www.itu.int/en/ITU-D/Statistics/Documents/publications/mis2013/MIS2013_without_Annex_4.pdf (last accessed on 23 December 2013).

———. (2013b). *The world in 2013: ICT facts and figures.* Report of the International Telecommunication Union Geneva, Switzerland. Retrieved from http://www.itu.int/en/ITU-D/Statistics/Documents/facts/ICTFactsFigures2013-e.pdf (last accessed on 6 July 2015).

Jameson, J. (2005). *Leadership in post-compulsory education: Inspiring leaders of the future.* London: David Fulton Publishers/Taylor & Francis Group.

———. (2013). Special issue on e-leadership. *British Journal of Educational* Technology, *44* (6): 883–888.

Meeker, M. (2013). Mary Meeker's 2013 internet trends report. Kleiner, Perkins, Caufield and Byers (KPCB). Retrieved from http://techcrunch.com/2013/05/29/mary-meeker-2013-internet-trends (last accessed on 23 December 2013).

Mitra, S. and Rana, V. (2001). Children and the Internet: Experiments with minimally invasive education in India. *British Journal of Educational Technology, 32*(2), 221–232.

Real Time Statistics (2014) Live Internet Statistics.Retrieved from http://www.internetlivestats.com/ (last accessed on 2 January 2014).

Super Monitoring (2013). *State of mobile 2013 (infographic)*. Retrieved from http://www.supermonitoring.com/blog/2013/09/23/state-of-mobile-2013-infographic/ (last accessed on 1 January 2014).

Trucano, M. (2012). *World Bank: ICTs in education*. Retrieved from http://blogs.worldbank.org/edutech/ict-education-policies (last accessed on 3 January 2014).

UNESCO. (2012). The future of mobile learning: implications for policy makers and planners. Retrieved from http://unesdoc.unesco.org/images/0021/002196/219637E.pdf (last accessed on 6 July 2015).

International Comparisons: Good or Misunderstood?

Alma Harris and Michelle S. Jones

As highlighted at the start of this book, the pressure to achieve better education outcomes and to raise performance for all young people is now stronger than ever. It is particularly acute in public education where improving school performance is now an expectation placed squarely on the shoulders of those who lead schools and classrooms. This expectation, however, does not come with any guaranteed solution or blueprint for an effective organizational change. It certainly does not come with any clear idea about how to integrate new technology and pedagogy to best effect, as Chapter 16 has argued. It is not accompanied with any fail-safe model for improving organizational performance. But one thing is clear, any organizational change and improvement is heavily dependent upon the action of leaders, at *all* levels in the system, and the quality of the collaborative cultures they create (Harris et al., 2014).

This book provides a range of pointers and ideas about future leaders and leading futures from a global perspective. There are some strong themes emanating from the chapters. First, connecting policy and practice more strongly and more effectively requires the involvement of school leaders in the policy-formation and policy-implementation stages in an active way. School leaders, it is argued, need to be the instigators and architects of change not just passive recipients. Second, effective professional learning for future leaders has to be focused on responding to challenges, risks and uncertainty not bound up with bureaucracy, stability and low-level management.

Third, the Generation X principals are in schools and are significantly recasting what is understood by leadership and what leaders do. These future leaders are redefining school leadership far more quickly than any mandate or training programme. Fourthly, the focus on leadership and leadership practice in Asian countries is an important theme throughout the book. Looking across the vast leadership literature there is a relative absence of studies and empirical accounts of leadership in the East with very little of the existing literature focusing upon Central Asia (Hallinger, 2015). Accounts of leadership in Asian countries are, therefore, essential not only recalibrate the knowledge base but also to offer in-depth and alternative accounts of leadership practice that are deeply contextualized. The chapters that focus on Russia, Hong Kong, Singapore and Malaysia provide alternative reference points and empirical sources that will inform the global debate about leadership.

Finally, for future educational leaders seeking organizational change and improvement, the message from this book is very clear: there has to be collective capacity building that is carefully designed and supported. The most effective education systems actively build the collective capacity for change and there is also a growing body of evidence pointing to the fact that they connect research, policy and practice in coherent, aligned and dramatically powerful ways (Leana, 2011; Hargreaves and Fullan, 2012; Hargreaves and Shirley, 2012). They also invest in an implementation science that defines, delineates and, ultimately, determines exceptional performance (Harris et al., 2014).

Good or Misunderstood?

This takes us back to the issues raised at the start of this book and to the question of how far international organizations are authentically helping the pursuit of better educational outcomes globally. The influence of the Organisation for Economic Cooperation and Development's (OECD's) education policy work depends, to a significant extent, on stressing the importance of policy factors over the effects of culture and social contexts. The cultural and historical explanations for the success of certain education systems cannot be used to advocate or justify reforms in other nations; therefore, they are factored out of any contemporary international debate about improving education systems. They are not part of any policy advice from the OECD.

While distilling the effects of a policy from other factors associated with better education outcomes is reasonable, insufficient attention to cultural and system-specific factors means that the resulting analyses could be misunderstood and misused (Sellar and Lingard, 2014). Clearly, going too far down the contextual argument is unwise as it then becomes impossible to say anything at all about relative educational performance, precisely because it is so culturally specific and embedded. Alternatively, ignoring context altogether means that the policies advocated might not have taken full account of important and pervasive influences on a system's performance. For example, one major influence upon educational performance is structural inequality, and although the equity of schooling is certainly part of Programme for International Student Assessment's (PISA's) analysis, measures of inequality beyond schooling are not considered.

While it is interesting and even comforting to learn from the success of other systems (Stewart, 2013; Tucker, 2011), doing so without taking full account of the complexity and multifaceted influences that shape the everyday experience of learners and teachers is not only naïve but also potentially dangerous. Evidence from the 7-system study shows that some of the existing explanations of system success are simplistically reflecting a shallow understanding of the context. It is also revealing that accounts of high or low performance are intrinsically bound up with the political, religious and economic landscapes of each country. It is important to reflect upon whether those advocating policy solutions based on 'high-performing' systems have actually spent any substantial time in those countries or systems. Have they visited schools, talked to teachers or listened to young people share their experiences of schooling? Without such direct experiences, it is unclear on what basis are they advocating certain improvement approaches over others.

One thing is crystal clear, future leaders in schools and school systems will have much greater demands placed upon them. That much we know. But the current choice before them is stark. It is *either* to comply with the PISA worldview with the robotic replication of the strategies of the 'best' systems *or* to build upon the strengths of their existing system, in context, with its cultural specific advantages in a deep and authentic way. This is not to suggest that the findings from the large-scale assessments are ignored, as taking a global comparative view is important, but rather to propose that this data is used wisely and critically to *inform* rather than to *prescribe* policy solutions.

Currently, PISA provides possibly the most important measure of educational performance across the globe. The 'policy lessons' drawn from PISA, however, remain at a very high level of generality (OECD, 2014; Schleicher, 2014) and, in part, reflect the extent to which the 'best-performing' systems are mostly homogeneous in their contextual make-up and educational provision. PISA has not only significant strengths but also significant weaknesses. Only by understanding the good and the misunderstood about PISA is it possible to interpret its data with any degree of accuracy (Rees and Taylor, 2015). In the words of T. S. Eliot, we may find that in time, the *centre cannot hold*, and the global policy grip of PISA and the other large-scale assessments will lessen and revert to being just measures, among many other measures of educational outcomes. In the interim, remembering that education is about *leading futures* and that high-quality education is more than just a set of numbers might be a timely and important reality check.

References

Eliot, T.S. (1989). The Waste Land. *The Complete Poems and Plays*. London: Faber and Faber, 59–80.

Hargreaves, A., and Fullan, M. (2012). *Professional capital: Transforming teaching in every school*. New York: Teachers College Press.

Hargreaves, A., and Shirley, D. (2012). *The global fourth way: The quest for educational excellence*. California: Corwin Press.

Harris, A., Jones, M., Adams, D., Perera, J. and Sharma, S. (2014). High Performing Education Systems in Asia: Leadership Art Meets Implementation Science. *Asia-Pacific Education Researcher, 23* (4), 861–869.

Hallinger, P., and Chen, J. (2015). Review of research on educational leadership and management in Asia: A comparative analysis of research topics and methods, 1995–2012. *Educational Management Administration and Leadership, 43*(1), 5–27.

Leana, C.R. (2011). The missing link in school reform. *Stanford Social Innovation Review, 9*(4), 34.

OECD. (2014). *Improving schools in Wales: An OECD perspective.* Paris: OECD.

Rees, G. and Taylor, C. (2015). *Is there a crisis in Welsh education? A review of the evidence.* A report prepared for the Honourable Society of Cymmrodorion, Wales Institute of Economic and Social Research, Data and Methods. Retrieved from http://orca.cf.ac.uk/id/eprint/72803 (accessed on 7 May 2015).

Schleicher, A.(2014). *Qualified for life: Embedding PISA skills into Welsh education.* Presentation at National Education Conference, Cardiff.

Sellar, S., and Lingard, B.(2014). The OECD and the expansion of PISA: New global modes of governance in education. *British Educational Research Journal, 40*(6), 917–936.

Stewart, V. (2013). *A World-Class Education: Learning from International Models of Excellence and Innovation.* Alexandria, VA: ASCD.

Tucker, M. (2014). *Standing on the Shoulders of Giants: An American Agenda for Education Reform.* National Centre on Education and the Economy: Washington, D.C.

About the Editors and Contributors

Editors

Alma Harris is Professor of Educational Leadership at the Institute of Educational Leadership, University of Malaya, Malaysia. Since September 2012, she has been the Director of the Institute of Educational Leadership at the University of Malaya (UM). In 2010–2012 she was a senior policy adviser to the Welsh Government. Professor Harris holds visiting professorial posts at Moscow Higher School of Economics, Nottingham Business School, University of Wales and the University of Southampton. She is currently Past President of the International Congress for School Effectiveness and School Improvement. Professor Harris has published many books including *Distributed Leadership Matters* (2013), and *Uplifting Leadership* (2014) with Andy Hargreaves and Alan Boyle.

Michelle S. Jones is Deputy Director at the Institute of Educational Leadership, UM, where she focuses upon academic development and internationalization. In 2008, she became a school effectiveness associate for the Welsh Government and subsequently a professional education adviser assisting teachers' and principals' professional learning in over 2,000 schools. Dr Jones has also been working with government agencies in England, Russia, Australia, Singapore and Malaysia to contribute to the design and delivery of their professional learning programmes.

Contributors

Donnie Adams is a PhD candidate under the supervision of Professor Harris and Dr Jones at UM. He's currently a BrightSparks scholarship holder—a special programme at UM to upgrade research and publications by selecting outstanding researchers (Bright Sparks) from within UM and other universities to serve with UM. His primary research interests are in the area of leadership in special educational needs and school-wide reformation of inclusive education agenda in Malaysia.

Albert Bertani is a Senior Adviser for the Urban Education Institute at the University of Chicago and a Senior International Associate with the Innovation Unit in London. He has designed, facilitated and evaluated leadership development programmes for districts, organizations and federally funded grants across the USA as well as internationally in Australia, Brazil, England, Qatar, South Africa and South Korea.

Carol Campbell is an Assistant Professor at the Ontario Institute for Studies in Education (OISE). She is particularly interested in whole-system reforms for large-scale change leveraging evidence of effective and promising practices within and across classrooms, schools, districts, provinces or states and countries.

Christopher Chapman is the Chair of Educational Policy and Practice at the University of Glasgow, Scotland and Co-Director of the Robert Owen Centre for Educational Change and What Works Scotland—a three year Economic and Social Research Council (ESRC), Scottish Government-funded programme of research—exploring public-sector reforms. Christopher's research focuses on the interaction between educational and public sector policy and practice, specifically in relation to the improvement of outcomes in disadvantaged settings. He has led research projects for research councils, charities and research and evaluations for national and local governments and their agencies.

Janet H. Chrispeels is Professor Emeritus of Education Studies, University of California, San Diego, where she served as the Director of Doctoral Programme in Educational Leadership. At present, she is the Director of Transformative Inquiry Designs for Effective Schools (TIDES), which provides professional development for schools and districts to strengthen teacher and principal leadership, data use and inquiry learning.

Karen Edge is Reader in Educational Leadership at UCL Institute for Education, a Research Fellow at the Western University in Canada, Editor-in-Chief of *Educational Assessment Evaluation and Accountability*. She is also on the six-person Advisory Panel for International School Leadership Principals and is involved in ESRC—an internationally funded research project. Karen's latest research has engaged 60+ Generation X school leaders in London, New York and Toronto.

Isak Froumin is Professor and Academic Advisor to the Institute of Education, National Research University–Higher School of Economics (NRU HSE) in Moscow. Since 2012, he has been Advisor to the Ministry of Education and Science of the Russian Federation. He is also Professor and Chair of the Educational Theory Department at Krasnoyarsk University, Siberia. Professor Froumin led the World Bank's education programme in Russia from 1999 to 2011. Since 2011, he has been the Vice-president of Skolkovo Foundation and a member of the Russian delegation at the Organisation for Economic Co-operation and Development's (OECD) Education Policy Committee. Professor Froumin is the author of more than 250 publications including articles and books in Russian and English.

Irina Grunicheva is Research Fellow at the Centre of Social and Economic School Development, Institution of Education, NRU HSE.

Jill Jameson is Professor of Education and Chair of the Centre for Leadership and Enterprise, Faculty of Education and Health,

University of Greenwich, London. Professor Jameson is the Convenor of the British Educational Research Association (BERA) Educational Technology SIG and has won the Chartered Management Institute (CMI) Award for Leadership and Management Achievement, 2011. She was the Guest Editor of the *British Journal of Educational Technology*'s special edition on e-Leadership in 2013.

Anatoly Kasprzhak is PhD in Pedagogy; Director of Institute of Education, Centre for Leadership Development in Education, NRU HSE; Professor of Department of Educational Programmes; Academic Supervisor of Master Programmes in Education Administration, Institute of Education, NRU HSE.

Serge Kosaretsky, is PhD and Director of the Centre for Social and Economic School Development, Institute of Education, NRU HSE, Russia.

Paula Kwan is Associate Professor at the Department of Educational Administration and Policy, The Chinese University of Hong Kong (CUHK). She is concurrently the Associate Director of the Hong Kong Institute of Educational Research at CUHK. She also serves on the editorial boards of several international refereed journals.

Zoe Lai-mei Leung received her BEd and MEd in Teaching English to Speakers of Other Languages (TESOL) from Queensland University of Technology, and her PhD from Hong Kong Polytechnic University. In 2007, she joined the Hong Kong Centre for the Development of Educational Leadership at CUHK and is presently working as School Development Officer.

Anthony Mackay is the CEO at the Centre for Strategic Education, Melbourne; Chair of the Global Education Leaders Partnership based at the Innovation Unit (IU), London and also the Board Director at IU; Chair of the National Institute for School Leadership at the National Centre for Education and the Economy, Washington, D.C. He was the inaugural chairperson of the Australian Institute for Teaching and School Leadership (AITSL).

Daniel Muijs is Professor of Education at the University of Southampton, UK. He is an expert in educational effectiveness and Co-editor of the journal *School Effectiveness and School Improvement*. He has published widely in areas of teacher effectiveness and research methods.

Vasu Muniandy had been working as a public school teacher in Malaysia since 13 years prior to becoming Senior Lecturer in the Department of Coaching and Monitoring, Institute of Aminuddin Baki, Genting Highlands, Ministry of Education, Malaysia. His expertise is in educational leadership. Currently, he is a PhD candidate in the field of creativity in curriculum leadership.

Pak Tee Ng is Associate Dean, Leadership Learning at the National Institute of Education (NIE), Nanyang Technological University (NTU), Singapore. He is also the Head of the Policy and Leadership Studies Academic Group at the NIE. He is the Executive Editor of Educational Research for Policy and Practice and also Associate Editor of several other internationally refereed journals.

Nicholas Sun-keung Pang serves as Professor and Chairperson, Department of Educational Administration and Policy; and as Director of the Hong Kong Centre for Development of Educational Leadership (HKCDEL), CUHK. Professor Pang has been leading a number of research projects in educational administration, management and leadership as well as school improvement projects in Hong Kong. He has been publishing locally and internationally.

Corinne Jacqueline Perera serves as Research Assistant at the Institute of Educational Leadership, University of Malaya, where she currently pursues her doctorate under the supervision of Professor Alma Harris and Dr Michelle Jones. Her research interests lie in areas of school improvement, leadership practices and mixed research methods. She has joint authorship in The Asia-Pacific Education Researcher journal publication namely *High-Performing Education Systems in Asia: Leadership Art Meets Implementation Science*.

Marina Pinskaya, a PhD candidate, is a Leading Research Fellow of the Centre of Social and Economic School Development, Institute of Education, NRU HSE, Russia.

Louisa Rennie is Director of the Australian Principal Certification Program at Principals Australia Institute (PAI). Prior to joining PAI, Louisa was Manager of the School Leadership team at AITSL. She has 18 years of experience in Catholic Education South Australia as teacher, education consultant, deputy principal and acting principal. Louisa has also worked internationally as teacher and education adviser in South America, Japan and the United Arab Emirates.

David Reynolds is Professor of Educational Effectiveness at the University of Southampton, UK. Professor Reynolds has published 23 books and over 200 papers, articles and shorter publications. He has lectured and consulted in over 40 countries across the world and has been heavily involved in educational policy-making in England and Wales.

James P. Spillane is the Spencer T. and Ann W. Olin Professor in Learning and Organizational Change at the School of Education and Social Policy at the Northwestern University, Illinois. He is also Professor of Human Development and Social Policy of Learning Sciences and of Management and Organizations, and Faculty Associate at Northwestern University's Institute for Policy Research. Professor Spillane has published extensively on issues of education policy, policy implementation, school reform and school leadership.

Yong Zhao is Presidential Chair and Director of Institute of Global Online Education at University of Oregon. He is also Senior Research Fellow at the Mitchell Institute, Victoria University, Australia. He is the author of the best-selling book, *Who's Afraid of the Big Bad Dragon: Why China Has the Best (and Worst) Education System in the World.*

Index